INDIE PRESSES
2016/17

The Mslexia guide to small and independent
book publishers and literary magazines in the
UK and the Republic of Ireland

First published 2016 by Mslexia Publications Ltd

PO Box 656, Newcastle upon Tyne NE99 1PZ
www.mslexia.co.uk

ISBN 978-0-9555111-9-6

Printed and bound in the UK by TJ International
Designed by Juliette Boisseau, www.outlinedesign.co.uk

Supported using public funding by
**ARTS COUNCIL
ENGLAND**

Contents

Back in the dim and distant past every serious writer had four reference books on her shelf: the *Writers' and Artists' Yearbook*, *Roget's Thesaurus*, *Chambers' Dictionary* (the only one worth having if you're a fan of cryptic crosswords) – and a little yellow directory entitled *The Small Press Guide*.

If you started writing in the last decade, chances are you've never even heard of *The Small Press Guide*. This is because the last edition was published in 2002, after which it retreated online where it limped along for a while, before creeping into a dark cave to expire.

The reason it disappeared was the reason it was so valuable in the first place: because there are literally hundreds of independent book publishers and literary magazines based on these islands, but they are incredibly difficult to catalogue. As fast as a new book publisher is launched, another one shuts up shop; new magazines appear every year and others disappear into the ether. The original *Guide* had to be updated every year, which was a truly daunting prospect in the days before websites, emails and smartphones were ubiquitous – not just because of the here-today-gone-tomorrow nature of indie presses, but also because the editors tend to be hard to track down. This is partly due to the way creative types tend to move around, following what few opportunities there are for paid employment – a residency here, a temporary lectureship there. But it's also because they tend to burn out and pass the baton to someone else – someone less wise and less jaded, at yet another address.

For years I was part of the editorial collective that ran *Writing Women* magazine, a chunky quarterly(-ish) A5 magazine that published short fiction, poetry and reviews by women. There were nominally five of us – or was it six? I was invited on board over pizza in a dark trattoria in a Newcastle backstreet.

Subscriber details were kept in a dog-eared card-index. We read thousands of submissions – I remember long evenings, heaps of paper clips and stamped-addressed envelopes (remember when they were essential?), arguing back and forth about shortlisted stories and poems. I remember lugging boxes of newly-printed magazines, stuffing envelopes, licking stamps (that's how long ago this was). We all had boxes of unsold magazines in wardrobes, attics and garages, and under tables, at our various houses.

None of us were paid. We used a PO box for all magazine communications. No telephone number; no email; no website. A few years after I got involved, we turned the magazine into an annual anthology,

The Virago Book of Writing Women. Were we still a magazine? Or had we become book publishers? We didn't know or care; we just wanted to showcase brilliant new writing by women. By this time three (or was it four?) of the original editors had bowed out (aka burned out) and two more had been recruited, over more pizza, in another dark trattoria…

Now imagine that situation multiplied more than 400 times (there are more than 400 indie presses listed in this book). That is why *The Small Press Guide* gave up the ghost. And why nothing has emerged in the meantime to replace it – until now.

Reinventing a definitive guide to small presses has been a cherished item on my 'to do' list ever since the original little yellow bible bit the dust back in 2002. But we've never before had the time or resources that would be needed at Mslexia to take on such a mammoth task. That changed at the end of 2014, when we received funding from Arts Council England to employ an Editorial Associate for a year to work on the project. Enter Françoise Harvey, who is responsible for the majority of the work involved in producing this book, and who has since become a permanent member of the Mslexia team.

We created *Indie Presses* 2016/17 primarily as a resource for writers, but we hope it will also act as a calling card for all the independent presses represented here too. Because they need, and deserve, our support. And we can guarantee – because we excluded presses set up solely to publish the work of the editors – that every publisher listed here is dedicated to bringing the writing they admire to as many readers as possible.

These are your magazines, your publishers. In fact the literary magazine sector is the only game in town if you're a poet or writer of short fiction. It's almost unheard for writers in these genres to see a first collection in print with a mainstream publisher without first gaining a track record of publication in literary magazines. And the careers of many novelists and writers of narrative non-fiction don't begin to take off until their debut manuscript emerges as a lovingly produced indie press paperback.

Independent presses are literature's Amazon rainforest, the oxygen that sustains new voices and helps them rise to the top of the mainstream's slush pile. Yet many presses teeter constantly on the brink of extinction, sustained mainly by the hard work and self-sacrifice of those who run them. If we don't buy what they publish, they will disappear. They need us as much as we need them. It's as simple as that.

Debbie Taylor
Editorial Director
Mslexia Publications Limited

In order to bring you the information in this Guide, we first gathered the names and contact details of as many of the UK's small(ish) independent book publishers and literary magazines as we could find. Then we sent them a survey, inviting them to answer as many (or few) of the survey questions as they liked. The results await you.

We've divided the Guide into book publishers and magazines (including e-zines), though there is some overlap. We have also separated the prose and poetry book publishers (presses that do both are listed in both sections), and magazines have been divided into poetry only, prose only and mixed poetry and prose.

Where the publisher didn't respond to our survey, we checked to ensure they did still exist then included them as a 'stub' entry, consisting of contact details and minimal information.

For publishers that did respond to our survey, we were able to generate entries that include much of the following information:

- The type of publications they produce. Please note that 'e-books' does not always mean *only* e-books.
- Contact details (including a postal address, a phone number, an email address and a website) and the name of the editor(s).
- The year the press was established, and where their publications are available (and how freely, if online) so that you, the writer, have an idea of where your work might end up. We've also tried to include details of any awards the press might have won.
- The genres published, where relevant.
- How to submit and where you can find further guidelines; any restrictions on eligibility; how long you can expect to wait for a response; whether the editor(s) can offer feedback; payment policy.
- A ☆ symbol indicates the press also runs one or more writing competitions – flip to the Competitions section on p211 for more information.
- There is an Index at the end of the book if you want to look up a particular publisher (p227).

We have also added a section entitled 'We say' to many of the entries so that we could give you a Mslexia perspective on the quality of production and what to expect from the press in question. For this we asked the presses to send us a sample of their output. Not every press was able to oblige, but we've tried to fill in the gaps with our own research – in libraries and on the internet – and hope we've managed to provide some perspective on most of the publishers listed. (If there is no 'We say' under an entry, check to see whether the press is listed in a different section, where the 'We say' might be included.)

Some presses also opted to include an image – a logo or an example book cover – and the chance to describe their aims, aesthetics and the kind of writing they are looking for. This is listed under 'They say'.

If you want to make sure you are submitting to an established and respected 'A-list' book press, check out the awards and prizes in the introductory section to each. But bear in mind that a lack of awards does not necessarily indicate a lesser press – sometimes it just means a less active marketing/PR department. The fee/royalty conditions, and where the books are available, are also good indicators.

You will notice that some entries state that a press does not accept 'unsolicited submissions'. This does not necessarily mean its doors are closed to you. It usually means that the editors' policy is to approach writers whose work they have seen elsewhere, often in a literary magazine – another indication, if one were needed, of how important it is to get your work out there.

We hope this information will set you firmly on the way to being able to find a small publisher or magazine that will be a good fit for your work.But please remember to treat these entries as signposts – our 'We say' opinion may not match yours. So before sending your work, we urge you to research the press yourself – go to their website and check their backlist.

Small presses and magazines start up and close down at the drop of a hat – compiling this Guide was a bit like playing whack-a-mole. In the time between this Guide going to press and your using it, the publishers may have opened a new imprint or launched a new competition. If you know of a press we have omitted, please contact us so we can include them in future editions.

Part 1:
Book Publishers

Submitting to small and indie presses

Some publishers listed here like to be referred to as 'indie presses'; others prefer the term 'small presses'. In general a small press is also an indie (independent) press.

The UK and Irish small press sector has been expanding in the past few years. A new generation of editors has swelled the ranks, and access to affordable printing and print-on-demand has improved financial viability. The growth of digital publishing has helped too, with stats showing that small presses are holding their own against the big publishers in terms of e-books sales.

There are pros and cons of approaching a small indie press with your work. On the plus side, small presses are often more willing to take a punt on experimental writing – indeed many were started precisely because their founders were frustrated that work they admired was rarely picked up by the big publishers. An open submission policy is another bonus; unlike with big publishers, you don't necessarily need to have an agent before a small press editor is willing to consider your manuscript. And because editors are more personally invested and passionate about the books they publish, they have a reputation for working more closely with authors they take on.

There are many instances where this risk-taking and passion has paid off. Eimear McBride approached many agents and publishers with her challenging novel *A Girl is a Half-formed Thing* – to no avail, until indie Galley Beggar Press spotted its potential. Several nominations and awards later, Faber reprint the book, and Galley Beggar Press has established a reputation for spotting top-notch writing.

What about the cons? Well, not surprisingly, small presses often lack the clout of the bigger publishers when it comes to marketing a book. So you may need to get involved in the marketing and publicity yourself, possibly including contacting distributors to try and get your book into bookshops.

The production values (design, proofing, paper quality, etc.) are also worth keeping an eye on. If you can, examine other titles published by the press you're considering approaching, and make sure you're happy with their output. In our 'We Say' comments, we have tried to give an idea of what to expect from each press, but these are only a starting point. Putting time into researching your options can save a lot of heartache later on.

Here are some basic guidelines to bear in mind when submitting:
- Do your research. We've given you enough information to help you

shortlist the right press for you, but ideally you should also check the websites, research books they've published, establish that your work is the kind of thing they are looking for.

- Also, make sure that the publisher offers what *you* are looking for. You don't want your manuscript to be accepted only to discover that the look and feel of their publications is not how you envisioned your work appearing – or that you've been taken on by an e-book-only publisher when you harbour dreams of ink and paper.
- Do not submit your manuscript until it is finished – i.e. redrafted and redrafted (and redrafted) and polished to a high gleam. No publisher will be interested in reading three chapters of an unfinished book, or a hastily written first draft.
- Several of the publishers in this section also run literary magazines. In this case, the anthologies/collections they publish may arise from writers submitting work to the magazine. So do check whether you need to have published in the magazine before a book manuscript can be considered.
- Follow the submission instructions. Most publishers have guidelines on their website, and they all vary from one another. You will irritate the editor if you don't read and follow them carefully. Don't send more than the requested number of words; don't submit outside the window for submissions if there is one; if they've requested a query email, don't send your manuscript without querying first. Don't email if they specify post; don't post your only copy if they specify email.
- Be patient. There will probably be a lot of submissions and not many people assessing them. So don't email or call after two weeks to chase your submission. Most presses in our Guide have indicated their usual response time. If that time passes and you still haven't heard, check their website or social media to see if there's a reason for the delay. Then, and only then, send a polite reminder.
- To reiterate: be polite. These people will be considering working closely with you; any spikiness will affect their decision. And bear in mind that the world of small presses is *small*. Editors talk to each other, and they remember the writers who have been rude.

Good luck!

Some of the publishers listed here cannot really be considered 'small' at all – Bloodaxe Books, for example, have been established for decades, publish many titles every year, and have an enormous backlist of titles. However, because all specialist poetry publishers are open to submissions by poets without agents, we felt it important to include them all.

Bear in mind that most publishers of poetry collections do expect you to have a history of publication in magazines and anthologies. So if you don't yet have a track record for publishing single poems, skip to page p123 and check out the magazine listings.

Also listed in this section are a number of presses that publish both poetry and prose. In these cases we have indicated, where appropriate, what their dominant area of publishing is.

ACUMEN PUBLICATIONS
COLLECTIONS AND CHAPBOOKS/
PAMPHLETS
info@acumen-poetry.co.uk
www.acumen-poetry.co.uk
Editor: Patricia Oxley
Established 1985. Publications
available direct from publisher
website, by post and email order,
at local literary events and through
Amazon.
Award-winning publishers.
SUBMISSIONS: Open to all, but
publication history required (must
have been published in *acumen
Literary Journal* for pamphlet
publication). Submit by post (6 The
Mount, Higher Furzeham Road,
Brixham, South Devon TQ5 8QY)
or by email (patriciaoxley6@gmail.
com). Guidelines at www.acumen-
poetry.co.uk. Usually responds
within four weeks. May occasionally
provide feedback on submissions,
but only on request. Authors
receive free copies of their book,
no fee or royalties.
WE SAY: We looked at poetry
pamphlet *Dragon Child*, by
Marina Sanchez: a slim, 32-page
pamphlet, with stiff, matt, dark
pink cover with a photographic
image of a dragon sculpture. It's a
well-produced publication, with the
poems carefully ordered to tell a
chronological story.
**See also: *acumen Literary Journal*
(poetry magazine) p179**

AESOP MAGAZINE
ANTHOLOGIES
18 and a half Sekforde Street,
London EC1R 0HL
editor@aesopmagazine.com
www.aesopmagazine.com
Editor: Max Raku
Established 2015. Primarily a
fiction magazine with some poetry;
occasional publishes poetry
anthologies.
SUBMISSIONS: Open to all.
Submit via the online form at www.
aesopmagazine.com/submissions.
Usually responds within one
to three months. Feedback on
submissions only if requested.
Contributors receive free copies of
the book; no fee or royalties.
**See also: prose publishers p65;
Aesop Magazine (prose magazine)
p199**

AGENDA EDITIONS
COLLECTIONS
The Wheelwrights, Fletching Street,
East Sussex TN20 6TL
editor@agendapoetry.co.uk
www.agendapoetry.co.uk
Editor: Patricia McCarthy
Established 1959.
SUBMISSIONS: See *Agenda* (p179).
WE SAY: Collections and
anthologies from Agenda tend to
have the same look and production
vaues as *Agenda* magazine – see
p179.
**For a fuller description of this press,
see *Agenda* (poetry magazine) p179**

ALBA PUBLISHING
COLLECTIONS, ANTHOLOGIES AND
CHAPBOOKS/PAMPHLETS
PO Box 266, Uxbridge UB9 5NX
01895 832444
info@albapublishing.com
www.albapublishing.com

Editor: Kim Richardson
Established 1990. Also publishes some prose (see p65). Publications available by post and email order; and from Amazon.
A title from Alba Publishing was shortlisted for the Haiku Foundation Touchstone Distinguished Book Award 2013.
GENRES: Spirituality and beliefs.
SUBMISSIONS: Publication history required. Submit by post (PO Box 266, Uxbridge UB9 5NX) or by email (info@albapublishing.com). Usually responds within four weeks, with submission feedback only if requested. Authors contribute to editorial/publication/marketing costs.
WE SAY: We looked at a PDF proof of *Initial Response* by Maeve O'Sullivan, a 33-page, perfect-bound pamphlet. The cover has a striking red and black design of scribbled calligraphy, which will look lovely in print, and the collection comprises 'an a-z of haiku moments'. Each letter of the alphabet has a title ('A is for Autumn', 'B is for Birds & Berries', etc.) and a six-haiku poem across a double-page spread, with some black, splashed-ink illustrations on the second half of their spreads. It's an uncluttered, eye-catching design.
See also: prose publishers p65

AND OTHER STORIES
COLLECTIONS
88 Easton St, High Wyecombe, Buckinghamshire HP11 1LT
07534 974322
nichola@andotherstories.org
www.andotherstories.org
Editors: Tara Tobler, Stefan Tobler, Sophie Lewis
Established 2010. Mainly publishes fiction (see p65). Publications available in chain bookshops nationwide; in independent bookshops; at local literary events; and from Amazon and other bookshop websites. Plans are in place for purchase direct from the publisher. Also offers a subscription: £20, £35 or £50 per year for two, four or six books per year.
And Other Stories was shortlisted for the 2013 IPG Newcomer Award. Its authors have also been shortlisted for and won awards.
SUBMISSIONS: Open to all, but submitters are required to show proof of purchase from the press. Submit by post to 88 Easton St, High Wycombe, Bucks HP11 1LT. Guidelines at www.andotherstories.org/about/contact-us/. Usually responds within one to three months. A standard rejection may occasionally include unsolicited feedback. Author payment is an advance/fee plus royalties.
For a fuller description of this press, see prose publishers p65

ANIMA POETRY PRESS
COLLECTIONS, ANTHOLOGIES AND CHAPBOOKS/PAMPHLETS
www.animapoetry.uk
Editor: Marcus Sly
Established 2014. Publications available direct from publisher website.
GENRES: Spirituality and beliefs.
SUBMISSIONS: Open to all. Submit through Submittable at anima.submittable.com/submit. Usually responds within four to six months. Rejection may occasionally include unsolicited feedback. Authors receive royalties.
WE SAY: Anima has recently started publishing books as

well as *Anima* magazine; its first collection, *Leaves Like Spindrift* by Isabel Chenot, is out in 2016. We can't comment on the quality of this publication (yet!), but we do like what we've seen of the cover design, which has photo-real autumn leaves falling across a textured grey background.

For a fuller description of this press, see *Anima* (poetry magazine) p180

ARACHNE PRESS ☆

COLLECTIONS AND ANTHOLOGIES
100 Grierson Road, London SE23 1NX
020 8699 0206
www.arachnepress.com
Editor: Cherry Potts
Established 2012. Mainly publishes fiction (see p65) but also some poetry. Publications available direct from publisher website; by post and email order; at chain bookshops and independent bookshops nationwide; at local literary events; and from Amazon and other bookshop websites, including distributor inpressbooks.co.uk.
SUBMISSIONS: During submissions windows, submit through Submittable at arachnepress.submittable.com/submit. Guidelines at arachnepress.com/submissions/. Usually responds within one to three months. Provides feedback on submissions where the editor thinks it would be useful to the author, unless explicitly asked not to. Authors receive royalties and/or free copies of their book.

For a fuller description of this press, see the extended entry under prose publishers p65

ARC PUBLICATIONS

E-BOOKS, COLLECTIONS, ANTHOLOGIES AND CHAPBOOKS/

PAMPHLETS
Nanholme Mill, Shaw Wood Road, Todmorden OL14 6DA
01706 812338
info@arcpublications.co.uk
www.arcpublications.co.uk
Editors: Tony Ward, Angela Jarman
Established 1969. Publications available direct from publisher website; by post and email order; at chain and independent bookshops nationwide; at national and local literary events; and from Amazon and other bookshop websites.
Shortlisted for the Griffin Poetry Prize 2015.
SUBMISSIONS: Publication history required. Submit by email to info@arcpublications.co.uk (hard copy submissions not accepted). Guidelines at www.arcpublications.co.uk/submissions. Usually responds within four to six months. Rejections may occasionally include unsolicited feedback. Authors are paid an advance/fee plus royalties, and receive free copies of their book.
WE SAY: We looked at *Indelible, Miraculous: the collected poems of Julia Darling*, edited by Bev Robinson. This is a posthumous collection from a much-loved poet. The print quality is high – a matt cover with a faded image of a handprint on a window. The poems have been selected from an archive and the book includes a preface explaining that process and an Introduction by poet Jackie Kay. The 168 pages span work across Darling's lifetime, beautifully presented and divided into chapters. The final poem, 'Entreaty', is a perfect sign off for both the book and for Darling. A well-made tribute from the heart.

ARETÉ BOOKS
E-BOOKS, COLLECTIONS
8 New College Lane, Oxford OX1 3BN
01865 289193
aretebooks@gmail.com
www.aretemagazine.com
Editor: Craig Raine
Book awards include *A Scattering*
by Christopher Reid winning the
2009 Costa Prize, which was also
shortlisted for The Forward Prize
and the T S Eliot prize in the same
year. Writers receive royalties only.
**For a fuller description of this press,
see *Areté Magazine* (mixed-form
literary magazine) p131**

AS YET UNTITLED ☆
ARTISTS' BOOKS
138 Erlanger Rd, London SE14 5TJ
ayupublishing@gmail.com
www.asyetuntitled.org
Editors: Rosie Sherwood,
Zelda Chappel
Established 2012. Mixed form:
artists' books. Publications
available direct from publisher
website; from selected/local chain
bookshops; from independent
bookshops; at local literary events;
and at Artists' Book Fairs (national),
and the Small Publishers Fair.
SUBMISSIONS: As Yet Untitled
books are in the early days of
production. See the website for
more information on submissions.
**For fuller descriptions of this press,
including what They Say, see prose
publishers p65 and *Elbow Room*
(mixed-form literary magazine) p140**

ASLS
COLLECTIONS
7 University Gardens, Glasgow
G12 8QH
0141 330 5309
office@asls.org.uk
www.asls.org.uk

Established 1970. Publications
available direct from publisher
website; by post and email order; at
chain bookshops; at independent
bookshops; at national and local
literary events; and from Amazon
and other bookshop websites.
**For a fuller description of this press,
see *New Writing Scotland* (mixed-
form literary magazine) p159 and
prose publishers p65**

AUGUR PRESS
COLLECTIONS AND ANTHOLOGIES
info@augurpress.com
www.augurpress.com
Established 2004. Books with an
emphasis on enabling the reader
'to reflect, and to look beyond
... that which is immediately
apparent'. Includes translated
collections.
See also: prose publishers p65

BARE FICTION ☆
COLLECTIONS AND
CHAPBOOKS/PAMPHLETS
177 Copthorne Road,
Shrewsbury SY3 8NA
info@barefiction.co.uk
www.barefictionmagazine.co.uk
Editor: Robert Harper
Established 2013. Publications
available direct from publisher
website; by post and email order;
and from independent bookshops.
SUBMISSIONS: Currently collection
publication is through the Bare
Fiction Debut Poetry Collection
competition, see p216. Writers
receive royalties and free copies of
their book.
WE SAY: The first full collection
from Bare Fiction is Zelda
Chappel's *The Girl in the
Dogtooth Coat*, which is a 72-
page paperback. Bare Fiction have
used the magazine's style (font

choice etc) with this book and the transition works well. The cover is matt, with a striking, ghostly, black-and-white image, the title font nodding to art-deco. The poems are well presented, and the quality of print high.
For a fuller description of this press, and what They Say, see also *Bare Fiction Magazine* (mixed-form literary magazine) p132

BIRLINN PRESS
COLLECTIONS AND ANTHOLOGIES
West Newington House,
10 Newington Road, Edinburgh
EH9 1QS
info@birlinn.co.uk
www.birlinn.co.uk
Managing director: Hugh Andrews
Poetry published under the Polygon imprint. Mixed form: also publishes fiction and non-fiction.
See also: prose publishers p65

BLACK & BLUE
ANTHOLOGIES AND
CHAPBOOKS/PAMPHLETS
33 Cheval Court, 335 Upper Richmond Road, London SW15 6UA
info@blackbluewriting.com
www.blackbluewriting.com
Editors: Dane Weatherman, Miriam Tobin, Beckie Stewart, Harriet Hill-Payne, Alice Popplewell, Peter Masheter
Established 2012. Anthologies tend to be a creative collection, and the press released a series of 'political-poetic' pamphlets in 2015. Publications available direct from publisher website; by post and email order; at selected/local chain bookshops and independent bookshops; and at local literary events and small press fairs.
SUBMISSIONS: Open to all during submissions windows.

Submit by email to submissions@ blackbluewriting.com. Usually responds within four to six months – rejections include free feedback.
For a fuller description of this press, see *Black & BLUE* (mixed-form literary magazine) p133

BLACK LIGHT ENGINE ROOM, THE
COLLECTIONS, ANTHOLOGIES AND CHAPBOOKS/PAMPHLETS
theblacklightenginedriver@hotmail.co.uk
Editor: P.A. Morbid
Established 2010. Subscription: two issues of *Dark Matter* chapbook per year £12 (UK), £16 (Europe), £20 (rest of the world). Publications available by post and email order; and at local literary events.
SUBMISSIONS: Open to all. Submit by email to theblacklightengine driver@hotmail.co.uk. Usually responds within one to three months. No feedback offered with rejections. Authors receive copies of their book.
For a fuller description of this press, see *The Black Light Engine Room* (poetry magazine) p181

BLACK PEAR PRESS ☆
COLLECTIONS AND ANTHOLOGIES
office@blackpear.net
www.blackpear.net
Editors: Rod Griffiths, Polly Robinson, Tony Judge
Established 2013. Publications available direct from publisher website; by post and email order; at local literary events; and from Amazon and other bookshop websites.
SUBMISSIONS: Usually by invitation only, but with occasional short submission windows open to all, which are advertised on the

website. Usually responds within one to three months. Rejections may occasionally include unsolicited feedback. Authors receive royalties, plus discounted copies of their books.
For a fuller description of this press, see prose publishers p65

BLOODAXE BOOKS

COLLECTION, ANTHOLOGIES, E-BOOKS WITH AUDIO, BOOKS WITH VIDEO DVDS AND AUDIO CDS
Eastburn, South Park, Hexham, Northumberland NE46 1BS
01434 611581
admin@bloodaxebooks.com
www.bloodaxebooks.com
Editor: Neil Astley
Established 1978. Publications available direct from publisher website; by post and email order; from chain bookshops nationwide; from independent bookshops; at national literary events; and from Amazon and other bookshop websites.

Bloodaxe is a multi-award-winning press: awards won by its poets in the past ten years include the Nobel Prize in Literature, T S Eliot Prize, Griffin International Poetry Prize, Queen's Gold Medal for Poetry, Pulitzer Prize (USA), National Book Award (USA), Somerset Maugham Award, Geoffrey Faber Memorial Prize, Edwin Morgan Poetry Award, Roland Mathias Poetry Award, Corneliu M. Popescu Prize for European Translation, Criticos Prize, Bernard Shaw Prize, and Cholmondeley Award – to name just a few.

SUBMISSIONS: Publication history required. Submit by post to Submissions, Bloodaxe Books, Eastburn, South Park, Hexham, Northumberland NE46 1BS. A sample of up to a dozen poems is preferable to a full manuscript, and don't forget to include return postage. Usually responds within one to three months. Usually no feedback if rejected, but very occasionally a standard rejection may include unsolicited feedback. Authors receive an advance/fee, plus royalties.

WE SAY: Bloodaxe is a major indie publisher with open submissions, a long history of successfully taking risks on poets, and beautifully produced publications. With their high-gloss covers and instantly recognisable black spine and logo, Bloodaxe books are quality products. Most collections have an uncluttered layout on bright white paper, but the press also stretches to thick shiny paper and a square format for Frieda Hughes' poems and paintings book *Alternative Values*, which wouldn't be out of place on a coffee table.

BRADSHAW BOOKS

COLLECTIONS AND ANTHOLOGIES, Civic Trust House, 50 Pope's Quay, Cork City T23 R6XC
0214 215175
info@bradshawbooks.com
www.bradshawbooks.com
Publishing director: Máire Bradshaw
Established 1985. Mainly publishes poetry, but also some prose (see p65). Publications available direct from publisher website; by post and email order; at independent bookshops and from Amazon. Publications from Bradshaw Books include work on the *Eurochild: Artwork and Poetry For Children by Children* annual anthology.
See also: *Cork Literary Review* (mixed-form literary magazine) p138 and prose publishers p65

BUNBURY PUBLISHING LTD
COLLECTIONS AND CHAPBOOKS/
PAMPHLETS
5 Chester Street, Bury, Lancashire
07446 025630
admin@bunburymagazine.com
www.bunburymagazine.com
Editors: Christopher Moriarty,
Keri-Ann Edwards
Established 2013. Book publishing
a new venture.
SUBMISSIONS: Open to all.
Guidelines at bunburymagazine.
com/submit-to-us/. Authors receive
royalties only.
**See also: prose publishers p65; for
a fuller description of this press,
see *Bunbury Magazine* (mixed-form
literary magazine) p135**

BURNING EYE BOOKS
COLLECTIONS, PAMPHLETS AND
ANTHOLOGIES
burningeyebooks.wordpress.com
Editors: Clive Birnie, Thommie Gillow
(poetry), Alice Furse (fiction)
Specialises in spoken word artists,
with a view to showing that
performance poetry can translate
to the page. A publisher for
poets for whom traditional poetry
publishers may not be a good fit.
See also: prose publishers p65

BUTCHER'S DOG
ANTHOLOGIES
c/o New Writing North, 3 Ellison
Place, Newcastle-upon-Tyne NE1 8ST
submissions@butchersdogmagazine.
com
www.butchersdogmagazine.com
Editors: Degna Stone, Luke Allan,
Sophie F Baker, Jake Campbell,
Amy Mackelden, Andrew Sclater
Established 2012. Publications
available direct from publisher
website; at selected/local chain
bookshops; at independent
bookshops; and at national and
local literary events.
Butcher's Dog was selected for The
Pushcart Prize 2016.
GENRES: Includes prose poetry.
**For a fuller description of this
press, including what They Say, see
Butcher's Dog Poetry Magazine
p182**

CANDLESTICK PRESS ☆
ANTHOLOGIES AND CHAPBOOKS/
PAMPHLETS
72 Nottingham Road, Arnold,
Nottingham NG5 6LF
0115 967 4455
info@candlestickpress.co.uk
www.candlestickpress.co.uk
Editors: Jenny Swann, Di Slaney
Established 2008. Publications
available direct from publisher
website; by post and email
order; from chain bookshops
and independent bookshops
nationwide; at national and local
literary events; from Amazon and
other bookshop websites; and from
some farm shops, gift shops and
non-book online retailers.
Candlestick Press won a Progress
Award from Nottingham's
'Cultivate' arts organisation in
2009.
SUBMISSIONS: Submissions by
invitation only – guidelines at
www.candlestickpress.co.uk/
submissions. Writers are paid a flat
fee and receive free copies of the
book.
WE SAY: Well-presented anthology
chapbooks that can be sent as gifts,
as Candlestick Press say, 'instead of
a card'. The A5 chapbook comes
complete with envelope, sticker and
bookmark. We looked at *Ten Poems
on Knitting* (Candlestick covers
many different topics): a quality
product printed on thick textured

paper with a bright cover and simple illustrations. Perfect as a light read for readers who enjoy quality over quantity.

CARCANET PRESS
COLLECTIONS AND ANTHOLOGIES
4th Floor, Alliance House,
30 Cross Street, Manchester M2 7AQ
0161 834 8730
info@carcanet.co.uk
www.carcanet.co.uk
Managing editor: Luke Allan
One of the UK's major poetry publishing houses, founded in the 1960s. Includes several imprints, and publishes a comprehensive and diverse list of modern and classic poetry in English and in translation.
SUBMISSIONS: Open to all. Hard-copy submissions only, which should include six to ten pages of work and an SAE – see the website for full details. Decisions usually taken within eight weeks. Please familiarise yourself with Carcanet's books before submitting.
See also: *PN Review* (poetry magazine) p188

CB EDITIONS
COLLECTIONS
146 Percy Road, London W12 9QL
0208 7432467
info@cbeditions.com
www.cbeditions.com
Editor: Charles Boyle
Established 2007. Publishes poetry, and short fiction and other prose (see p65). Publications available direct from publisher website; at chain and independent bookshops nationwide; at national and local literary events; and from Amazon and other bookshop websites.
A multi-award-winning publisher: titles have won the Aldeburgh First Collection Prize (2009, 2011, 2013);

the Scott Moncrieff Translation Prize (2014); the McKitterick Prize (2008) and the *Guardian* First Book Award (2014), as well as being shortlisted for the Goldsmiths Prize (2014).
SUBMISSIONS: Open to all. Submit by post (146 Percy Road, London W12 9QL) or by email (info@cbeditions.com). No guidelines available, so read publications by CB Editions to be sure your work will be a good fit. Usually responds within one to three months. No feedback offered with rejection. Authors are paid an advance/fee plus royalties, and receive free copies of the book.
WE SAY: We looked at Dan O'Brien's *War Reporter*, a 134-page paperback, printed on high quality materials. The cover design adheres to the CB brand, which is a textured grey/brown background, with another single colour (red in this case) accenting the design. The text (long-line poems, based on interviews, conversations and transcripts) is well laid out.
See also: prose publishers p65 and *Sonofabook* (mixed-form literary magazine) p169

CIRCAIDY GREGORY PRESS
COLLECTIONS
Creative Media Centre, 45 Robertson Street, Hastings, East Sussex TN34 1HL
sales@circaidygregory.co.uk
www.circaidygregory.co.uk
Mixed form: poetry as well as various prose (see p65).
See also: prose publishers p65

CLUTAG PRESS
COLLECTIONS AND CHAPBOOKS/PAMPHLETS
PO Box 154, Thame OX9 3RQ
info@clutagpress.com
www.clutagpress.com

CINNAMON PRESS ☆

COLLECTIONS, ANTHOLOGIES,
AND CHAPBOOKS/PAMPHLETS
Meirion House, Glan yr afon, Blaenau
Ffestiniog, Gwynedd LL41 3SU
01766 832112
jan@cinnamonpress.com
www.cinnamonpress.com
Editors: Jan Fortune, Adam Craig

Established 2005. Mixed form:
alongside poetry, also publishes
novels, short stories and creative
non-fiction (p65). Cinnamon Book
Club: £30 per annum for six brand-
new books. Publications available
direct from publisher website; at
chain and independent bookshops
nationwide; at local literary events;
from Amazon and from Inpress
Books. Titles from Cinnamon Press
have won Scottish Arts Best First
Book of the Year; Wales Book of
the Year; and Wales Book of the
Year Readers' Vote. Also shortlisted
for Wales Book of the Year and
the Forward Prize for Best First
Collection.
SUBMISSIONS: Submit only during
submissions periods. See www.
cinnamonpress.com/index.php/
about-cinnamon-press/submissions
for full details. Usually responds
within one to three months.
Submissions that came close to
publication may receive some
feedback with rejection. Authors
are paid royalties only.
WE SAY: We looked at the *Lost
Voices* anthology: not strictly
a poetry pamphlet, as it also
contains (very) short fiction. Perfect
bound despite being slim, this A5
pamphlet anthology is elegant,
with a minimalist black-and-white
cover design and cream pages. The

THEY SAY

Based in North Wales,
Cinnamon Press is a family
team selecting books we feel
passionate about: fiction,
poetry, prose-poetry and
creative non-fiction. We aim
to find distinctive voices and
have a significant list of Welsh
writers, whilst also providing
a centre of excellence for
literature from the UK and
the world. Our new Liquorice
Fish Books imprint exists to
develop more experimental and
cross-genre publications. We
are keen to support emerging
writers: publishing *Envoi Poetry
Journal* as well as running
courses, competitions in several
genre and a mentoring scheme
that has seen 70% of students
go on to publication.

writing is sharp and succinct, and
veers towards slipstream in terms
of genre. We also enjoyed the
extracts from forthcoming titles
– Cinnamon are good promoting
their writers and wares.
**See also: *Envoi Poetry Journal*
p183 and prose publishers p65**

Not currently accepting unsolicited manuscripts.
See also: *Archipelago Magazine* (poetry magazine) p131

CRINKLE CRANKLE
CHAPBOOKS/PAMPHLETS
crinklecrankle@gmail.com
Editor: Eleanor Margolies
Established 2014. Mixed form: also publishes non-fiction (see p65) Publications available by post and email order, or by download from the sales site.
GENRES: Society, education and politics.
SUBMISSIONS: By invitation only.
See also: prose publishers p65

CRO MAGNON, THE ☆
COLLECTIONS AND ANTHOLOGIES
51 Wakefield House, Goldsmith Road, London SE15 5SU
www.thecromagnon.com
Editor: Henry Tobias Jones
Established 2015. Mixed form: also produces short story anthologies and collections (see p65).
SUBMISSIONS: Open to all. Submit by email to editors@ thecromagnon.com. See guidelines on the website. May charge for submissions. Usually responds within one to three months, with feedback only if requested.
For a fuller description of this press see *The Cro Magnon* (mixed-form e-zine) p138. See also prose publishers p65

CULTURED LLAMA
COLLECTIONS AND ANTHOLOGIES
11 London Road, Teynham, Sittingbourne, Kent ME9 9QW
07800 522724
info@culturedllama.co.uk
www.culturedllama.co.uk

Editors: Maria C McCarthy, Bob Carling
Established 2011. Mixed form: poetry, short fiction and cultural non-fiction (see p65). Publications available direct from publisher website; at national and local literary events; and from Amazon and other bookshop websites.
SUBMISSIONS: A publication history is required. Poetry submissions are not always open – check the guidelines at www. culturedllama.co.uk/publishing/ submission to find out when and how to submit your work. Usually responds within one to three months. A rejection may occasionally include unsolicited feedback, but usually not. Authors are paid royalties only and receive free copies of the book.
For a fuller description of this press, see prose publishers p65

DEAD INK
COLLECTIONS AND CHAPBOOKS/PAMPHLETS
dead.ink.books (skype)
www.deadinkbooks.com
Editor: Nathan Connelly
Established 2011. Mainly publishes fiction (see p65). Publications available direct from publisher website; by post and email order; from chain bookshops nationwide; from independent bookshops; and from Amazon.
Among many award long- and shortlistings, Dead Ink- poetry title *Kissing Angles* by Sarah Fletcher was shortlisted for Best Poetry Collection in the 2015 Saboteur Awards.
SUBMISSIONS: Open to all, but check that the submissions windows are open. Submit by email to nathan@deadinkbooks.

com. Guidelines at deadinkbooks. com/submissions/. Usually responds within one to three months. Will give feedback on submissions for a fee, though on occasion a rejection may include unsolicited feedback. Authors receive free copies of the book, but no fee or royalties.

WE SAY: We looked at Saboteur Award-shortlisted book *Kissing Angles* by Sarah Fletcher, a perfect-bound 34-page pamphlet with a matt cover. The writing is bold, sexy and funny and the wrap-around cover design features sketches of a kissing couple; there is a lot of blurb in tiny text.

See also: prose publishers p65

DEDALUS PRESS

E-BOOKS / COLLECTIONS AND ANTHOLOGIES
13 Moyclare Road, Baldoyle, Dublin 13, Ireland
+35 318 392034
www.dedaluspress.com
office@dedaluspress.com
Editor: Pat Boran
Established 1985. Publications are available direct from publisher website; by post and email order; at chain bookshops nationwide; at independent bookshops; at local literary events; and from Amazon and other bookshop websites.
GENRES: Poetry; music, stage and screen.
SUBMISSIONS: Submissions open to all, but only during submission windows. Guidelines at dedaluspress.com/submissions/. Submit by post to The Editor, Dedalus Press, 13 Moyclare Road, Baldoyle, Dublin 13, Ireland. Strictly no submissions by email. Usually responds within one to three months. Rejections may

occasionally include unsolicited feedback. Authors are paid royalties only, although an advance may be offered in particular cases.
WE SAY: Grace Wells' book *Fur* has a timeless look to it, with a white matt cover featuring an image of a sculpture: striking and classical without being stuffy. The production values are high. Themes in Wells' poetry include transformation, nature and Irish folklore (Dedalus has a particular focus on Irish writing, or translations by Irish writers).

DIAMOND TWIG

COLLECTIONS
9 Eversley Place,
Newcastle-upon-Tyne NE6 5AL
0191 276 3770
www.diamondtwig.co.uk
diamond.twig@virgin.net
Editor: Ellen Phethean
Established 1992. Predominantly publishes poetry, but also publishes short story collections (see p65). Publications available direct from publisher website, and by post and email order.
Diamond Twig title *The Ropes: poems to hold on to*, an anthology of poems for teenagers, was shortlisted for the 2009 CLPE Poetry Award (Centre for Literacy in Primary Education) (www.clpe. co.uk).
SUBMISSIONS: Submissions for book publication are by invitation only. Usually decides within one to three months. Rejection may include occasional unsolicited feedback. Authors are paid a flat fee and receive free copies of the book.
See also: *Diamond Twig* (poetry e-zine) p183 and prose publishers p65

DIRT PIE PRESS
ANTHOLOGIES
editors@riptidejournal.co.uk
www.riptidejournal.co.uk
Editors: Dr Virginia Baily, Dr Sally Flint
Established 2006. Mainly fiction
(see p65), but also some poetry.
Publications available direct from
publisher website; by post and
email order; from independent
bookshops; and at local literary
events. All stockists are listed on
the website.
SUBMISSIONS: Open to all,
guidelines on the website. Submit
by email to editors@riptidejournal.
co.uk. Usually responds within four
to six months. No feedback offered
with rejections. Contributors
receive a flat fee.
**For a fuller description of this press
see also *Riptide Journal* (mixed-
form literary magazine) p166. See
also prose publishers p65**

DOG HORN PUBLISHING ☆
COLLECTIONS, ANTHOLOGIES AND
CHAPBOOKS/PAMPHLETS
45 Monk Ings, Birstall,
Batley WF17 9HU
01924 466853
editor@doghornpublishing.com
www.doghornpublishing.com
Editor: Adam Lowe
Established 2005. Also publishes
prose (short stories, non-fiction,
novels), see p65. Publications
available direct from publisher
website; by post and email order;
from chain bookshops nationwide;
from independent bookshops; at
national and local literary events;
and from Amazon and other
bookshop websites, including
lulu.com.
Titles from Dog Horn have won the
Guardian First Book Award (reader
nomination); the Noble (*not* Nobel)

Book Prize; and have had multiple
honourable mentions in the Year's
Best Horror.
SUBMISSIONS: Submissions
by invitation only. If invited,
submit by email to editor@
doghornpublishing.com.
Guidelines at
www.doghornpublishing.com/
wordpress/about. Usually responds
in over six months. Rejections may
occasionally include insolicited
feedback. Authors are paid
royalties only and receive free
copies of the book.
WE SAY: We looked at an e-book of
Bite Me, Robot Boy, an anthology
of short stories and poems by
new writers who were winners of a
competition run by the press. The
cover is bright and abrasive, which
is in keeping with Dog Horn's
slogan 'books with bite'. The
poetry and stories are modern, fun
and definitely have teeth – this is
not a collection for delicate souls.
Editor Adam Lowe makes it clear
that the press is looking for writers
he can rescue from the conventions
of the publishing market.
See also: prose publishers p65

DOIRE PRESS
COLLECTIONS AND ANTHOLOGIES
Aille, Inverin, County Galway, Ireland
+353 091 593290
www.doirepress.com
Editor: John Walsh
Established 2007. Publishes poetry
and short stories equally (see p65).
Publications available direct
from publisher website; from
independent bookshops; at
national literary events; and from
Amazon and kennys.ie.
Doire Press title *Waiting for the
Bullet* by Madeleine D'Arcy won
the 2015 Edge Hill Readers' Prize.

SUBMISSIONS: Only open to writers living in Ireland, and not actively seeking submissions (though open to being approached by writers familiar with Doire's books who sure their work will be a good fit). Submit by post (Aille, Inverin, County Galway, Ireland) or by email (doirepress@gmail.com). Guidelines at www.doirepress.com/submissions/. Usually responds within one to three months. No feedback offered with rejections. Book deals vary: authors may be paid royalties only; may be paid an advance/fee plus royalties; and/or may receive free copies of book – the deal depends on grant funding received.

WE SAY: *The Woman on the Other Side* by Stephanie Conn is an 80-page poetry collection – we looked at a PDF version. The cover design is a photo of a snowy road. The poetry, largely free verse, explores feelings of alienation in language, place and relationships. Well designed, with well-ordered poems that conduct the reader on a journey through the Netherlands. **See also: prose publishers p65**

DREADFUL PRESS, THE ☆
COLLECTIONS
Clonmoyle House, Coachford, Cork
the.p.dreadful@gmail.com
www.thepennydreadful.org
Editors: Marc O'Connell,
John Keating
Mixed form: also publishes prose (see p65). Publications available direct from publisher website; from selected/local chain bookshops; from independent bookshops; and at local literary events.
SUBMISSIONS: Open to all – see guidelines at thepennydreadful. org/index.php/submit/. Usually

responds within four weeks. Rejections may occasionally include unsolicited feedback. Writers are currently unpaid. **For a fuller description of this press see *The Penny Dreadful* (mixed-form literary magazine) p164. See also prose publishers p65**

EGG BOX PUBLISHING
COLLECTIONS, ANTHOLOGIES AND CHAPBOOKS/PAMPHLETS
nathan@eggboxpublishing.com
www.eggboxpublishing.com
Editor: Nathan Hamilton
Established 2006. Publications available direct from publisher website; by post and email order; from chain bookshops nationwide; from independent bookshops; at national literary events; and from Amazon and other bookshop websites.
SUBMISSIONS: Open to all. Submit by email to submissions@eggboxpublishing.com. Guidelines at eggboxpublishing.com/contact. If no response after one month, assume a rejection and feel free to submit elsewhere. Authors are paid royalties only, and receive free copies of the book.
WE SAY: Egg Box publish the annual UAE MA anthologies, as well as various poetry pamphlets, printed on quality paper. Their cover designs are uncluttered and brightly coloured. *Falseweed* by Bill Manhire (a long-poem pamphlet) has a matt cardboard cover and stapled spine.

ENITHARMON PRESS
E-BOOKS, COLLECTIONS, ANTHOLOGIES, CHAPBOOKS/PAMPHLETS, ART BOOKS
10 Bury Place, London, WC1A 2JL
020 7430 0844

EMMA PRESS, THE

ANTHOLOGIES, CHAPBOOKS/
PAMPHLETS AND CHILDREN'S
POETRY COLLECTIONS
Spectacle Works, 16-24 Hylton Street,
Jewellery Quarter, Birmingham B18 6HN
queries@theemmapress.com
www.theemmapress.com
Editors: Emma Wright, Rachel Piercey

Established 2012. Primarily
publishes poetry, but also prose
(see p65). Publications available
direct from publisher website; from
chain bookshops and independent
bookshops nationwide; at national
and local literary events; and from
Amazon and other bookshop
websites. The Emma Press was
shortlisted for the 2014 and 2015
Michael Marks Award for Poetry
Pamphlet Publishers.
SUBMISSIONS: Open to all, during
submissions windows. Submitters
required to show proof of purchase
from the press. Submit by email
– there's a different address
for each call. See guidelines
at theemmapress.com/about/
submissions. Usually responds
within four to six months. Rejections
may occasionally include unsolicited
feedback. Authors are paid royalties
only, and receive free copies of the
book.
WE SAY: We looked at anthology
Slow Things, a slightly smaller than
A5 paperback, 53 pages long.
Made from quality materials, with
a lovely, quirky cover that has
an illustration of a sloth having a
picnic, and blue end papers. A
clean layout, plenty of biog space
and illustrated with sketches. Top
notch.

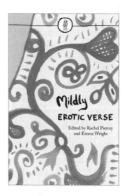

THEY SAY

The Emma Press is an
independent publisher
dedicated to producing
beautiful, thought-provoking,
often illustrated books. They
have been awarded funding
by Arts Council England
to run two national poetry
tours, in 2013 and 2015, and
their publishing programme
features themed poetry
anthologies and single-
author poetry and prose
pamphlets. In 2015, *Oils* (a
poetry pamphlet by Belfast
poet Stephen Sexton) was
selected as the PBS Pamphlet
Choice and the Emma
Press began an ambitious
publishing programme for
children's poetry anthologies
and collections. The Emma
Press was shortlisted for the
Michael Marks Awards for
Poetry Pamphlet Publishers
in 2014 and 2015.
See also: prose publishers p65

info@enitharmon.co.uk
www.enitharmon.co.uk
Established 1967. Publishes art
and poetry. Publications available
direct from publisher website; by
post and email order; from chain
bookshops nationwide; from
independent bookshops; and from
Amazon.
SUBMISSIONS: Submissions by
invitation only.
WE SAY: Enitharmon Press have
had 40 years of experience
publishing poetry – longevity
achieved by the production of
first-rate publications. The quality
of materials used remains high.
Recent poetry collections favour
bold, uncluttered graphic cover
designs. We are particular fans of
Maureen Duffy's *Pictures from an
Exhibition*, which features different
coloured eyes staring out from a
dark blue background.

ERBACCE-PRESS ☆

COLLECTIONS, ANTHOLOGIES AND
CHAPBOOKS/PAMPHLETS
erbacce@blueyonder.co.uk
erbacce-press.com
Editor: Alan Corkish
Established 2004. Publications
available direct from publisher
website; by post and email order;
from independent bookshops; at
national and local literary events;
on and from Amazon. Note:
erbacce is a cooperative, in which
poets volunteer to support other
poets via their royalties.
SUBMISSIONS: Open to all. Submit
by post (Dr Andrew Taylor, 5
Farrell Close, Melling, Liverpool,
L31 1BU) or by email (erbacce@
blueyonder.co.uk). Guidelines are
on the website. Usually responds
within four weeks. Rejections may
occasionally include unsolicited

feedback. Authors are paid 20%
royalties and receive free copies of
the book.
WE SAY: We saw the PDF proofs of
Blood Orange by Maroula Blades,
the 2012 'erbacce-prize for poetry'
winner. This will be a 128-page
perfect-bound publication with
a simple, bold black and orange
cover. Unusually, *Blood Orange*
begins with an interview with the
author, which helps contextualise
the work. The poetry is followed
by a few short stories. Editor
Alan Corkish has produced
a professional, high-quality
publication.
**See also: erbacce (poetry magazine)
p184**

ESC ZINE

SHORT FICTION AND POETRY
ANTHOLOGIES
escpeople@gmail.com
esczine.com
Editors: Jessica Maybury, Aine Belton
Established 2011. Mixed form:
fiction (see p65) and poetry.
Publications available direct from
publisher website; and at national
and local literary events.
GENRES: Literary fiction;
slipstream, experimental; art,
fashion and photography.
SUBMISSIONS: During submissions
windows, submit by email to
escpeople@gmail.com. Guidelines
at esczine.com/submissions/.
Usually responds within four
weeks. Rejections may occasionally
include unsolicited feedback.
Contributors receive print copy/ies.
See also: prose publishers p65

ETRUSCAN BOOKS

COLLECTIONS AND ANTHOLOGIES
Flat 2, 9 Maze Hill, St Leonards-on-
Sea, East Sussex TN38 0BA

01424 433412
etruscanpublishing@gmail.com
llpp.ms11.net/etruscan/index2.html
Primarily a poetry publisher,
though now looking into prose.
Publications include visual and
verbal poems and translated works.

EYEWEAR PUBLISHING ☆
COLLECTIONS, ANTHOLOGIES AND
CHAPBOOKS/PAMPHLETS
info@eyewearpublishing.com
www.eyewearpublishing.com
Editors: Dr Todd Swift, Kelly Davio
Established 2012. Mainly publishes
poetry, but does extend to non-
fiction and fiction (see p65).
Publications available direct from
publisher website; by post and
email order; at chain bookshops
nationwide; at independent
bookshops; at local literary events;
and from Amazon and other
bookshop websites.
Eyewear won The Pegasus Award
for Poetry Criticism, 2015 (from the
Poetry Foundation).
SUBMISSIONS: Open to all.
Submit by email to info@
eyewearpublishing.com.
Sometimes charges a readers'
fee – check guidelines at www.
eyewearpublishing.com/about-us/
submission-guidelines/. Usually
responds within one to three
months. No feedback offered
with rejections. Authors are paid
royalties only.
WE SAY: Perfect-bound paperbacks,
mainly poetry collections, though
there's a healthy handful of prose
titles available too, and the press is
expanding so check out their prose
entry in this Guide. Jan Owen's *The
Offhand Angel*, the collection we
considered, had a sleek appearance
with unusually positioned page
numbers and several experimental

poetic forms (even the dedication
page had a funky layout). The
pages felt thick and Eyewear covers
are matt-laminate, with instantly
recognisable designs.
See also: prose publishers p65

FAIR ACRE PRESS ☆
COLLECTIONS, ANTHOLOGIES,
CHAPBOOKS/PAMPHLETS
fairacrepress@gmail.com
www.fairacrepress.co.uk
Editor: Nadia Kingsley
Established 2011. Predominantly
publishes poetry, but with
increasing focus on fiction (see
p65). Publications available direct
from publisher website; and at
national and local literary events.
Represented by Signature Books
and expects books to be more
widely available soon.
GENRES: Some focus on art,
photography, popular science and
nature.
SUBMISSIONS: Solicited work
only, apart from submissions
arising from competitions or other
opportunities announced on the
website. Usually responds within
one to three months. Rejections
may occasionally include
unsolicited feedback. Writers are
paid royalties only and receive free
copies of the book.
**For a fuller description of this press
see prose publishers p65**

FISH PUBLISHING ☆
ANTHOLOGIES
Durrus, Bantry, Co. Cork, Ireland
info@fishpublishing.com
www.fishpublishing.com
Editors: Clem Cairns, Jula Walton,
Mary-Jane Holmes
Established 1995. Poetry is
published only as part of mixed-
content anthologies, alongside

short stories and memoir. Please see p65 (prose publishers) for more details.

For a fuller description of this press, including what They Say, see prose publishers p83

FITZCARRALDO EDITIONS ☆
COLLECTIONS
243 Knightsbridge, London SW7 1DN
info@fitzcarraldoeditions.com
www.fitzcarraldoeditions.com
Editor: Jacques Testard
Established 2014. Mixed-form publisher: primarily publishes literary fiction and non-fiction/essays (see p65). Publications available direct from publisher website; by post and email order; from chain bookshops and independent bookshops nationwide; at national and local literary events; and from Amazon. Offers a books subscription: £70 for eight books, £35 for four. Fitzcarraldo title *My Documents*, by Alejandro Zambra, was shortlisted for the 2015 Frank O'Connor Short Story Award.
SUBMISSIONS: Open to all. Usually responds within one to three months. Rejections may occasionally include unsolicited feedback. Authors are paid an advance/fee plus royalties.
For a fuller description of this press see prose publishers p65

FIVE LEAVES PUBLICATIONS
COLLECTIONS
Five Leaves Bookshop, 14a Long Row, Nottingham NG1 2DH
info@fiveleaves.co.uk
www.fiveleaves.co.uk
Editor: Ross Bradshaw
Established 1995. Primarily non-fiction, but also publishes fiction (see p65) and poetry. Publications available direct from publisher website; by post and email order; from selected/local chain bookshops; from independent bookshops; at local literary events; from Amazon and other bookshop websites; and from Inpress.com.
GENRES: Literary fiction; history; society, education and politics; Jewish interest.
SUBMISSIONS: Solicited work only. Authors are paid an advance/fee plus royalties. Any unsolicited submissions receive a standard rejection.
WE SAY: A glance through Five Leaves' most recent publications reveals a press in touch with current affairs, and that responds quickly to them (*Over Land, Over Sea* is a 142-page poetry anthology 'for those seeking refuge'; there's also a look at Nottingham's council houses and a pamphlet on Harper Lee and the American South). Production design standards seem to vary (some of the photo-background cover designs look less than polished), but the pamphlet series and other books (such as the anthology *Maps*) look fantastic.
See also: prose publishers p65

FLAPJACK PRESS
E-BOOKS, COLLECTIONS AND ANTHOLOGIES
6 Chiffon Way, Salford, Greater Manchester M3 6AB
mail@flapjackpress.co.uk
www.flapjackpress.co.uk
Editor: Paul Neads
Established 2008. Publications available direct from publisher website; by post and email order; at independent bookshops; at local literary events; and from Amazon and other bookshop websites.

Flapjack Press title *Selkie Singing at the Passing Place* by Sarah Miller and Melanie Rees was runner-up for Best Collaborative Work, Saboteur Awards 2015. *We Are Poets!* by Helên Thomas won the Book of the Month Award from The Poetry Kit, 2008.

SUBMISSIONS: Priority is for northwest-based performance poetry and debut collections. Currently closed to unsolicited submissions. Usually responds within one to three months. No feedback offered with rejection. Authors receive a flat fee or advance/fee plus royalties, and free copies of the book.

WE SAY: With the focus on performance, rather than traditional poetry, Flapjack Press's publications have a distinctly punk, anti-establishment tone and design, which we love. We looked at the e-book of Jackie Hagan's *Some People Have Too Many Legs*, which is the script of a show written and performed by Hagan after she had to have a leg amputated. From the intro and acknowledgements to the poem/script and cover design, this is a well-produced book with a strong voice.

FLARESTACK POETS
CHAPBOOKS/PAMPHLETS
flarestackpoets@gmail.com
www.flarestackpoets.co.uk
Editor: Meredith Andrea
Established 2009. Publications available direct from publisher website; at independent bookshops; and at national and local literary events.
Flarestack won Publisher of the Year at the 2013 Michael Marks Awards for Poetry Pamphlets.
SUBMISSIONS: Open to all, during submissions windows. Submit by email to flarestackpoets@gmail.co.uk. Guidelines on the website. Usually responds within one to three months. No feedback offered with rejections. Authors receive free copies of the book, and are able to buy more copies at 33% discount. Pamphlets are promoted: sent to an extensive review list, plus a limited number of places nominated by the writer; submitted to PBS for Pamphlet Choice; and entered for the Michael Marks Award.
WE SAY: Pamphlets from Flarestack all have the same look: a stapled card cover in a plain colour, with the pamphlet title in a heavy silver font, with the poems inside printed on quality white paper. A striking design and instantly recognisable.

FLIPPED EYE PUBLISHING
COLLECTIONS, ANTHOLOGIES AND CHAPBOOKS/PAMPHLETS
Free Word Centre, 60 Farringdon Road, London, EC1R 3GA
books@flippedeye.net
www.flippedeye.net
Established 2001. Predominantly publishes poetry, but also some fiction (see p65). Publications available direct from publisher website; from selected/local chain bookshops; from independent bookshops; from Amazon; and at book launches and readings. Titles from Flipped Eye have won the PBS Pamphlet Choice award (2015) and been shortlisted for the Michael Marks Award (2014).
SUBMISSIONS: Submit by email to newwork@flippedeye.net. Guidelines at www.flippedeye.net/blog/2009/08/thesubs/. A response is not guaranteed, but may be sent within one to three months. Rejections may

occasionally include unsolicited feedback. Authors are paid royalties only and receive free copies of the book.

WE SAY: Another poetry press with distinctive pamphlet designs. Flipped Eye pamphlets have cream card covers, with the faint outline of an F as the central decoration, plus a small photograph of the poet and the title across the bar of the F. Thick quality paper makes up the inner pages.

See also: prose publishers p65

FOR BOOKS' SAKE

ANTHOLOGIES

www.forbookssake.net

Mixed-form publisher. Publishes poetry but also a lot of fiction and non-fiction prose (see pages 65 and 143). Publications available direct from publisher website; from selected/local chain bookshops; from independent bookshops; and at national and local literary events. For Book's Sake title *Furies: A poetry anthology of women warriors* was runner-up for the Best Anthology prize at the 2015 Saboteur Awards.

SUBMISSIONS: Open to self-identifying women, and especially encouraged from women of colour, disabled women, queer women, trans women and women from low-income backgrounds. Submit, during submissions windows only, via Submittable (forbookssake. submittable.com/submit – guidelines at same address). Usually responds within four weeks.

WE SAY: We checked out *Furies: A Poetry Anthology of Women Warriors*, which is one of a handful of For Books' Sake's cherry-picked titles. A perfect-bound hardcover with a sleek black and silver design,

the collection has a luxurious feel – made edgy and current by the content itself. A fierce product for a fierce campaign: the collection raised money for the charity Rape Crisis. We approve.

See also: For Books' Sake mixed-form e-zine p143 and prose publishers p65

FREIGHT BOOKS

COLLECTIONS AND ANTHOLOGIES

49 Virginia Street, Glasgow G1 1TS

info@freightbooks.co.uk

www.freightbooks.co.uk

Editor: Henry Bell

Established 2011. Mainly publishes fiction, but also some non-fiction (see p65) and poetry. Publications available direct from publisher website; from chain bookshops nationwide; from independent bookshops; at national and local literary events; and from Amazon and other bookshop websites. Shortlisted for The Saltire Society's Scottish Publisher of the Year Award (2013, 2014).

SUBMISSIONS: No unsolicited poetry manuscripts. Authors are paid an advance/fee plus royalties. Guidelines on the website. Usually responds in over six months, with feedback only if requested.

For a fuller description of this press see *Gutter Magazine* (mixed-form literary magazine) p145. See also prose publishers p65

GATEHOUSE PRESS ☆

COLLECTIONS AND CHAPBOOKS/ PAMPHLETS

90 Earlham Road, Norwich, Norfolk NR2 3HA

admin@gatehousepress.com

www.gatehousepress.com

Editors: Meirion Jordan, Andrew McDonnell, Julia Webb,

Philip Langeskov, Anna de Vaul,
Jo Surzyn, Angus Sinclair,
Scott Dahlie, Iain Robinson,
Zoe Kingsley
Established 2006. Mainly publishes
poetry, but also some fiction (short
stories and novellas – see p65).
Publications available direct
from publisher website; from
selected/local chain bookshops;
from independent bookshops; at
national and local literary events;
and from bookshop websites.
SUBMISSIONS: Submit during
submissions windows. Usually
responds within one to three
months. No feedback offered
with rejections. Writer payment/
remuneration varies according to
publication.
**For a fuller description of this press
see *Lighthouse* (mixed-form literary**

GREEN BOTTLE PRESS

COLLECTIONS AND
CHAPBOOKS/PAMPHLETS
83 Grove Avenue, London N10 2AL
jennifer@greenbottlepress.com
www.greenbottlepress.com
Editor: Jennifer Grigg

Established 2014. Publications
available direct from publisher
website; from selected/local
chain bookshops; and from
independent bookshops.
SUBMISSIONS: Publication
history required – must have
a record of publishing in
magazines and journals. Submit
by post to 83 Grove Avenue,
London, N10 2AL. Guidelines
at www.greenbottlepress.com/
submit. Usually responds within
one to three months. The
press aims to provide positive
comments and feedback as
part of rejection letters. Authors
are paid royalties only and
receive free copies of the book.
WE SAY: Green Bottle Press
has arrived with a bang. The
pamphlet *The Withering Room*
by Sarah Sibley was named as

THEY SAY

We are looking for poetry
written in English from
anywhere in the world.
Currently, our brief is to
publish first collections and
first pamphlets. Our books
are produced to a very high
standard (buy one and see!).
Covers are designed with
images chosen in consultation
with the poet. We want you to
be happy with your book and
then to work hard to help us
sell it.

the *London Review of Books*'
pamphlet of the year. Containing
20 (mostly short) poems, this
is a disconcerting collection, a
feeling echoed in the beautiful
cover image, which features lovely
wallpaper with mould creeping
across it. The layout is clear and
uncluttered and the production
values very high indeed. Any poet
would be proud to have a pamphlet
produced by this press.

magazine) p151. See also prose publishers p65

GRAFT POETRY

COLLECTIONS
Frizingley Hall, Frizinghall Road, Bradford BD9 4LD
01274 541015
www.graftpoetry.co.uk
Editor: Nicholas Bielby
Established 2008. Publications available direct from publisher website; by post and email order; at local literary events; and from Amazon and other bookshop websites.
SUBMISSIONS: Submissions by invitation only – Graft Poetry publishes people who have achieved a good track record in *Pennine Platform* (open submissions, see p187) and who the editor thinks are ready for book publication. Writers receive free copies of the book.
For a fuller description of this press see *Pennine Platform* (poetry magazine) p187

GRIND, THE

COLLECTIONS AND CHAPBOOKS/
PAMPHLETS
07714 735500
thegrindjournal@gmail.com
www.the-grind.co.uk
Editor: Gordon Robert Johnstone
Established 2013. Mixed form. Publications available direct from publisher website.
SUBMISSIONS: Open to all. Submit by email to thegrindsubmissions@gmail.com. Usually responds within one to three months. Rejections may occasionally include unsolicited feedback.
For a fuller description of this press see *The Grind* (mixed-form magazine) p145

HAFAN BOOKS (REFUGEES WRITING IN WALES)

ANTHOLOGIES AND CHAPBOOKS/
PAMPHLETS
c/o Tom Cheesman, Dept of Languages, Swansea University SA2 8PP
t.cheesman@swansea.ac.uk
sbassg.wordpress.com
Editors: Tom Cheesman, Jeni Williams
Established 2003. Mixed form: publishes poetry and prose, and various refugee-related books and booklets (see p65). Publications available direct from publisher website; by post and email order; at local literary events; and from Amazon.
SUBMISSIONS: By invitation only, depending on the publication. Author contributions needed. Submit by email to t.cheesman@swansea.ac.uk. Usually responds within four weeks. Rejections may occasionally include unsolicited feedback. Authors receive free copies of the book; no fee or royalties.
WE SAY: Hafan Books is part of local community efforts to support asylum seekers and refugees. All proceeds from sales go to Swansea Bay Asylum Seekers Support Group.
See also: prose publishers p65

HAPPENSTANCE PRESS

COLLECTIONS, ANTHOLOGIES AND CHAPBOOKS/PAMPHLETS
21 Hatton Green, Glenrothes, Fife KY7 4SD
nell@happenstancepress.com
www.happenstancepress.com
Editor: Helena Nelson
Established 2005. Predominantly publishes poetry, as well as literary essays, and online interviews and reviews. Publications available direct from publisher website;

by post and email order; from independent bookshops; at national and local literary events; and from Amazon.

Happenstance won the 2010 Michael Marks Award for Poetry Pamphlet Publishing.

SUBMISSIONS: Publication history required. Submit during submissions windows, by post to 21 Hatton Green, Glenrothes, Fife KY7 4SD. Usually responds within four weeks. Rejections are personalised and include feedback, often detailed. Authors receive free copies of the book.

WE SAY: We looked at *Notes for Lighting a Fire* by Gerry Cambridge, a perfect-bound 68-page poetry collection, with a matt black cover and the title text coloured as flames – a compelling design. The inner formatting is simple and uncluttered; an effortless read that focuses on light and nature throughout, taking the reader from 'the winter fire' to 'the fire of the sun'.

HEARING EYE
COLLECTIONS
Box 1, 99 Torriano Avenue,
London NW5 2RX
020 7482 0044
info@hearingeye.org
www.hearingeye.org
Established 1987. Poetry ranging from haiku to epic translations.

HIGH WINDOW PRESS, THE
COLLECTIONS, ANTHOLOGIES AND CHAPBOOKS/PAMPHLETS
submissions@the highwindow.uk
thehighwindowpress.com
Established in 2015. Publishes anthologies and chapbooks from up-and-coming talent, alongside collections from established poets.

See also: *The High Window Journal* **(poetry magazine) p184**

INFLUX PRESS
COLLECTIONS
Unit 3a, Mill Co Project,
3 Gaunson House, Markfield Road,
London N15 4QQ
www.influxpress.com
Editors: Kit Caless, Gary Budden
Established 2012. Mixed form: fiction and non-fiction (p65) as well as poetry. Publications available direct from publisher website; from chain bookshops nationwide; from independent bookshops; at local literary events; and from Amazon and other bookshop websites. Influx title *Above Sugar Hill* by Linda Mannheim was nominated for the Edge Hill Short Story Prize.

SUBMISSIONS: During submissions windows, otherwise agent submissions or submissions by invitation only. Submit by email to submissions@influxpress.com. Guidelines at www.influxpress.com/submissions/. Usually responds within four to six months. No feedback offered with rejections. Authors are paid royalties only or an advance/fee plus royalties, and receive free copies of the book. **For a fuller description of this press see prose publishers p65**

INK, SWEAT & TEARS PRESS ☆
ANTHOLOGIES
ink-sweat-and-tears.blogharbor.com/
Editor: Helen Ivory
Established 2007. Publications available from Amazon.
SUBMISSIONS: Open to all. Submit by email to www.inksweatandtears.co.uk. Usually responds within one to three months. No feedback offered with rejections. Writers are unpaid.

INDIGO DREAMS ☆

COLLECTIONS, ANTHOLOGIES AND
CHAPBOOKS/PAMPHLETS
24 Forest Houses, Halwill, Beaworthy,
Devon EX21 5UU
publishing@indigodreams.com
www.indigodreams.co.uk
Editors: Ronnie Dyer, Dawn Bauling

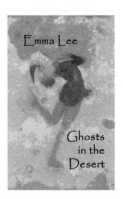

Emma Lee

Ghosts
in the
Desert

Established 2005 (ltd company
2010). Publications available
direct from publisher website; by
post and email order; from chain
bookshops and independent
bookshops nationwide; and from
Amazon. The Indigo Dreams
editors won the Ted Slade Award
for Services to Poetry (2015),
organised by Poetry Kit.
SUBMISSIONS: Open to all, but
a publication history is required.
Complete the appropriate
publication enquiry form at
www.indigodreams.co.uk/
submissions/4591467549
(guidelines are at the same
address). Submit the form by email
to publishing@indigodreams.
co.uk. Usually responds within four
weeks. Rejections may occasionally
include unsolicited feedback.
Authors are paid royalties only and
receive free copies of the book.
WE SAY: We looked at *Ghosts in
the Desert* by Emma Lee, a 72-
page A5 paperback with a glossy
finish – very high quality as with
all IDP publications. The poems
inside are contemporary in style
and deal with themes of loss and
international unrest, seen from a
personal perspective.
**See also: *Reach Poetry* p191; and
Sarasvati p167 and *The Dawntreader*
p139 (mixed-form literary magazines)**

THEY SAY

Award-winning publishers
Indigo Dreams consider
work from both new and
established poets. We publish
around 40 poetry collections/
pamphlets a year, plus
Reach Poetry, *Sarasvati* and
The Dawntreader magazines.
There are also publication
opportunities through two
competitions. IDP won the
'The Ted Slade Award for
Services to Poetry 2015'
and *The Morning Star* quoted
us as one of four 'shining
examples' of presses who
'keep the doors open for
different kinds of voices
and experiences.' We have
a reputation for high
production qualities – and for
being nice people work with!
Currently, the majority of our
poets are female.

For a fuller description of this press, including what They Say, see *Ink, Sweat and Tears* (mixed-form literary e-zine) p149

IRON PRESS
E-BOOKS / COLLECTIONS, ANTHOLOGIES AND CHAPBOOKS/ PAMPHLETS
5 Marden Terrace, Cullercoats, North Shields NE30 4PD
0191 2531901
ironpress@blueyonder.co.uk
www.ironpress.co.uk
Editor: Peter Mortimer
Established 1973. Primarily publishes poetry, but also releases some prose (fiction, drama etc) – see 65. Publications available direct from publisher website; by post and email order; from selected/local chain bookshops; from independent bookshops; and via Inpress Ltd.
Iron Press's 2014 Iron Age Literary Festival won Best Event: Tyneside in The Journal Culture Awards.
GENRES: All poetry including haiku.
SUBMISSIONS: Contact the press before submitting work: see the website for guidelines. Submit by post (5 Marden Terrace, Cullercoats, North Shields NE30 4PD) or by email (ironpress@blueyonder. co.uk). Usually responds within one to three months. Rejections may occasionally include unsolicited feedback. Authors are paid a flat fee.
WE SAY: *Limehaven* by Vicky Arthurs. A professionally designed poetry collection, 71 pages long, printed on quality cream paper and illustrated with detailed images. With its lyrical form, the poetry is inspired by childhood memory, exploring themes of love, nature, war and innocence. A very relatable collection and a recommended read for poets seeking nostalgia. Beautifully presented by the press.
See also: prose publishers p65

KATABASIS
COLLECTIONS, ANTHOLOGIES, CHAPBOOKS/PAMPHLETS
10 St Martin's Close, London NW1 0HR
020 7485 3830
katabasis@katabasis.co.uk
www.katabasis.co.uk
Publishes both poetry and prose. Poetry focus is English and bilingual editions of Latin American poetry.
See also: prose publishers p65

KETTILLONIA
COLLECTIONS AND CHAPBOOKS/ PAMPHLETS
Sidlaw House, South Street, Newtyle, Angus PH12 8UQ
Tel: 01828 650615
www.kettillonia.co.uk
Editor: James Robertson
Established 1999. New Scottish writing. The press aims 'to put "original, adventurous, neglected and rare writing" into print'.

KNIVES FORKS AND SPOONS
E-BOOKS, COLLECTIONS, ANTHOLOGIES AND CHAPBOOKS/ PAMPHLETS
theknivesforksandspoonspress@ hotmail.com
www.knivesforksandspoonspress.co.uk
Editor: Alec Newman
Established 2010. Publications available direct from publisher website; by post and email order; from chain bookshops and independent bookshops nationwide; at national and local

literary events; and from Amazon and other bookshop websites. Some online content (videos and audio) is also freely available to all. Knives Forks and Spoons was shortlisted for the Michael Marks Publisher of the Year Award (2010). **SUBMISSIONS:** During submissions windows, submit by email to theknivesforksandspoonspress@hotmail.com. Usually responds in over six months. No feedback offered with rejections. Authors receive free copies of the book. **WE SAY:** We saw *Oh-Zones* by Elizabeth-Jane Burnett, a 20-page pamphlet. The cover design, which prominently features tree bark, appears ambiguous until you've read the pamphlet, at which point it's revealed as simple yet effective. Contemporary environmental poetry with an urban edge.

LAGAN PRESS
COLLECTIONS
Verbal Arts Centre, Stable Lane & Mall Wall, Bishop Street Within, Derry-Londonderry BT48 6PU
028 7126 6946
info@laganpress.co
www.laganpress.co
Mixed form: also publishes non-fiction and novels. Looks for work of 'literary, artistic, social and cultural importance to the north of Ireland'. Irish and Ulster-Scots language work also welcomed.
See also: prose publishers p65

LAPWING PUBLICATIONS
COLLECTIONS AND CHAPBOOKS/PAMPHLETS, E-BOOKS
1, Ballysillan Drive, Belfast BT14 8HQ
lapwing.poetry@ntlworld.com
www.lapwingpoetry.com
Editor: Dennis Greig
Established 1988. Primarily

a poetry publisher, but does occasionally produce autobiographical memoirs and novellas. Publications available direct from publisher website; by post and email order and at author events, self-organised or in partnership. PDF books available for requested £5 donation.
SUBMISSIONS: Open to all within Western Europe (due to logistical costs). Submit by email to lapwing.poetry@ntlworld.com, ideally using Word doc format. Guidelines at www.lapwingpoetry.com/submissiondetails.htm. Usually responds within four weeks. Rejections may occasionally include unsolicited feedback. Authors receive free copies of the book.
WE SAY: We looked at the previews available on the Lapwing website. A very small press, the designs are kept simple and as a result are classic and contemporary (the covers are white, with the title, a small image, and some line art) and the press has varying style of poetry appearing in its pages, including some rather striking concrete poetry.

LEAFE PRESS
COLLECTIONS AND CHAPBOOKS/PAMPHLETS
xeqalan@hotmail.com
www.leafepress.com
Editor: Alan Baker
Established 2000. Publications available direct from publisher website; by post and email order; from chain bookshops nationwide; from independent bookshops; at national and local literary events; and from Amazon and other bookshop websites.
SUBMISSIONS: Submissions

currently by invitation only. Usually responds within four weeks. No feedback offered with rejections. Authors receive free copies of the book.

WE SAY: For an idea of the type of poetry that appeals to the editors, see what we say about *Litter Magazine*, p185.

For a fuller description of this press, see *Litter Magazine* (poetry magazine) p185

LIBERTIES PRESS

COLLECTIONS AND ANTHOLOGIES
140 Terenure Road North,
Dublin 6W, Ireland
01 905 6072
info@libertiespress.com
www.libertiespress.com
Founded in 2003 and billed as Ireland's leading independent publisher. Mostly publishes non-fiction and fiction (see p65) but also some poetry. Open to unsolicited submissions. See the website for full details.

See also: prose publishers p65

LONGBARROW PRESS

COLLECTIONS, ANTHOLOGIES AND CHAPBOOKS/PAMPHLETS
76 Holme Lane, Sheffield S6 4JW
longbarrowpress@gmail.com
www.longbarrowpress.com
Titles range across various formats, including pamphlets, boxes and CDs – not currently open to unsolicited submissions.

MARISCAT PRESS

COLLECTIONS, ANTHOLOGIES AND CHAPBOOKS/PAMPHLETS
10 Bell Place, Edinburgh EH3 5HT
0131 332 3451
hamish.whyte@btinternet.com
www.mariscatpress.com
Editors: Hamish Whyte, Diana Hendry

Established 1982. Publications available direct from publisher website; by post and email order; from selected/local chain bookshops; from independent bookshops; and at local literary events.

Mariscat Press won the 2015 Callum Macdonald Memorial Award for poetry pamphlet publishing.

SUBMISSIONS: Open to all. Submit by post (10 Bell Place, Edinburgh EH3 5HT) or by email (hamish.whyte@btinternet.com). Usually responds within one to three months. Rejections may occasionally include unsolicited feedback. Authors are paid royalties only, or an advance/fee plus royalties.

WE SAY: *The Empathetic Store* by Jackie Kay is a 35-page stapled A5 pamphlet. A plain textured card cover and simple design with quality cream paper for the contents. Kay's poems provide a narrative approach and transformative pieces. Ideal for commuters or readers who prefer quality over quantity. This pamphlet demonstrates Kay's poetry at its best.

MELOS PRESS

COLLECTIONS AND CHAPBOOKS/ PAMPHLETS
melos.press@btinternet.com
www.melospress.blogspot.co.uk
Editor: William Palmer
Established 2007. Publications available direct from publisher website; by post and email order; in chain bookshops nationwide; in independent bookshops; and on Amazon and other bookshop websites. Strictly poetry only.

SUBMISSIONS: Publication history

required. Submit by email to melos.press@btinternet.com. Usually responds within one to three months. Rejections may occasionally include unsolicited feedback. Authors receive free copies of their book.

WE SAY: Saddle-stitched pamphlets with plain card covers and white printer paper inside. We flicked through *Black and Blue*, a sequence of sonnets by Cathy Galvin, which was clean and clear – focusing on the words themselves as opposed to the aesthetic. With just six titles, the Melos range isn't the most diverse, but they're actively seeking submissions.

MICA PRESS
COLLECTIONS
47 Belle Vue Road, Wivenhow, Colchester, Essex CO7 9LD
info@micapress.co.uk
micapress.co.uk
Editor: Leslie Bell
Good quality press with worldwide distribution. Submissions welcome, but publications infrequent.

MUDFOG PRESS
COLLECTIONS AND ANTHOLOGIES

MOTHER'S MILK BOOKS
☆
E-BOOKS, COLLECTIONS, ANTHOLOGIES AND CHAPBOOKS/ PAMPHLETS
Based in Nottingham
teika@mothersmilkbooks.com
www.mothersmilkbooks.com
Editor: Teika Bellamy

Established 2011. Mixed form: also publishes fiction (short and long) and non-fiction – see p65. Publications available direct from publisher website; from independent bookshops; at local literary events; and from Amazon.

SUBMISSIONS: Open to all. During submissions windows, submit by email to teika@mothersmilkbooks. com. Submitters required to show proof of purchase from press. Usually responds within one to three months. The editors try to give as much useful feedback

with rejections as is possible within time constraints. Authors are paid a flat fee; royalties only; or an advance/fee plus royalties. They also receive free copies of the book.

For a fuller description of this press see prose publishers p65

c/o Beacon Guest, Chop Gate,
Stokesley TS9 7JS
contact@mudfog.co.uk
www.mudfog.co.uk
Editors: Pauline Plummer, Jo Heather
Established 1993. Mixed form: also
publishes prose (see p65).
Publications available direct from
the publisher website.
GENRES: Environmental writing.
SUBMISSIONS: Favours writers
in the Tees Valley, stretching
from Whitby to Sunderland,
west to Darlington. However
also occasionally publishes
writers outside this area. Submit
by post (Beacon Guest, Chop
Gate, Stokesley TS9 7JS) or by
email (contact@mudfog.co.uk).
Guidelines at www.mudfog.co.uk/
submissions/. Usually responds
within one to three months.
Rejections may occasionally
include unsolicited feedback.
Authors are able to buy a number
of their books at cost-price and sell
them at sales price.
**For a fuller description of the press,
see prose publishers p65**

NEGATIVE PRESS
COLLECTIONS
info@neg-press.com
www.neg-press.com
Publishes both poetry and prose
books. Visual and verbal creations,
and photobooks.
See also: prose publishers p65

NEON BOOKS
E-BOOKS, COLLECTIONS,
ANTHOLOGIES AND CHAPBOOKS/
PAMPHLETS
info@neonmagazine.co.uk
neonmagazine.co.uk
Editor: Krishan Coupland
Established 2006. Mixed form:
also publishes prose (see p65).
Publications available direct
from publisher website; from
independent bookshops; at local
literary events; and from Amazon.
All online content is freely available
to all. Neon chapbook *The
Mesmerist's Daughter* by Heidi
James won the 2015 Saboteur
Award for Best Novella.
GENRES: Literary and slipstream;
magical realism; experimental
forms.
SUBMISSIONS: Open to all. Submit
by email to subs@neonmagazine.
co.uk. Usually responds within one
to three months. Feedback given
to donors to/subscribers of *Neon*.
Writers are paid royalties only and
receive free copies of the book.
**For a fuller description of the
press, see *Neon Literary Magazine*
(mixed form) p158. See also prose
publishers p65**

NEW ISLAND
COLLECTIONS
16 Priory Office Park, Stillorgan,
County Dublin
+353 1 278 42 25
info@newisland.ie
newisland.ie/
Mixed form: also publishes drama,
fiction and Irish-focussed non-
fiction.
See also: prose publishers p65

NEXT REVIEW, THE
CHAPBOOKS/PAMPHLETS
Basement Flat, 116 Offord Road,
London N1 1PF
thenextreview@gmail.com
www.thenextreview.co.uk
Editor: Patrick Davidson Roberts
Available direct from publisher
website, at chain bookshops
nationwide, independent
bookshops and local literary events.
SUBMISSIONS: Publishes poets

discovered through *The Next Review* magazine. See p161.
WE SAY: The design of The Next Review poetry pamphlets are even simpler that of the magazine – similar paper, similar style, but stripped bare to let the words speak for themselves. See what We Say about *The Next Review* on p161.
For a fuller description of the press see *The Next Review* (mixed-form literary magazine) p161

NINE ARCHES PRESS ☆
E-BOOKS, COLLECTIONS AND ANTHOLOGIES
mail@ninearchespress.com
www.ninearchespress.com
Editors: Matt Merritt, Jane Commane
Established 2008. Publications available direct from publisher website; by post and email order; from chain bookshops and independent bookshops nationwide; at national and local literary events; and from Amazon and other bookshop websites. Nine Arches Press won the 2014 Saboteur Award for Most Innovative Publisher.
SUBMISSIONS: Open to all, during submissions windows. Submit through Submittable at ninearchespress.submittable. com/submit. Guidelines at ninearchespress.com/submissions. html. Usually responds within one to three months. No feedback offered with rejections. Contracts vary.
WE SAY: Nine Arches produce excellent books. *Kith* by Jo Bell is a perfect-bound, 74-page publication complete with a high-quality dust-cover. It has an abstract artistic cover design that lends itself well to the title:

the more you read, the more you understand. Made from quality materials and containing engaging poetry inspired by Bell's community and friends. Ideal for readers who wish to be immersed in various poetry techniques.
See also: *Under the Radar* (poetry magazine) p173

OFFA'S PRESS
COLLECTIONS AND ANTHOLOGIES
info@offaspress.co.uk
www.offaspress.co.uk
Publishes and promotes work by West Midland poets.

ORIGINAL PLUS
COLLECTIONS AND CHAPBOOKS/ PAMPHLETS
17 High Street, Maryport, Cumbria CA15 6BQ
smithsssj@aol.com
thesamsmith.webs.com
Editor: Sam Smith
Established 1996. Publications available direct from publisher website; and by post and email order.
SUBMISSIONS: Poets should preferably have some history of publication in *The Journal*. Submit by post (17 High Street, Maryport, CA15 6BQ) or by email (smithsssj@ aol.com). Usually responds within four weeks. Rejections may occasionally include unsolicited feedback. Writers can buy copies of their publication for resale at 33% discount.
For a fuller description of the press, see *The Journal* (poetry magazine) p185

OVERSTEPS BOOKS LTD
COLLECTIONS
6 Halwell House, South Pool, nr Kingsbridge, Devon TQ7 2RX

01548 531969
alwynmarriage@overstepsbooks.com
www.overstepsbooks.com
Editor: Alwyn Marriage
Established 1992. Publications available direct from publisher website; by post and email order; independent bookshops; at national and local literary events; and from bookshop websites.
SUBMISSIONS: Publication history required. Guidelines at www.overstepsbooks.com/submissions/. Usually responds within one to three months. Rejections may occasionally include unsolicited feedback. Authors receive free copies of the book.
WE SAY: *Lighting the Fire* by John Daniel is a 58-page poetry collection with an artistic, fun design – a red cover with a cartoon sketch of a fireplace. Oversteps' focus is on contemporary poetry, and they produce this to a high standard with contemporary design.

OYSTERCATCHER PRESS
CHAPBOOKS/PAMPHLETS
4 Lighthouse Close, Hunstanton, Norfolk PE36 6EL
oystercatcherpress@gmail.com
www.oystercatcherpress.com
Editor: Peter Hugh
Established 2007. Publications available direct from publisher website, and by post and email order. All online content is available to all. Offers an annual subscription of £25 for six pamphlets.
Oystercatcher Press won the 2008 Michael Marks Award for Outstanding UK Publisher of Poetry in Pamphlet Form.
SUBMISSIONS: Submissions by invitation only. Usually responds within one to three months. Rejections may occasionally include unsolicited feedback. Authors receive initial free copies of the book, plus a discount on all further copies.

PAEKAKARIKI PRESS
COLLECTIONS, ANTHOLOGIES AND CHAPBOOKS/PAMPHLETS
4 Mitre Ave, Walthamstow, London E17 6QG
07836 785505
matt@paekakarikipress.com
www.paekakarikipress.com
Established 2010. Publications available direct from publisher website; by post and email order; and from Amazon.
SUBMISSIONS: Open to all, but for a single author collection poems must be mostly unpublished. Submit by email to poetry@paekakarikipress.com.
Guidelines at paekakarikipress.com/?content=poetrysubmissions.html. Usually responds within four weeks. No feedback offered with rejections. Authors receive a small number of copies free of charge and others at trade price. If sales enter profit, then a 10% royalty pool is shared between creators, e.g. author, illustrator etc.
WE SAY: Paekakariki was originally established as a letterpress printer, in an effort to keep the skill of letterpress printing alive. They now produce all of their poetry publications through letterpress printing, which means that each book has a unique, handmade quality, made extremely well and with care.

PANKHEARST
COLLECTIONS, ANTHOLOGIES AND CHAPBOOKS/PAMPHLETS
editor@pankhearst.com
www.pankhearst.com

Editors: Evangeline Jennings, Lucy Middlesmass, Kate Garrett Established 2012. Mixed form: also publishes short stories and novels (see p65). Publications available in independent bookshops; at local literary events; and from Amazon and other bookshop websites. Also publishes one poem and one short story a week online.

Pankhearst was shortlisted for the 2015 Saboteur Award for Excellence in Independent Publishing: Best Novella.

SUBMISSIONS: Open to all. Guidelines at pankhearst.wordpress.com/general-information/ (the submission process varies, project to project). Usually responds within four weeks. Rejections may occasionally include unsolicited feedback. Writer payment varies by project, but writers are never asked to pay anything.

WE SAY: This publisher's products range from Kindle shorts to full-length collections and the odd novel or two. We had a nosey through one of their slim volumes, *No Love Lost*, which was a perfect-bound paperback brimming with delicious poetry and flash fiction – and we thought the black and white cover worked well. The lovely thing about this bunch is that they reinvest all revenue from your work into promotion and publicity, so despite the lack of advances and royalties, it's a great place to grow your platform.

See also: prose publishers p65

PARTHIAN BOOKS

E-BOOKS, COLLECTIONS, ANTHOLOGIES AND CHAPBOOKS/PAMPHLETS
426 Grove Building, Swansea University, Singleton Park, SA2 8PP
01792 606605
susieparthian@gmail.com;
c.houguez@gmail.com
www.parthianbooks.com
Editors: Susie Wild, Claire Houguez
Established 1993. Mixed form: also publishes fiction and non-fiction (see p65). Publications available direct from publisher website; from chain bookshops nationwide; from independent bookshops; at local literary events; and from Amazon and other bookshop websites.

Parthian Books' title *Forgotten Footprints* by John Harrison won the British Guild of Travel Writers' Best Narrative Award, 2014, and *Rhys Davies: A Writer's Life* by Meic Stephens won Wales Book of the Year 2014. Jemma King's *The Shape of a Forest* was shortlisted for the Dylan Thomas Prize in 2014.

SUBMISSIONS: Open to all. Submit by post to 426 Grove Building, Swansea University, Singleton Park, Swansea, SA2 8PP. Guidelines at www.parthianbooks.com/contact. Usually responds within one to three months. Rejections may occasionally include unsolicited feedback. Authors are paid an advance/fee plus royalties.

For a fuller description of this press see prose publishers p65

PATRICIAN PRESS

COLLECTIONS AND CHAPBOOKS/PAMPHLETS
51 Free Rodwell House, School Lane, Mistley, Manningtree CO11 1HW
07968 288651
patricia@patricianpress.com
www.patricianpress.com
Editor: Patricia Borlenghi
Established 2012. Mainly publishes fiction, but also some poetry books (see p65). Publications available direct from publisher website; from

selected/local chain bookshops; from independent bookshops; at local literary events; and from Amazon and other bookshop websites, including The Great British Bookshop website.
SUBMISSIONS: Open to new and unpublished writers without agents. Submit during submissions windows, by email (patricia@patricianpress.com) or via the form at www.patricianpress.com/submissions/ (guidelines at the same address). Usually responds within one to three months. Rejections may occasionally include unsolicited feedback. Author contributions are needed for publications. Authors are paid royalties only.
For a fuller description of this press, including a cover image, see prose publishers p65

PEEPAL TREE PRESS
COLLECTIONS, ANTHOLOGIES AND CHAPBOOKS/PAMPHLETS
contact@peepaltreepress.com
www.peepaltreepress.com
Editors: Jeremy Poynting, Kwame Dawes, Jacob Ross, Kadija Sesay
Established 1986. Mixed form: also publishes short stories and novels (see p65). Specialises in Caribbean and Black British writing. Publications available direct from publisher website; by post and email order; from chain bookshops and independent bookshops nationwide; at national and local literary events; and from Amazon and other bookshop websites. Peepal Tree title *Sounding Ground* by Vladimir Lucien was overall winner for The OCM Bocas Prize for Caribbean Literature 2015.
SUBMISSIONS: Open to all, specialising in Caribbean and Black

British writing. Submit through Submittable at peepaltreepress.submittable.com (guidelines at same address). Usually responds within four to six months. Rejections may occasionally include unsolicited feedback, and some manuscripts by UK-based authors are offered a (free) in-depth reader report through the press's Inscribe Writer Development Programme Authors are paid royalties only.
WE SAY: A prolific publisher of exclusively Caribbean and Black British writing with over 300 titles to its name, from memoir and fiction to historical studies and literary criticism. We looked at *Wife*, a poetry collection by Tiphanie Yanique, which was formatted beautifully inside but admittedly had a few cover Issues, in the form of low resolution stock photography and poorly aligned blurb text. The submission guidelines are buried on the website, and there are several submission portals depending on what genre an author writes – and whether they're based in the UK or not.
See also: prose publishers p65

PENNED IN THE MARGINS
COLLECTIONS AND ANTHOLOGIES
Toynbee Studios, 28 Commercial Street, London E1 6AB
020 7375 0121
info@pennedinthemargins.co.uk
www.pennedinthemargins.co.uk
Editor: Tom Chivers
Established 2006. Mixed form: also publishes prose (see p65). Publications available direct from publisher website; by post and email order; from selected/local chain bookshops; from independent bookshops; at local literary events; and from Amazon.

Penned in the Margins won Most Innovative Publisher at the Saboteur Awards 2015.

SUBMISSIONS: Publication history required. Submit by email to submissions@pennedinthemargins.co.uk. Usually responds within one to three months. Rejections may occasionally include unsolicited feedback. Authors are paid royalties only.

WE SAY: High-concept cover art, unique titles and an effortlessly cool website make this high on our list of favourite indie presses. The perfect-bound paperbacks are slim and elegant – we admired *The Story Of No*'s funky cover and its handbag-friendly size (smaller than A5). The poetry within is experimental, modern and appropriates pop culture to great effect. Thick creamy paper tops off the stylish package.

See also: prose publishers p65

PINDROP PRESS

COLLECTIONS

Gardoussel, 30940 St Andre de Valborgne, France

pindroppress@gmail.com

www.pindroppress.com

Editor: Sharon Black

Established 2010. Publications available direct from publisher website; from independent bookshops; at national and local literary events; and from Amazon. Originally based in the UK, Pindrop Press editor Jo Hemmant passed the reins to France-based Sharon Black in early 2016.

SUBMISSIONS: Publication history required. Submit during submissions windows, by email to pindroppress@gmail.com. Usually responds within one to three months. No feedback offered with rejections. Authors receive free copies of the book.

PLATYPUS PRESS

E-BOOKS, COLLECTIONS

enquiries@platypuspress.co.uk

www.platypuspress.co.uk

Editors: Michelle Tudor, Peter Barnfather

Established 2015. Primarily a poetry press, but does also publish short story collections (see p65). Publications available from Amazon and other bookshop websites.

SUBMISSIONS: Open to all. Submit by email to submissions@platypuspress.co.uk. Usually responds within four weeks. No feedback offered with rejections. Writers are paid royalties only and receive free copies of the book.

WE SAY: The relatively new Platypus Press has an eye for design. A browse through the catalogue shows elegant photo covers with judicious use of accented covers, slim modern fonts and a preference for strong contemporary writing. We weren't able to get our hands on a print version, but we hope the materials live up to the designs.

See also: prose publishers p65

POETRY LONDON ☆

ANTHOLOGIES

The Albany, Deptford

London SE8 4AG

admin@poetrylondon.co.uk

www.poetrylondon.co.uk

Editors: Jess Chandler, Ahren Warner, Tim Dooley, Martha Kapos

Established 1988. Publications available direct from publisher website and from chain bookshops nationwide.

For a fuller description of this

press, see *Poetry London* (poetry magazine) p189

POETRY SPACE ☆
COLLECTIONS, ANTHOLOGIES AND CHAPBOOKS/PAMPHLETS
www.poetryspace.co.uk
Editor: Susan Sims
Publications available direct from publisher website and from Amazon.
SUBMISSIONS: Open to all. Submit by email to susan@poetryspace.co.uk. Guidelines at www.poetryspace.co.uk/about/. Usually responds within one to three months. Rejections may occasionally include unsolicited feedback. Authors receive free copies of the book.
For a fuller description of this press see *Poetry Space Showcase* (poetry e-zine) p189

PS PUBLISHING
COLLECTIONS, ANTHOLOGIES AND CHAPBOOKS/PAMPHLETS
Grosvenor House, 1 New Road, Hornsea, East Yorkshire
01964 537575
nickycrowther@pspublishing.co.uk
www.pspublishing.co.uk
Editor: Nicky Crowther
Established 1991. Mainly publishes fiction (see p65), but also some poetry. Publications available direct from publisher website; from Amazon and other bookshop websites; and at the British Science Fiction Convention and British Fantasy Convention.
PS Publishing won The Karl Wagner Award at the British Fantasy Awards 2012.
SUBMISSIONS: Submissions welcome by invitation only or from agents, during submissions windows. Submit by email to nickycrowther@pspublishing.co.uk. Usually responds within one to three months. Rejections may occasionally include unsolicited feedback. Authors may receive a flat fee; royalties only; an advance/fee plus royalties; and/or free copies of the book (depending on agreement).
See also: prose publishers p65

RACK PRESS
CHAPBOOKS/PAMPHLETS
The Rack, Kinnerton, Presteigne, Powys, Wales LD8 2PF
07817 424560
rackpress@nicholasmurray.co.uk
www.rackpress.blogspot.com
Editor: Nicholas Murray
Established 2015. Primarily publishes poetry, but also publishes some criticism (see p65). Publications available direct from publisher website; by post and email order; from chain bookshops and independent bookshops nationwide; at national and local literary events; and from bookshop websites.
Rack Press won the 2014 Michael Marks Award for Publisher of the Year.
SUBMISSIONS: Open to all. Submit by post (The Rack, Kinnerton, Presteigne, Powys, Wales LD8 2PF) or by email (rackpress@nicholasmurray.co.uk). Guidelines at www.nicholasmurray.co.uk/About_Rack_Press.html. Usually responds within four weeks. Rejections may occasionally include unsolicited feedback. Authors receive free copies of the book., plus other copies at discount price for sale at readings etc.
WE SAY: Rack Press pamphlets are simple affairs, with clean, cream covers; and a bold font for the

title and poet name. The name of the press takes a backseat in the branding, as they focus on the poetry. However, the press does also sell limited sets of pamphlets, signed by the poets and numbered accordingly, which we think adds a 'must read now' edge.

See also: prose publishers p65

RED CEILINGS PRESS, THE

E-BOOKS, CHAPBOOKS/
PAMPHLETS
53 High Street, New Mills, High Peak, Derbyshire SK22 4BR
theredceilings@gmail.com
www.theredceilingspress.co.uk
Editor: Mark Cobley
Publications available direct from publisher website and from the poets themselves.
SUBMISSIONS: Chapbooks from UK poets only; e-books open to all. Publication history required. Submit by email to theredceilings@gmail.com. Guidelines on the website. Author contributions needed. Usually responds within one to three months. No feedback offered with rejections. Authors receive at least ten copies of the book.
WE SAY: We looked at the PDF version of *anyone for anymore* by Rufo Quintavalle. A simple design with an abstract photograph on the cover, reflecting its content. The publication is modern and experimental, the poem building up by one word, and one line per page to begin with. An experimental piece that challenges conventional poetry and is smartly presented. Similar to the works of Gertrude Stein. A press that's ideal for poets whose work doesn't fit the traditional mould.

RED SQUIRREL PRESS

COLLECTIONS, ANTHOLOGIES AND CHAPBOOKS/PAMPHLETS
Briery Hill Cottage, Stannington, Morpeth NE61 6ES
info@redsquirrelpress.com
www.redsquirrelpress.com
Editor: Sheila Wakefield
Established 2006. Mainly publishes poetry, but also some prose (see p65). Publications available direct from publisher website; by post and email order; from chain bookshops nationwide; from independent bookshops; at national and local literary events; from Amazon and other bookshop websites; and from Inpress.com. Red Squirrel was shortlisted for the Callum Macdonald Memorial Award 2015.
SUBMISSIONS: Open to all. Submit by post to Briery Hill Cottage, Stannington, Morpeth NE61 6ES. Guidelines at www.redsquirrelpress.com/submissions. Usually responds in over six months. No feedback offered with rejections. Authors receive free copies of the book.
WE SAY: Red Squirrel press has a reputation for promoting its poets well, and working with local groups to create events. Its print output doesn't have a strong branded feel – title design varies from book to book – but the formatting is well done and the materials good quality.
See also: prose publishers p65

RIALTO, THE/BRIDGE PAMPHLETS ☆

PAMPHLETS/CHAPBOOKS
PO Box 309 Aylsham, Norwich NR11 6LN
info@therialto.co.uk
www.therialto.co.uk

Editor: Michael Mackmin.
Assistant Editors: Rishi Dastidar, Holly Hopkins, Fiona Moore, Abigail Parry
Established 1984. Publications available direct from publisher website; from selected/local chain bookshops; and from independent bookshops.
Rialto title *What I Saw* by Laura Scott won the 2014 Michael Marks Pamphlet Award.
SUBMISSIONS: Currently by invitation only, but with plans to open a submission programme for pamphlets. Please keep checking the website, www.therialto.co.uk. Chapbook authors receive all profits.
WE SAY: We looked at *What I Saw* by Laura Scott. Printed on quality cream paper, with a line sketch of the Thames and London skyline on the cover. A light, but compelling look that matches a light but compelling selection of poems. Stapled spine and lovely texture to the paper.
See also: *The Rialto* **(poetry magazine) p192**

ROCKINGHAM PRESS
COLLECTIONS
11 Musley Lane, Ware, Herts SG12 7EN
01920 467 868
rockpress@ntlworld.com
www.inpressbooks.co.uk
Editor: David Perman
Established 1991. Primarily publishes poetry, but also some non-fiction on Hertfordshire local history. Publications available by post and email order; at local literary events; from Amazon; and from www.inpressbooks.co.uk.
SUBMISSIONS: Submissions by invitation only, to rockpress@ntlworld.com. Usually responds within one to three months. Rejections may occasionally include unsolicited feedback. Authors are paid royalties only.
WE SAY: *More new and collected poems* by Lotte Kramer is a perfect-bound 411-page poetry publication with a simple design. Plain cover, with a photo of the poet, and plentry of blurb on the back. This collection is a nostalgic tour of Germany and England, with poems focussing on family and nature within both countries. The book includes a good introduction, some marketing of other titles and well-formatted poems.

ROUTE PUBLISHING LTD
COLLECTIONS
34 Banks Avenue, Pontefract WF8 4DR
01977 793442
info@route-online.com
www.route-online.com
Editor: Ian Daley
Established 2000. Primarily publishes non-fiction above other prose (see p65) and poetry. Publications available direct from publisher website; by post and email order; from chain bookshops nationwide; from independent bookshops; at national and local literary events; and from Amazon and other bookshop websites. Route has been shortlisted for the Pen/Ackerley Prize (2008); the James Tait Black Memorial Prize for Fiction (2011); NME Book of the Year (2015); and the Penderyn Prize (Music Book of the Year) (2015).
GENRES: Literary fiction; biography and true stories; music, stage and screen; and sports and leisure.
SUBMISSIONS: During submissions windows. Guidelines at www.route-online.com/submissions. Usually responds within four to six months,

with feedback only if an SAE is provided. No feedback offered with rejections. Authors receive a flat fee, or royalties only, or an advance/fee plus royalties.
For a fuller description of this press, see prose publishers p65

SACRISTY PRESS

COLLECTIONS
PO Box 612, Durham DH1 9HT
0191 303 8 313
enquiries@sacristy.co.uk
www.sacristy.co.uk
Editor: Thomas Ball
Established 2011. Primarily publishes non-fiction, but also some novels (see p65) and poetry. Publications available direct from publisher website; from selected/local chain bookshops; from independent bookshops; at local literary events; and from Amazon and other bookshop websites.
GENRES: Historical fiction; history; spirituality and beliefs.
SUBMISSIONS: Open to all. All submission information at www.sacristy.co.uk/info/authors. Author contributions needed. Usually responds within one to three months. Rejections may occasionally include unsolicited feedback. Authors are paid royalties only.
See also: prose publishers p65

SALMON POETRY

E-BOOKS, COLLECTIONS AND ANTHOLOGIES, LITERARY CRITICISM
Knockeven, Cliffs of Moher, County Clare, Ireland
info@salmonpoetry.com
www.salmonpoetry.com
Editor: Jessie Lendennie
Established 1981. Publications available direct from publisher website; by post and email order; from chain bookshops and independent bookshops nationwide; at national and local literary events; and from Amazon and other bookshop websites. Salmon Poetry was one of five finalists for the 2015 AWP Small Press Publisher Award.
SUBMISSIONS: Publication history required. During submissions windows, submit by post (Knockeven, Cliffs of Moher, Co. Clare, Ireland) or by email (info@salmonpoetry.com). Usually responds within four to six months. Rejections may occasionally include unsolicited feedback. Authors are paid royalties only and receive free copies of the book.

SEIN UND WERDEN BOOKS

COLLECTIONS
9 Dorris Street, Manchester M19 2TP
seinundwerden@gmail.com
www.kissthewitch.co.uk/seinundwerden/sein.html
Editor: Rachel Kendall
Established 2004. Mixed form: also publishes prose (see p65). Publications available from website.
GENRES: Crime/thriller/mystery; fantasy/sci-fi; horror; literary fiction; surreal; art, fashion and photography; music, stage and screen; travel.
SUBMISSIONS: Open to all. Submit by email to seinundwerden@gmail.com. Guidelines at www.kissthewitch.co.uk/seinundwerden/submissions.html. Usually responds within one to three months. Rejections may occasionally include unsolicited feedback.
For a fuller description of this press see *Sein und Werden* (e-zine) p167. See also prose publishers p65

SEREN BOOKS ☆

COLLECTIONS, ANTHOLOGIES AND
CHAPBOOKS/PAMPHLETS
57 Nolton Street, Cardiff,
Wales CF31 3AE
01656 663018
seren@serenbooks.com
serenbooks.com
Editor: Amy Wack
Established 1963. Mixed form: also
publishes fiction and non-fiction
(see p65). Publications available
direct from publisher website;
by post and email order; from
chain bookshops nationwide;
from independent bookshops; at
national and local literary events;
and from Amazon.
Winner of the Costa Poetry Award
2014.
SUBMISSIONS: Open to all. Submit
by post to 57 Nolton Street,
Bridgend CF31 3AE. Guidelines
at www.serenbooks.com/seren/
submissions-policy. Usually responds
within one to three months.
Rejections may occasionally include
unsolicited feedback. Authors are
paid an advance/fee plus royalties
and receive free copies of the book,
as well as other copies at a discount
price.
WE SAY: Seren is one of the most
established and respected poetry
publishing houses, and certainly
one for poets to aspire to. *My
Family and Other Superheroes* by
Jonathan Edwards is a 72-page
award-winning publication with an
artistic design, available in both
print and digital format. Provides
nostalgia and naivety through the
poet's voice. Various poetic forms
are used throughout, including
free-verse; ideal for readers who
wish to escape into a good book.
Mslexia recommends.
See also: *Poetry Wales* (poetry
magazine) p190 and prose
publishers p65

SHEARSMAN BOOKS LTD

COLLECTIONS, ANTHOLOGIES AND
CHAPBOOKS/PAMPHLETS
50 Westons Hill Drive, Emersons
Green, BS16 7DF
0117 957 2957
editor@shearsman.coom
www.shearsman.com
Editor: Tony Frazer
Established 1981/2003. Publications
available direct from publisher
website; by post and email
order; from selected/local chain
bookshops; from independent
bookshops; and from Amazon
and other bookshop websites.
Shearman Books is a multi-award-
nominated press, and has been
nominated for the Forward Prize
for Best First Collection (2011,
2012); the Forward Prize for Best
Collection (2012, 2015); Jerwood
Aldeburgh First Collection Prize
(2007); the Popescu Translation
Prize (2009, 2001, 2013); the
Michael Murphy Award for First
Collections (2015) and the Michael
Marks Awards for Pamphlets
(Publisher Award) (2013, 2014).
SUBMISSIONS: Publication
history required. Submit during
submissions windows, by post
(Shearsman Books Ltd, 50
Westons Hill Drive, Emersons
Green, Bristol BS16 7DF), by
email (editor@shearsman.com) or
via the online PDF submissions
portal (www.shearsman.com/
how-to-contact-shearsman-books).
Usually responds within four to
six months. No feedback offered
with rejections. Authors are paid
royalties only and receive free
copies of the book.
For a fuller description of this

press, including what They Say, see *Shearsman Magazine* (poetry magazine) **p193**

see *Shearsman Magazine* (poetry magazine) **p193**

SHOESTRING PRESS
COLLECTIONS, ANTHOLOGIES AND CHAPBOOKS/PAMPHLETS
19 Devonshire Avenue, Beeston,

SIDEKICK BOOKS
ANTHOLOGIES, CHAPBOOKS/ PAMPHLETS, POETRY-BASED MIXED CONTENT
contact@drfulminare.com
www.sidekickbooks.com
Editors: Kirsten Irving, Jon Stone

Established 2009. Primarily publishes poetry, with mixed content including poems with essays, poets teamed with illustrators, poetry comics etc. Publications available direct from publisher website; from independent bookshops; and at local literary events. All online content is available to all. Sidekick title *Riotous* won Best Collaboration at the Saboteur Awards 2014.
SUBMISSIONS: Open during submissions windows. Usually responds within four to six months. Rejections may occasionally include unsolicited feedback. Writers receive a flat fee and free copies of the book.
WE SAY: We looked at *Birdbook: Farmland, Heathland, Mountain, Moorland*, in which poets 'poemify' birds of Britain. The book is printed on high quality materials with a striking silhouette image cover, and filled with glorious illustrations and poems in a range of styles.
See also: *Fuselit* (poetry magazine) **p184**

THEY SAY

Bubbling up from the infernal book lab of mad alchemist Dr Fulminare, Sidekick Books publish collaborations and innovative anthologies – volatile fusions that blend poetry with visual art and critical writing, taking in pop culture, the natural world, science, dinosaurs, comics, video games and more besides, with a dash of formal experimentation for good measure. Poets Kirsten Irving and Jon Stone are the commissioning editors, but the writers who've contributed to the Sidekick catalogue are multifarious and ever-increasing in number.

Nottingham NG9 1BS
0115 925 1827
info@shoestringpress.co.uk
www.shoestring-press.com
Editor: John Lucas
Mainly publishes poetry, but also some prose (see p65). Publications available direct from publisher website; by post and email order; from independent bookshops; at national and local literary events; and from Amazon.
Shoestring titles have been shortlisted for Vondel Prize for Translation and for the Cricket Club Writers Book of the Year.
SUBMISSIONS: Submit by invitation only. Usually responds within four weeks. No feedback offered with rejections. Authors are paid royalties only and receive free copies of the book.
WE SAY: A stalwart of poetry publishing, Shoestring has recently levelled up in terms of design and quality – which is not to say that the publications were ever low quality (they weren't). But there's a notable difference between the more recent books published (eg *A Night of Islands* by Angus Martin) and the older ones. The design is more modern and cleaner, with clearer formatting that looks more stylish on the page. This is a press widely acknowledged to be publishing important work, and doing it well.
See also: prose publishers p65

SILHOUETTE PRESS
COLLECTIONS AND CHAPBOOKS/ PAMPHLETS
ICE, Parkside, Coventry CV1 2NE
adam.steiner@silhouettepress.co.uk
www.silhouettepress.co.uk
Editor: Gary Sykes-Blythe
Established 2012. Publishes fiction (see p65) and poetry. Publications available direct from publisher website; by post and email order; from independent bookshops; and from bookshop websites.
SUBMISSIONS: Open to all. Submit through Submittable at silhouettepress.submittable.com/submit/40008. Guidelines at same address. Usually responds within four to six months. Rejections may occasionally include unsolicited feedback. Authors are paid royalties only.
For a fuller description of this press, see *Here Comes Everyone* (mixed-form literary magazine) p146. See also prose publishers p65

SMITH|DOORSTOP BOOKS ☆
E-BOOKS, COLLECTIONS, ANTHOLOGIES AND CHAPBOOKS/ PAMPHLETS
The Poetry Business, Bank Street Arts, 32-40 Bank Street, Sheffield S1 2DS
0114 346 3037
office@poetrybusiness.co.uk
www.poetrybusiness.co.uk
Editors: Ann Sansom, Pete Sansom
Established 1986. Publications available direct from publisher website; by post and email order; and at Cornerhouse (Manchester) and Salts Mill (Saltaire). smithldoorstop won the 2012 Michael Marks publisher award.
SUBMISSIONS: Open to all, during submissions windows.
Submit by post to The Poetry Business, Bank Street Arts, 32-40 Bank Street, Sheffield, S1 2DS. Online submissions accepted only from overseas writers (see www.poetrybusiness.co.uk/north-menu/international-submissions). Full guidelines at www.poetrybusiness.co.uk/north-menu/submissions. Usually responds within one to

three months. No feedback offered with rejection. Authors receive free copies of their books. Only book authors (not pamphlet) receive royalties.

WE SAY: Long-established, with some big names on its author list,

smithldoorstop's publications have a design formula that works, with a look and feel to them that speak of excellent materials. The formatting is tidy and the covers have plenty of white space, with images restricted to the lower half of the

SINE WAVE PEAK

COLLECTIONS, ANTHOLOGIES AND CHAPBOOKS/PAMPHLETS
114 Sandy Lane, Cholton, Manchester M21 8TZ
www.sinewavepeak.com
Editor: Luke Allan

Established 2011. Poetry and philosophy/criticism. Available direct from publisher website and at independent bookshops. Winner of the Creative Futures Award, NALD, 2012.
GENRES: Emphasis on philosophy and typography.
SUBMISSIONS: Open to all. Submit by post (114 Sandy Lane, Cholton, Manchester M21 8TZ) or by email (luke@sinewavepeak. com). Usually responds within four weeks. A rejection may occasionally include unsolicited feedback. Authors receive copies of the book.
WE SAY: Extremely high quality publications. Both hardcover and paperback have very simple, white designs on the cover, with folded flaps. The paper is thick and textured, and the formatting clean and sophisticated, with light illustration on occasion.
See also: *Quait* **(poetry magazine) p191**

THEY SAY

sine wave peak specialises in formally innovative and experimental poetry. The press was founded in 2012 by Luke Allan and currently publishes from Manchester (before that Edinburgh, and before that Newcastle). Recent titles include works by Jerome Rothenberg, Hannah Lowe, and Thomas A Clark; books by Tom Betteridge, Kathryn Gerard, Sam Riviere, and Kathleen Jamie are forthcoming. Hand-sewn in limited editions, each edition is 'rested' in the weeks leading up to publication in a place chosen by the poet. There is a particular attention to typography, design, and the book as a multisensory experience.

page while the title and author text appears at the top. The books look rather more academic than many of the presses these days, but haven't dated.
See also: *The North Magazine* (poetry magazine) p187

SMOKESTACK BOOKS
POETRY COLLECTIONS AND ANTHOLOGIES
1 Lake Terrace, Grewelthorpe, Ripon, North Yorkshire HG4 3BU
01765 658917
info@smokestack-books.co.uk
www.smokestack-books.co.uk
Editor: Andy Croft
Established 2003. Publications available direct from publisher website; by post and email order; at chain bookshops and independent bookshops nationwide; at national and local literary events; and from Amazon and other bookshop websites. Smokestack poet Steve Ely's collection, *Oswald's Book of Hours*, was shortlisted for the 2013 Forward Best First Collection and shortlisted for the 2014 Ted Hughes Award.
SUBMISSIONS: Publication history required. Submit by post (1 Lake Terrace, Grewelthorper, Ripon, North Yorkshire HG4 3BU) or by email (info@smokestack-books. co.uk). Guidelines at smokestack-books.co.uk/publish.php. Usually responds within four weeks. Rejections may occasionally include unsolicited feedback. Author payment in the form of free copies of the book.
WE SAY: Smokestack Books looks for work that is out of fashion, radical and left-field, and champions poets 'working a long way from the metropolitan centres of cultural authority'. Very much a publisher for the people, but without the bells and whistles of looking a bit punk about it. In fact, the Smokestack design is rather staid, with glossy covers and decent quality materials, and a cover design that is usually an image topped and tailed by the title (top of the page) and author (bottom of the page) against a grey background. This text can sometimes look a little clunky and squashed, but the formatting within the publications is smart and uncluttered.

SOARING PENGUIN PRESS
COLLECTIONS, ANTHOLOGIES AND CHAPBOOKS/PAMPHLETS
4 Florence Terrace, London SW15 3RU
submissions@soaringpenguinpress.com
www.soaringpenguinpress.com
Editors: John Anderson, Ruth O'Callaghan
Established 2012. Mainly publishes fiction (see p65). Publications available direct from publisher website; by post and email order; from selected/local chain bookshops; from independent bookshops; at national literary events; and from Amazon and other bookshop websites. Title *To End All Wars* was nominated for two Eisner Awards: Best Anthology and Best Non-fiction Title.
SUBMISSIONS: Open to all. Submit by post (4 Florence Terrace, London SW15 3RU) or by email (submissions@ soaringpenguinpress. com). Guidelines at www. soaringpenguinpress.com/ submissions/. Usually responds within four to six months or more. Rejections may occasionally

include unsolicited feedback. Writers are paid royalties only, and receive free copies of the books and discount purchase price on future copies.

See also: *Meanwhile* (mixed-form literary magazine) p155 and prose publishers p65

SOUNDSWRITE PRESS

COLLECTIONS, ANTHOLOGIES, AND CHAPBOOKS/PAMPHLETS
52 Holmfield Road,
Leicester LE2 1SA
0116 270 2661
soundswrite@ntlworld.com
www.soundswritepress.co.uk
Editors: varies

Established 2005. Publications available direct from publisher website and at local literary events.
SUBMISSIONS: Currently accepts submissions by invitation only – further information at soundswritepress. co.uk/submissions.html. Rejections may include occasional unsolicited feedback. Author payment in the form of free copies of the book.
WE SAY: We looked at *Beyond the Tune* by Sarah James, a 31-page A5 chapbook with a simple design. The poems are printed on high-quality cream paper; the cover is glossy and attrative. The poems are subtly nostalgic, referring to past experiences and stories, and the writing is contemporary and descriptive.

sounds*write*
Anthology of contemporary poetry

THEY SAY

SOUNDSWRITE PRESS is a small independent women's poetry press based in Leicester, which promotes first collections and anthologies. The press was established in 2005 by Karin Koller and Pat Corina. Over the past ten years the press has published four anthologies featuring poets attending Soundswrite, an open group for women in the East Midlands enthusiastic about all aspects of poetry. In addition the press has published one full collection and four single-author poetry pamphlets, all of which have received positive reviews. Further information can be found on the website: www. soundswritepress.co.uk

58

SOUTHWORD EDITIONS ☆
CHAPBOOKS/PAMPHLETS
Munster Literature Centre, Frank
O'Connor House, 84 Douglas Street,
Cork, Ireland
+353 21 431 2955
info@munsterlit.ie
www.munsterlit.ie
Editors: Patrick Cotter,
Danielle McLaughlin,
Matthew Sweeney, Colm Breathnach
Established 2001. Publications
available direct from publisher
website; by post and email order;
at national and local literary events;
and from Amazon.
SUBMISSIONS: Open to all, during
submissions windows – chapbook
publication comes as part of
the Fool for Poetry competition.
Guidelines at www.munsterlit.ie/
Fool%20for%20Poetry.html. Usually
responds within one to three
months. No feedback offered with
rejections. Authors are paid a flat
fee and receive free copies of the
book.
**For a fuller description of this press,
see *Southword Journal* (mixed-
output literary e-zine) p169**

STONEWOOD PRESS
COLLECTIONS, ANTHOLOGIES AND
CHAPBOOKS/PAMPHLETS
97 Benefield Road, Oundle,
Peterborough PE8 4EU
0845 456 4838
stonewoodpress@gmail.com
www.stonewoodpress.co.uk
Editor: Martin Parker
Established 2011. Publications
available direct from publisher
website; from chain bookshops
and independent bookshops
nationwide; and from Amazon and
other bookshop websites.
SUBMISSIONS: Open to all.
Submit by post to 97 Benefield

Road, Oundle, Peterborough,
PE8 4EU. See guidelines at www.
stonewoodpress.co.uk/about/
submissions/. Usually responds
within one to three months.
Rejections may occasionally
include unsolicited feedback.
Authors are paid royalties only and
receive free copies of the book.
WE SAY: A boutique publisher
with a petite catalogue of a dozen
titles. *Small Grass*, the special
edition poetry collection we pored
over, was a perfect-bound, A6
hardcover in a striking slipcase. The
vivid orange cover with silver title
and grass graphic was incredibly
eye-catching, and the short
poetry inside, paired with black
and white illustrations, was dainty
and satisfying. Exceptionally well
presented.
See also: prose publishers p65

STRUCTO PRESS
CHAPBOOKS/PAMPHLETS
editor@structomagazine.co.uk
www.structomagazine.co.uk
Editor: Euan Monaghan
Established 2008. Mixed form:
also publishes fiction chapbooks
(see p65). Publications available
direct from publisher website; from
independent bookshops; and from
bookshop websites.
GENRES: Slipstream.
SUBMISSIONS: Open to all, during
submissions windows only. See
guidelines at structomagazine.
co.uk/submissions/.
**For a fuller description of this
press, see *Structo* (mixed-output
literary e-zine) p171. See also prose
publishers p65**

SYNCHRONISE WITCHES PRESS
ANTHOLOGIES AND CHAPBOOKS/
PAMPHLETS

16 Mayfield Road, Manchester
M16 8FT
07876 410543
www.cherrystyles.co.uk
Editor: Cherry Styles
Established 2012. Mixed form:
also publishes fiction (see p65).
Publications available direct from
publisher website; by post and
email order; from independent
bookshops; at national and local
literary events; at zine fairs; and in
art bookshops.
The press was shortlisted for the
Turn The Page artists' book award,
2015.
GENRES: Poetry; art, fashion and
photography; biography and true
stories; music, stage and screen;
society, education and politics.
SUBMISSIONS: Open to women
writers only. Submit by email
(thechapess@gmail.com) or via
online form (cherrystyles.co.uk/the-
chapess/). Usually responds within
one to three months. Rejections
may occasionally include
unsolicited feedback.
**For a fuller description of this
press, see *The Chapess* (mixed-form
magazine) p137. See also prose
publishers p65**

TALL-LIGHTHOUSE PRESS
COLLECTIONS AND CHAPBOOKS/
PAMPHLETS
22 Twigden Court, Luton LU3 2RL
01582 848797
tall.lighthouse@outlook.com
www.tall-lighthouse.co.uk
Editor: Gareth Lewis
Established 1999. Primarily
publishes pamphlets. Publications
available direct from publisher
website. Titles from tall-lighthouse
have been on various Michael
Marks shortlists for Best Pamphlet
of the Year over the course of the

award, including in 2012 for Ben
Parker's *The Escape Artists*. Harry
Man's *Lift* (2013) has also won or
been nominated for various poetry
awards.
SUBMISSIONS: Open to all, during
submissions windows. Submit by
post (22 Twigden Court, Luton LU3
2RL) or by email (tall.lighthouse@
outlook.com). Guidelines at www.
tall-lighthouse.co.uk/submissions.
html. Authors are paid royalties
only and receive free copies of
the book. Usually responds within
one to three months, and tries to
offer feedback with all rejections,
especially to work of exceptional
quality.
WE SAY: tall-lighthouse's
pamphlets are neat affairs, and
somewhat surprising. We looked
at Josephine Corcoran's *The
Misplaced House*, 36 pages long
with a glossy cover and perfect
bound. The materials are high
quality – higher than you'll often
see for pamphlets – and the
formatting is clean and accessible.
The cover design includes
professional blurb and a photo
image that gives the impression
of a more domestic collection
of poems than this is (a couple
of reviews note that they were
wrongfooted by this, and pleased
to discover politically charged,
darker poems than expected).

TANGERINE PRESS
COLLECTIONS
18 Riverside Road, Garratt Business
Park, London SW17 0BA
michael@eatmytangerine.com
www.eatmytangerine.com
Mixed form, including
photography, poetry and fiction
(see p65).
See also: prose publishers p65

TELLTALE PRESS

ANTHOLOGIES AND CHAPBOOKS/
PAMPHLETS
The Hive, 66 High Street,
Lewes BN7 1XG
editors@telltalepress.co.uk
www.telltalepress.co.uk
Established 2014. First pamphlets
only. Publications available direct
from publisher website; by post
and email order; from independent
bookshops; and at readings.
SUBMISSIONS: Submission by
invitation only – all poets are
members of the press. Full
details of this unusual model
on the website. Responses are
always personal, depending on
circumstances, but feedback on
work is not given.
WE SAY: Saddle-stitched A5
pamphlets on plain white printer
paper, wrapped in nicely illustrated
sleeves with quirky collage designs.
The production cost was probably
quite low, but since the pamphlets
are designed to be used as poetry
calling cards, this makes sense –
the main benefit of this press is in
the sense of community among the
Telltale authors, and in the way it
acts as a stepping stone to larger
deals.

TEMPLAR POETRY

COLLECTIONS, ANTHOLOGIES AND
CHAPBOOKS/PAMPHLETS
58 Dale Road, Matlock, Derbyshire
DE4 3NB
01629 582500
info@templarpoetry.com
www.templarpoetry.com
Regular pamphlet publication as
part of their Templar Quarterly
Portfolio awards, with launches at
Keats House.
See also: *Iota Poetry* **(poetry
magazine) p185**

TEST CENTRE

COLLECTIONS AND ANTHOLOGIES
77a Greenwood Road, London
E8 1NT
07870 646488
admin@testcentre.org.uk
www.testcentre.org.uk
Editors: Jess Chandler, Will Shutes
Established 2011. Mainly publishes
poetry, but also some prose (see
p65). Publications available direct
from publisher website; from
selected/local chain bookshops;
from independent bookshops; and
at local literary events.
Test Centre was nominated for
Most Innovative Publisher at the
Saboteur Awards 2015.
SUBMISSIONS: Open to all.
Submit by post (77a Greenwood
Road, London E8 1NT) or by
email (admin@testcentre.org.
uk). Guidelines at testcentre.
org.uk/about/submissions/.
Usually responds within one to
three months. Rejections may
occasionally include unsolicited
feedback. Authors are paid a flat
fee and royalties, and receive free
copies of their book.
WE SAY: A boutique publisher,
producing high quality publications
in limited editions. While pamphlets
are basic prints, of folded paper
and stapled spines, the paperback
perfect-bound books are
increasingly attractive: litho-printed,
with French flaps and beautifully
formatted. We particularly loved the
dark and minimalist design of Jen
Calleja's collection *Serious Justice*.
See also: *Test Centre* **(poetry
magazine) p185**

UNBOUND

E-BOOKS, COLLECTIONS AND
ANTHOLOGIES
2nd Floor, 19 Buckingham Gate,

London SW1E 6LB
020 7802 5413
www.unbound.co.uk
Established 2011. Mixed form:
also publishes prose (see p65).
Publications available direct
from publisher website; by
post and email order; at chain
and independent bookshops
nationwide; at national and local
literary events; and through
Amazon and other bookshop
websites. Publications are
subsidised by crowdfunding.
Multi-award-winning: Unbound title
The Wake won Book of the Year
at the 2015 Bookseller Industry
Awards and the 2014 Gordon Burn
Prize; was shortlisted for the 2014
Goldsmiths Prize; and longlisted
for the Man Booker Prize 2014, the
Desmond Elliott Prize 2014, and
The Folio Prize 2014. Unbound
won Best Publisher Website 2014
at the FutureBook Innovation
Awards and British Book Design
and Production Awards, and Best
Start-Up at the 2011 FutureBook
Innovation Awards. The press also
won the Literature Award 2013, for
26 Treasures, at the British Book
Design and Production Awards.
SUBMISSIONS: Open to all. Submit
via the online form at unbound.
co.uk/authors/work-with-us.
Guidelines at the same address.
Usually responds within one to
three months. Rejections may
occasionally include unsolicited
feedback. Authors are paid
royalties: a 50/50 profit share from
crowdfunding.
**For a fuller description of this press
see prose publishers p65**

UNTITLED FALKIRK ☆
CHAPBOOKS/PAMPHLETS
untitledfalkirk@gmail.com

untitledfalkirk.blogspot.co.uk
Editor: Craig Allan
Established 2012. Publications
available direct from publisher
website; by post and email
order; from selected/local chain
bookshops; from independent
bookshops; and at local literary
events.
SUBMISSIONS: During submissions
windows, submit by email to
untitledfalkirksubmissions@gmail.
com. As with *[Untitled]* (see p173),
only writers working, living in or
originally from Falkirk can submit.
Guidelines at untitledfalkirk.
blogspot.co.uk/2015/07/
untitledsix.html. Usually responds
within four weeks. Rejections may
occasionally include unsolicited
feedback. Authors receive no fee
or royalties at this time.
**For a fuller description of this press
see *[Untitled]* (mixed-form literary
magazine) p173**

V. PRESS
COLLECTIONS, ANTHOLOGIES AND
CHAPBOOKS/PAMPHLETS
vpresspoetry@hotmail.com
vpresspoetry.blogspot.co.uk
Editor: Sarah Leavesley
Established 2013. Mainly publishes
poetry, but is branching out
into flash fiction as of 2016.
Publications available direct from
publisher website; at national and
local literary events; and from
Amazon.
SUBMISSIONS: During submissions
windows, submit by email to
vpresspoetry@hotmail.com
but only when the submissions
window is open. Guidelines at
vpresspoetry.blogspot.co.uk/p/
submissions.html. Usually responds
within one to three months.
Rejections may occasionally

include unsolicited feedback. Authors receive initial free copies of the book, followed by copies at a discount rate.

WE SAY: V. Press's poetry pamphlets are eye-catching – the colours are dark, bold and solid, and the titles designed in a way that hearkens back to chapbooks Xeroxed in a basement, though the final product is actually high-quality print. The press favours experimental verse and flash fiction. We particularly loved the design and concept of Jacqui Rowe's *Ransom Notes*, which consists of fragments of text combined to look like ransom notes. Original works from a team unafraid to experiment.

VALLEY PRESS
COLLECTIONS, ANTHOLOGIES AND CHAPBOOKS/PAMPHLETS
Woodend, The Crescent, Scarborough YO11 2PW
jamie@valleypressuk.com
www.valleypressuk.com
Editor: Jamie McGarry
Established 2008. Mixed form: also publishes fiction and non-fiction (see p65). Publications available direct from publisher website; by post and email order; from chain bookshops and independent bookshops nationwide; at national and local literary events; and from Amazon and other bookshop websites. Valley Press title *Love and Eskimo Snow* by Sarah Holt was shortlisted for the People's Book Prize 2014.
SUBMISSIONS: During submissions windows, submit by post to Valley Press, Woodend, The Crescent, Scarborough, YO11 2PW. Guidelines at www.valleypressuk.com/contact/submissions.html.

Submitters are required to show proof of purchase from the press. Usually responds within four to six months. Rejections may occasionally include unsolicited feedback. Writers are paid royalties only and receive free copies of the book.

WE SAY: We looked at an e-book of *The Wild Gods* by Malene Engelund. A dark, disconcerting and intriguing cover – a black flower made of wings, on a shadowy background. The matt look, artistry and lovely formatting appear to be standard for Valley Press. The poems are contemporary free verse, for the most part, concerned with movement, freedom (and loss of), nature, love and haunting.
See also: prose publishers p65

VANE WOMEN PRESS
COLLECTIONS, ANTHOLOGIES AND CHAPBOOKS/PAMPHLETS
vane.women@ntlworld.com
www.vanewomen.co.uk
Editors: SJ Litherland, Marilyn Longstaff (assistant editor), Pat Maycroft (art editor)
Established 1993. Mainly publishes poetry, but also short stories (see p65). Publications available direct from publisher website; by post and email order; at local literary events; and at Vane Women events and workshops.
Vane Women title *The Spar Box* by Pippa Little was the 2006 Poetry Book Society Pamphlet choice.
SUBMISSIONS: Open to previously unpublished women in North East England. Contact by email (submissions@vanewomen.co.uk) in the first instance, and a postal address to send poems and short stories to will be provided

if appropriate. Full submission guidelines at www.vanewomen.co.uk/submissions.html. Usually responds in up to six months. Rejections may occasionally include unsolicited feedback. Authors receive free copies of their book. **WE SAY:** We looked at Lisa Matthews' *The Eternally Packed Suitcase*. Matt laminate cover, with a bright, modern, elegant design and a clear fresh typeface. With the professional blurb on the back and clean, spacious formatting inside, all on quality paper, this had the appearance of something from a much larger press. The Vane Women collective are a supportive group who do much to market their poets.
See also: prose publishers p65

VEER BOOKS
COLLECTIONS AND PAMPHLETS
School of English & Languages
FAHS, University of Surrey,
Surrey, Guildford GU2 7XH
020 8521 0907
veerbooks@gmail.com
www.veerbooks.com
Radical and experimental poetry.

WARD WOOD PUBLISHING
COLLECTIONS AND ANTHOLOGIES
6 The Drive, Golders Green, London NW11 9SR
adele@wardwoodpublishing.co.uk
www.wardwoodpublishing.co.uk
Mixed form publisher, established in 2010. Looking for 'innovative good reads of a high literary standard'. Submissions preferred by invitation only.
See also: prose publishers p65

WAYWISER PRESS ☆
COLLECTIONS AND ANTHOLOGIES
Christmas Cottage, Church Enstone,

Oxfordshire OX7 4NN
01608 677492
waywiserpress@aol.com
www.waywiser-press.com
Editors: Philip Hoy, Joseph Harrison, Dora Malech, V Penelope Pelizzon, Eric McHenry, Greg Williamson, Clive Watkins, Matthew Yorke
Established 2001. Also publishes some prose (see p65). Publications available direct from publisher website; by post and email order; at chain bookshops and independent bookshops nationwide; and from Amazon and other bookshop websites, including Inpress Books.
SUBMISSIONS: Poetry can be submitted only during submission windows. Submit by post to Christmas Cottage, Church Enstone Chipping Norton OX7 4NN. Guidelines at waywiser-press.com/authors.html. Usually responds within one to three months. No feedback offered if rejected. Authors receive royalties and free copies of their book.
WE SAY: We looked at a PDF of *How to Avoid Speaking* by Jaimee Hills, a 96-page publication with a simple cover design (slightly unpolished – the title runs close to the edge) and clean layout. The collection won the Anthony Hecht award, and includes a foreword from prize judge Anthony Thwaite. Includes both contemporary free poetry and more traditional forms, all experimenting with and confronting language.
See also: prose publishers p65

WORPLE PRESS
COLLECTIONS
Achill Sound, 2b Dry Hill Road, Tonbridge, Kent TN9 1LX
theworpleco@aol.com

www.theworplepress.com
Co-directors: Peter Carpenter,
Amanda Carpenter
Looks for excellence and
diversity of format and approach.
International submissions
welcomed.

WRECKING BALL PRESS ☆
COLLECTIONS, ANTHOLOGIES AND
CHAPBOOKS/PAMPHLETS
44-46 High Street, Danish Buildings,
Hull HU1 1PS
01482 211499
editor@wreckingballpress.com
www.wreckingballpress.com
Editors: Shane Rhodes, Russ Litten
Established 1997. Also publishes
prose (see p65). Publications
available direct from publisher
website; by post and email
order; at chain and independent
bookshops nationwide; at literary
events; and from amazon.co.uk.
Some online content available to
all.
Wrecking Ball Press title *The Scene
of My Former Triumph* by Matthew
Caley was nominated for Best
First Collection, The Forward Prize
2005.
SUBMISSIONS: Open to all. Submit
by post (Wrecking Ball Press, 44-46
High Street, Danish Buildings, Hull,
HU1 1PS) or by email (editor@
wreckingballpress.com). Guidelines
on the website. Usually responds
within one to three months.
Rejection may occasionally include
unsolicited feedback. Authors
receive royalties and free copies of
the book.
WE SAY: Wrecking Ball favours
muted dark colours and stark
illustrations reminiscent of 1970s
dystopian fiction, in conjunction
with textured matt paper –
pleasing to the eye and to the

touch. Design and formatting
is modern and thoroughly
professional.
See also: prose publishers p65

Listed in this section are publishers of every kind of prose, including full-length fiction, short stories, non-fiction, essays, memoir and other types of creative non-fiction. There are more fiction than non-fiction publishers listed, but many of the presses cover a range of prose publishing. Also listed are a number of presses that publish both poetry and prose. We've indicated, where possible, which is their dominant field of publishing.

ACCENT PRESS
NOVELS / NON-FICTION
Tŷ Cynon House, Navigation Park,
Abercynon CF45 4SN
01443 800354
info@accentpress.co.uk
www.accentpress.co.uk
Managing director: Hazel Cushion
Editors: Rebecca Lloyd, Greg Rees,
Alex Davies
Established 2003. Award-winning
independent publisher, now a
major name in trade publishing.
Includes imprints Xcite, Cariad and
YA Café.
Named Specialist Publisher
of the Year and shortlisted for
Independent Publisher of the Year
at the IPG Awards.
GENRES: Crime and psychological
thrillers; women's contemporary
fiction; YA; historical fiction;
romance; human interest and
self-help non-fiction. Strictly no
short stories or poetry.
SUBMISSIONS: Open to all, during
submissions windows. Guidelines
at www.accentpress.co.uk/
submission-guidelines.

AESOP MAGAZINE
SHORT STORY ANTHOLOGIES
18 and a half Sekforde Street,
London EC1R 0HL
editor@aesopmagazine.com
www.aesopmagazine.com
Editor: Max Raku
Established 2015. Primarily a
fiction magazine, but publishes the
occasional anthology.
SUBMISSIONS: Open to all. Submit
through the online form at www.
aesopmagazine.com/submissions

Usually responds within one to
three months, with feedback on
submissions only if requested.
Contributors receive free copies of
the book; no fee or royalties.
**See also: poetry publishers p13 and
Aesop Magazine (prose magazine)
p199**

AESTHETICA MAGAZINE ☆
ANTHOLOGIES
PO Box 371, York, North Yorkshire
YO23 1WL
01904 527560
info@aestheticamagazine.com
www.aestheticamagazine.com
Editor: Cherie Federico
Established 2003. Stunning
anthology resulting from the
Aesthetica Creative Writing
Award. Publications available
direct from publisher website
and at chain bookshops
nationwide.

ALBA PUBLISHING
SHORT STORY COLLECTIONS AND
ANTHOLOGIES / NON-FICTION
PO Box 266, Uxbridge UB9 5NX
01895 832444
info@albapublishing.com
www.albapublishing.com
Editor: Kim Richardson
Established 1990. Mainly publishes
poetry (see p13). Publications
available by post and email order;
and from Amazon.
A title from Alba Publishing
was shortlisted for the Haiku
Foundation Touchstone
Distinguished Book Award 2013.
GENRES: Spirituality and beliefs.
SUBMISSIONS: Publication history

required. Submit by post (PO Box 266, Uxbridge UB9 5NX) or by email (info@albapublishing.com). Usually responds within four weeks, with submission feedback only if requested. Authors contribute to editorial/publication/marketing costs.

For a fuller description of this press, see also poetry publishers p13

ALCHEMY PRESS

E-BOOKS / NOVELS / SHORT STORY COLLECTIONS AND ANTHOLOGIES
alchemypress@gmail.co.uk
alchemypress.wordpress.com
Established in the late 1990s. Fiction: fantasy and horror. Produces award-nominated titles (*Rumours of the Marvellous* by Peter Atkin) and winner of the British Fantasy Society's Best Small Press Award, 2014.

ALMOND PRESS ☆

E-BOOKS / SHORT STORY COLLECTIONS AND ANTHOLOGIES
79 Dumbiedykes Road, Edinburgh EH8 9UT
office@almondpress.co.uk
www.almondpress.co.uk
Editor: Marek Lewandowski
Established 2012. Primarily publishes fiction. Publications available from Amazon and other bookshop websites.
GENRES: Fantasy/sci-fi; horror; dystopian. No non-fiction.
SUBMISSIONS: Submissions take place during competition time, with competitions being the submissions windows (see p215). Usually responds within one to three months. No feedback offered. Authors receive an advance/fee plus royalties and free copies of the book.
WE SAY: Almond Press publishes short stories that are accessible in digital format. Specialising in dystopian fiction, the cover designs are appropriately bleak and atmospheric, and the stories are gripping and suspenseful.

AN SAGART

NON-FICTION
www.ansagart.ie
Editor: Pádraig Ó Fiannachta
Non-fiction (Irish language). including literary criticism and history, journals, poetry, drama and biography.

ANARCHY BOOKS

E-BOOKS
anarchy-books@hotmail.co.uk
www.anarchy-books.com
Editors: Phil Ambler, Mongrel Jones
Digital fiction publishing company, with a focus on 'multi-strand publishing projects' that combine different media.
GENRES: Fantasy/sci-fi; horror.

AND OTHER STORIES

E-BOOKS / NOVELS / SHORT STORY COLLECTIONS AND ANTHOLOGIES / NON-FICTION
88 Easton St, High Wyecombe, Bucks HP11 1LT
07534 974322
nichola@andotherstories.org
www.andotherstories.org
Editors: Tara Tobler, Stefan Tobler, Sophie Lewis
Established 2010. Mainly publishes fiction. Publications available in chain bookshops nationwide; from independent bookshops; at local literary events; and from Amazon and other bookshop websites. Plans are in place for purchase direct from the publisher. Also offers a subscription: £20, £35 or £50 per year for two, four or six

books per year.
And Other Stories was shortlisted for the 2013 IPG Newcomer Award. Its authors have also been shortlisted for and won awards.
GENRES: Literary fiction and literary non-fiction (subjects have included death, family and community).

ARACHNE PRESS ☆

E-BOOKS / NOVELS / SHORT STORY COLLECTIONS AND ANTHOLOGIES / NON-FICTION
100 Grierson Road, London SE23 1NX
020 8699 0206
arachnepress.com
Editor: Cherry Potts

Established 2012. Mainly publishes fiction (particularly children's/YA), but also publishes some poetry (see p13). Publications available direct from publisher website; by post and email order; at chain bookshops and independent bookshops nationwide; at local literary events; and from Amazon and other bookshop websites, including distributor inpressbooks.co.uk.
Arachne Press title *Devilskein & Dearlove* by Alex Smith was nominated for the Carnegie Medal 2015, and title *Weird Lies*, edited by Cherry Potts and Katy Darby, won Best Anthology in the 2014 Saboteur Awards.
GENRES: Children's fiction; fantasy/sci-fi; literary fiction; poetry; YA; art, fashion and photography.
SUBMISSIONS: During submissions windows, submit through Submittable at arachnepress.submittable.com/submit.
Guidelines at arachnepress.com/submissions. Usually responds within one to three months, and provides feedback on submissions where the editor thinks it would be useful to the author, unless explicitly asked not to. Authors receive royalties and/or free copies of the book.
WE SAY: Commissioned and edited by founder Cherry Potts, each title from this self-professed 'micro-publisher' is printed on eco-friendly wood-free paper. We looked at Kate Foley's *The Don't Touch Garden*, which was slightly smaller than A5, nicely laid out and designed with a glossy colour cover (an amateur photograph of a garden). It arrived with a nicely branded promotional postcard, featuring a puff from another author, plus a sweet note from Cherry herself. Well thought-out and lovingly put together.
See also: poetry publishers p13

SUBMISSIONS: Open to all, but submitters are required to show proof of purchase from the press. Submit by post to 88 Easton St, High Wycombe, Bucks HP11 1LT. Guidelines at www.andotherstories. org/about/contact-us/. Usually responds within one to three months. A standard rejection may occasionally include unsolicited feedback. Author payment is an advance/fee plus royalties.
WE SAY: We looked at *Southeaster* by Haroldo Conti, translated by Jon Lindsay Miles. And Other Stories produces top-rate paperbacks, using quality materials: thick cream paper

and a distinct brand. Cover designs usually consist of a funky modern graphic illustration. Writing is fresh and contemporary.
See also: poetry publishers p13

ANGRY ROBOT
NOVELS
Lace Market House, 54-56 High Pavement, Nottingham NG1 1HW
incoming@angryrobotbooks.com
angryrobotbooks.com
A global imprint dedicated to modern adult sci-fi, fantasy 'and everything in between'. E-books, print books and audio books all available.

AS YET UNTITLED ☆
ARTISTS' BOOKS
138 Erlanger Rd, London SE14 5TJ
ayupublishing@gmail.com
www.asyetuntitled.org
Editors: Rosie Sherwood, Zelda Chappel

Established 2012. Mixed form: artists' books. Publications available direct from publisher website; from selected/local chain bookshops; from independent bookshops; at local literary events; and at Artists' Book Fairs (National) and the Small Publishers Fair.
GENRES: Fantasy/sci-fi; graphic/ comics; historical fiction; literary fiction; poetry. Strictly no non-fiction.
SUBMISSIONS: As Yet Untitled books are in the early days of production. See the website for more information on submissions.

WE SAY: As Yet Untitled books are works of art, exploring the concept of space within pages. The first publications include a photobook containing tissue-thin, loose-leaf pages that can be reordered; and a short comic/photography/poetry book. All materials are of high quality.
See also: *Elbow Room* (mixed-form literary magazine) p140 and poetry publishers p18

ARLEN HOUSE
NOVELS / SHORT STORY
COLLECTIONS
arlenhouse@gmail.com
arlenhouse.blogspot.co.uk
One of Ireland's leading presses,
a literary publisher with a focus on
'works of cultural importance'.

ASLS
PRINT
ASLS, 7 University Gardens,
Glasgow G12 8QH
0141 330 5309
office@asls.org.uk
www.asls.org.uk
Editors: Gerry Cambridge,
Diana Hendry
Established 1970. Publications
available direct from publisher
website; by post and email order;
from chain bookshops nationwide;
from independent bookshops; at
national and local literary events;
and from Amazon and other
bookshop websites.
An ASLS title was shortlisted for
the Saltire Society Scottish Book of
the Year award, 2011.
GENRES: Short fiction; reprints of
classic Scottish texts; collections of
scholarly papers; study guides.
SUBMISSIONS: Submit by proposal
form at asls.arts.gla.ac.uk/contact.
html#A1. Usually responds within
four to six months. No feedback
offered with rejections. Authors
are paid a flat fee and receive print
copy/ies of the book.
WE SAY: We looked at *A Portable
Shelter* by Kirsty Logan: a
beautiful, limited edition hardback,
clothbound with silver embossed
text on the cover, and thick inner
paper for the 13 short stories in the
collection. A high art production,
worthy of the Folio Society.
See also: poetry publishers p13 and

New Writing Scotland **(mixed-form
literary magazine) p159**

ASTON BAY PRESS
NOVELS
Daniel Goldsmith Associates,
Dallam Court, Dallam Lane WA2 7LT
www.astonbay.co.uk
Publishes crime and historical
fiction; detective stories with
female leads. Welcomes
submissions from agents and
authors.

AUGUR PRESS
NOVELS / NON-FICTION
info@augurpress.com
www.augurpress.com
Non-fiction and fiction. Books
with an emphasis on enabling
the reader 'to reflect, and to
look beyond ... that which is
immediately apparent'.
See also: poetry publishers p13

BIRLINN PRESS
E-BOOKS / NOVELS / NON-FICTION
West Newington House,
10 Newington Road,
Edinburgh EH9 1QS
info@birlinn.co.uk
www.birlinn.co.uk
Managing director: Hugh Andrews
One of the larger independent
presses, with a wide range of
publications. Mixed form, fiction
and non-fiction. Imprints include
John Donald, Arena Sport and BC
Books.
See also: poetry publishers p13

BITTER LEMON PRESS
E-BOOKS / NOVELS / NON-FICTION
47 Wilmington Square,
London WC1X 0ET
books@bitterlemonpress.com
www.bitterlemonpress.com
Fiction and non-fiction crime,

thriller and mystery, 'exploring the darker side of foreign places'.

BLACK & WHITE PUBLISHING ☆

E-BOOKS / NOVELS / NON-FICTION
29 Ocean Drive, Edinburgh EH6 6JL
0131 625 4500
submissions@blackandwhite
                      publishing.com
www.blackandwhitepublishing.com
Editor: Karyn Millar

Established 1992. Mainly publishes fiction. Publications available from chain bookshops nationwide; from independent bookshops; at local literary events; and from Amazon and all other UK bookshop websites.
GENRES: Crime/thriller/mystery; historical fiction; literary fiction; romance; YA; biography and true stories; humour; sports and leisure.
SUBMISSIONS: Open to all. Submit by email to submissions@ blackandwhitepublishing. com. Guidelines at www. blackandwhitepublishing.com/ index.php/infopages/submissions. Usually responds within one to three months. If no response after three months, assume rejection. Individual contracts for each writer.
WE SAY: Black & White – one of the larger 'small' presses in this Guide – produces titles on a par with the larger presses in terms of quality. A glance over their website shows a full understanding of cover design and genre tropes. This is a press that knows how to market its wares.

BLACK DOG

NON-FICTION
10A Acton Street, London
WC1X 9NG
info@blackdogonline.com

www.blackdogonline.com
Publishes art, fashion and photography; and music, stage and screen.

BLACK PEAR PRESS ☆

E-BOOKS / NOVELS / SHORT STORY ANTHOLOGIES
office@blackpear.net
www.blackpear.net
Editors: Rod Griffiths, Polly Robinson, Tony Judge

Established 2013. Mixed form. Publications available direct from publisher website, by post and email order, at local literary events, on Amazon and on other bookshop websites.
GENRES: Crime/thriller/mystery; literary fiction; poetry; YA. No non-fiction.
SUBMISSIONS: Welcome during submissions windows, otherwise submissions are by invitation only. Guidelines at blackpear.net/ submissions/. Usually responds within one to three months. Rejections may occasionally include unsolicited feedback. Authors receive royalties and a discount on the price of the book.
WE SAY: We looked at a PDF of *Seeds of Destruction* by Frances Bennett: a perfect-bound, 216-page publication, also available in digital format. A black cover with a coloured pencil sketch of a dandelion clock against stormy cliffs, and a rounded font. The layout is tidy and professional. Cover and blurb are slightly amateurish, but the writing is tight and well-presented.
See also: poetry publishers p13

BLUEMOOSE BOOKS

E-BOOKS / NOVELS / NON-FICTION
25 Sackville Street, Hebden Bridge,

Yorkshire HX7 7DJ
01422 842731
kevin@bluemoosebooks.com
www.bluemoosebooks.com
Editors: Lin Webb, Leonore Rustamov,
Hetha Duffy

Established 2006. Mainly publishes
fiction. Publications available
direct from publisher website;
by post and email order; at
chain bookshops nationwide;
at independent bookshops; at
national and local literary events;
and from Amazon and other
bookshop websites.
Authors at Bluemoose books have
won The Gordon Burn Prize 2013
(Faber & New Writing North) and
Northern Writers' Award 2014
(New Writing North) and been
shortlisted for The Jerwood Fiction
Uncovered Award 2015.
GENRES: Crime/thriller/mystery;
literary fiction; biography and true
stories.
SUBMISSIONS: Open to all.
Submit by email to kevin@
bluemoosebooks.com. Guidelines
at bluemoosebooks.com/about.
Usually responds within four
to six months. Rejections may
occasionally include unsolicited
feedback. Authors receive royalties
only, or advance/fee plus royalties,
and free copies of the book.
WE SAY: Another small press
that can hold its own alongside
the best in the mainstream. We
looked at Sarayu Srivatsa's *If You
Look For Me, I Am Not There.*
Quality materials and a beautiful
cover design with a vibrant layered
image. Bluemoose has a quirky
logo, but its books are literary and
well produced. It is particularly
supportive of women writers and
translated works.

BOOKOUTURE
NOVELS
www.bookouture.com
Commerical fiction.
GENRES: Crime/thriller/mystery;
erotica; literary fiction; romance; YA.
SUBMISSIONS: Submit by email to
www.bookouture.com/pitch.

BRADSHAW BOOKS
NOVELS / SHORT STORY
ANTHOLOGIES / NON-FICTION
Civic Trust House, 50 Pope's Quay,
Cork City T23 R6XC
0214 215175
info@bradshawbooks.com
www.bradshawbooks.com
Editor: Eugene O'Connell
Established 1985. Mainly publishes
poetry (see p13). Publications
available direct from publisher
website; by post and email order;
from independent bookshops and
from Amazon. Publications from
Bradshaw Books include work on
the *Eurochild: Artwork and Poetry
For Children by Children* annual
anthology.
GENRES: Literary fiction.
**See also: *Cork Literary Review*
(mixed-form literary magazine)
p138 and poetry publishers p13**

BUNBURY PUBLISHING LTD
E-BOOKS / SHORT STORY
COLLECTIONS
07446 025630
admin@bunburymagazine.com
www.bunburymagazine.com
Editors: Christopher Moriarty,
Keri-Ann Edwards
Established 2013: book publishing
a new venture.
SUBMISSIONS: Open to all.
Guidelines at bunburymagazine.
com/submit-to-us/. Authors are
paid royalties only.
See also: poetry publishers p13; for

74

a fuller description of this press, see *Bunbury Magazine* (mixed-form literary magazine) p135

BURNING EYE BOOKS
NOVELS
burningeyebooks.wordpress.com
Editors: Clive Birnie, Thommie Gillow (poetry), Alice Furse (fiction)

'Never knowingly mainstream'. Primarily publishes poetry, but also indie fiction.
See also: poetry publishers p13

CATNIP PUBLISHING
NOVELS / PICTURE BOOKS
320 City Road, London EC1V 2NZ
020 7138 3650
liz.bankes@catnippublishing.co.uk
www.catnippublishing.co.uk
Editor: Liz Bankes
Established 2005. Fiction only, Publications available from chain bookshops nationwide; from independent bookshops; at national and local literary events; from Amazon and other bookshop websites; and direct from Bounce Sales and Marketing. Schools and libraries can order through wholesalers.
Catnip title *Girl with a White Dog* was shortlisted for the Waterstones Children's Book Prize 2015.
GENRES: Children's fiction; YA; picture books.
SUBMISSIONS: Agent submissions only. Submit by post (320 City Road, London EC1V 2NZ) or by email (liz.bankes@catnippublishing.co.uk). Unsolicited submissions are not guaranteed a response. Usually responds within one to three months. Rejections may occasionally include unsolicited feedback, but not guaranteed. Authors are paid an advance/fee plus royalties.

CB EDITIONS
E-BOOKS / NOVELS / SHORT STORY COLLECTIONS / NON-FICTION
146 Percy Road, London W12 9QL
020 8743 2467
info@cbeditions.com
www.cbeditions.com
Editor: Charles Boyle
Established 2007. Publishes poetry (see p13), short fiction and other prose. Publications available direct from publisher website; at chain and independent bookshops nationwide; at national and local literary events; and from Amazon and other bookshop websites.
A multi-award-winning publisher: titles have won the Aldeburgh First Collection Prize (2009, 2011, 2013); the Scott Moncrieff Translation Prize (2014); the McKitterick Prize (2008) and the Guardian First Book Award (2014), as well as being shortlisted for the Goldsmiths Prize (2014).
GENRES: Literary fiction; history; travel.
SUBMISSIONS: Open to all. Submit by post (146 Percy Road, London W12 9QL) or by email (info@cbeditions.com). No guidelines available, so read publications by CB Editions to be sure your work will be a good fit. Usually responds within one to three months. No feedback offered with rejection. Authors are paid an advance/fee plus royalties, and receive free copies of the book.
For a fuller description of this press, see poetry publishers p13. See also *Sonofabook* (mixed-form literary magazine) p169

CHOC LIT ☆
E-BOOKS / NOVELS / SHORT STORY COLLECTIONS AND ANTHOLOGIES
Penrose House, Crawley Drive, Camberley, Surrey GU15 2AB

01276 27492
info@choc-lit.co.uk
www.choc-lit.co.uk
Established 2009. Fiction.
Publications available from chain
bookshops nationwide; from
independent bookshops; and
from Amazon and other bookshop
websites.
Winner of the Romance Writers'
of New Zealand Koru Award
2015 and History Novel of the
Year Award from the Romantic
Novelists' Association 2014.
GENRES: Crime/thriller/mystery;
fantasy/sci-fi; historical fiction;
romance.
SUBMISSIONS: Open to all.
Submit through www.
choclitpublishing.com/html/
submissions. Usually responds
within one to three months,
with feedback only if requested.
Authors are paid royalties only.
WE SAY: These perfect-bound
paperbacks feel like Big Five titles:
glossy embossed cover, intriguing
blurb (we looked at *How I Wonder
What You Are* by Jane Lovering)
and nicely formatted, despite
the slightly-too-close page trims.
The Surrey-based publisher's key
criteria are swoon-worthy heroes
('irresistible like chocolate') and
romance-driven plots with or
without other genre elements,
such as mystery or fantasy. They
also require authors to have a
stellar web presence, either a
popular blog or heaps of followers
across the major social media
platforms.

CILLIAN PRESS
E-BOOKS / NOVELS
83 Ducie Street, Manchester M1 2JQ
0161 864 2301
info@cillianpress.co.uk

www.cillianpress.co.uk
Established 2012. Fiction publisher.
Publications available direct from
publisher website; by post and
email order; from chain bookshops
nationwide; from independent
bookshops; and from Amazon and
other bookshop websites.
GENRES: Literary fiction.

CINNAMON PRESS ☆
NOVELS / SHORT STORY
COLLECTIONS AND ANTHOLOGIES
Meirion House, Glan yr afon, Blaenau
Ffestiniog, Gwynedd LL41 3SU
01766 832112
jan@cinnamonpress.com
www.cinnamonpress.com
Editors: Jan Fortune and Adam Craig
Established 2005. Mixed form:
alongside novels, short stories
and creative non-fiction, it also
publishes poetry, see p13.
Cinnamon Book Club: £30 per
annum for six brand-new books.
Publications available direct from
publisher website; from chain
and independent bookshops
nationwide; at local literary events;
from Amazon; and from Inpress
Books.
Titles from Cinnamon have won
Scottish Arts Best First Book of the
Year; Wales Book of the Year; and
Wales Book of the Year Readers'
Vote. They've been shortlisted
for Wales Book of the Year and
the Forward Prize for Best First
Collection.
GENRES: Historical fiction;
literary fiction; experimental; cross-
genre; literary crime/thriller; literary
exploratory fiction/sci-fi; landscape;
creative biography; creative writing
related.
SUBMISSIONS: Submit only during
submissions periods. See www.
cinnamonpress.com/index.php/

about-cinnamon-press/submissions for full submissions details. Usually responds within one to three months. Submissions that came close to publication may receive some feedback with rejection. Authors are paid royalties only.
WE SAY: The fiction arm of Cinnamon sells well-produced paperbacks, belying the fact it's a small, family-run operation. The poetry and non-fiction titles are of a similar standard. Recent novel covers are infinitely cooler than earlier examples (we checked out *The Crocodile Princess* by Ian Gregson), and both the editing quality and paper weight give the illusion of a bigger publishing house. 'Sticker offers' on covers in the online shop offer titles at temporarily reduced prices to boost sales. Clever.
For a description of this press, including what They Say, See also poetry publishers p13 and *Envoi Poetry Journal* p183

CIRCAIDY GREGORY PRESS
E-BOOKS / NOVELS
Creative Media Centre, 45 Robertson Street, Hastings, Sussex TN34 1HL
sales@circaidygregory.co.uk
www.circaidygregory.co.uk
Mixed form: non-fiction, short stories, childrens' fiction, plays and novels as well as poetry (see p13).
See also: poetry publishers p13

COMMA PRESS ☆
E-BOOKS / SHORT STORY COLLECTIONS AND ANTHOLOGIES
Studio 510a, Fifth Floor, Hope Mill, 113 Pollard Street, Manchester M4 7JA
info@commapress.co.uk
www.commapress.co.uk
Editors: Ra Page, Jim Hinks, Sarah Hunt

Established 2007. Fiction only. Publications available direct from publisher website; from chain bookshops nationwide; from independent bookshops; at national and local literary events; and from Amazon and other bookshop websites.
Comma Press title *Tea at the Midland*, a short story collection by David Constantine, won the 2013 Frank O'Connor International Short Story Prize, and the short story of the same name won the 2010 BBC National Short Story Prize. *The Iraqi Christ* by Hassan Blasim, translated by Jonathan Wright, won the 2014 Independent Foreign Fiction Prize.
GENRES: Crime/thriller/mystery; fantasy/sci-fi; literary fiction. No non-fiction.
SUBMISSIONS: Open to all. Submit by email to info@ commapress.co.uk. Guidelines at commapress.co.uk/resources/ submissions/. Usually responds in over six months. Rejections may occasionally include unsolicited feedback. Authors are paid a flat fee or royalties, depending on the type of book/funding.
WE SAY: As a mainstay of the short story publishing world, the pressure's on Comma to maintain stellar quality across all of their titles. And they deliver. *Spindles* (a collection of 'stories from the science of sleep') is a perfect-bound paperback with a weighty, expensive feel. The cover art is surreal and carefully chosen, the fonts are edgy, and there are academic elements to the work – introductions and afterwords with immaculately referenced bibliographies. A class act.

COPY PRESS

NOVELS / SHORT STORY
COLLECTIONS / NON-FICTION
51 South Street, Ventnor, Isle of Wight
PO38 1NG
info@copypress.co.uk
www.copypress.co.uk
Publishes ranges including
'Common intellectual' (100-page
paperbacks that make propositions
for thinking, living and enjoyment)
and 'Loop' (short mixed-form
anthology volumes).

CRINKLE CRANKLE

NON-FICTION
crinklecrankle@gmail.com
Editor: Eleanor Margolies
Established 2014. Mixed form:
also publishes poetry (see p13).
Publications available by post and
email order, or by download from
sales site.
GENRES: Society, education and
politics.
SUBMISSIONS: By invitation only.
See also: poetry publishers p13

CRO MAGNON, THE ☆

SHORT STORY COLLECTIONS
AND ANTHOLOGIES
51 Wakefield House, Goldsmith Road,
London SE15 5SU
www.thecromagnon.com
Editor: Henry Tobias Jones
Established 2015. Mixed form: also
produces poetry anthologies and
collections (see p13).
SUBMISSIONS: Open to all.
Submit by email to editors@
thecromagnon.com. See
guidelines on the website. May
charge for submissions. Usually
responds within one to three
months, with feedback only if
requested.
**For a fuller description of this
press see *The Cro Magnon* (mixed-**

form e-zine) p138. See also poetry
publishers p13

CROOKED CAT PUBLISHING

NOVELS
enquiries@crookedcatpublishing.com
crookedcatpublishing.com
Fiction including crime/thriller/
mystery; historical fiction; literary
fiction; romance; YA.

CULTURED LLAMA

SHORT STORY COLLECTIONS AND
ANTHOLOGIES
11 London Road, Teynham,
Sittingbourne, Kent ME9 9QW
07800 522724
info@culturedllama.co.uk
www.culturedllama.co.uk
Editors: Maria C McCarthy,
Bob Carling
Established 2011. Mixed form:
short fiction and cultural non-
fiction, and poetry (see p13).
Publications available direct from
publisher website; at national and
local literary events; and from
Amazon and other bookshop
websites.
SUBMISSIONS: A publication
history is required. Check the
guidelines at www.culturedllama.
co.uk/publishing/submission to
find out when and how to submit
your work. Usually responds within
one to three months. Rejections
may occasionally include
unsolicited feedback, but usually
not. Authors are paid royalties
only, and receive free copies of the
book.
WE SAY: Perfect-bound short story
anthologies, non-fiction works
and poetry collections printed on
cream paper. We looked at Emma
Timpany's *The Lost of Syros*, a
short story collection with abstract
cover art and well-edited prose.

The whole product felt simple and polished, from the back cover text (a succinct blurb, author bio and puff quote) to the chic sans serif font used for the chapter headings – though the cover title was rather inelegant. Cultured Llama requests more in-depth submissions than other publishers, asking for detailed insights into the author's background and publicity plans, but their stringency seems to yield quality results.

See also: poetry publishers p13

DAUNT BOOKS PUBLISHING

E-BOOKS / NOVELS / SHORT STORY COLLECTIONS / NON-FICTION
158-164 Fulham Road, London
SW10 9PR
020 7373 4997
publishing@dauntbooks.co.uk
www.dauntbookspublishing.co.uk
The publisher behind the bookshops – vibrant books and international authors. Unsolicited manuscripts welcomed.

DEAD INK

E-BOOKS / NOVELS / SHORT STORY COLLECTIONS / NON-FICTION
dead.ink.books (skype)
www.deadinkbooks.com
Editor: Nathan Connelly
Established 2011. Mainly publishes fiction. Publications available direct from publisher website; by post and email order; from chain bookshops nationwide; from independent bookshops; and from Amazon. Titles from Dead Ink have been listed for multiple awards: *Brick Mother* by SJ Bradley and *Wild Ink* by Richard Smyth were longlisted for the 2014 Guardian First Book and 2014 Guardian Not The Booker awards. *Controller* by Sally Ashton was shortlisted for the 2013 Saboteur Awards, Best Novella.
GENRES: Literary fiction; criticism and cultural commentary.
SUBMISSIONS: Open to all, but check that submissions windows are open. Submit by email to nathan@deadinkbooks.com. Guidelines at www.deadinkbooks.com/submissions/. Usually responds within one to three months. Will give feedback on submissions for a fee, though on occasion a rejection may include unsolicited feedback. Authors receive free copies of the book, but no fee or royalties.
For a fuller description of this press, see poetry publishers p13

DEDALUS LTD

E-BOOKS / NOVELS / SHORT STORY ANTHOLOGIES / NON-FICTION
24-26, St Judith's Lane, Sawtry, Cambridgeshire PE28 5XE
01487 832382
info@dedalusbooks.com
www.dedalusbooks.com
Editors: Eric Lane, Timothy Lane, Marie Lane
Established 1983. Mainly publishes fiction. Publications available from chain bookshops nationwide; from independent bookshops; at national literary events; and from Amazon and other bookshop websites.
Titles from Dedalus Books have won the Read Russia Prize 2015, the Oxford-Weidenfeld Translation Prize 2012, the Portuguese Translation Prize 2013, and the Polish Translation Prize 2014.
GENRES: Crime/thriller/mystery; historical fiction; literary fiction; biography and true stories; food and drink; travel.
SUBMISSIONS: Open to all. Submit by post, sending a covering letter

about the author with three sample chapters to Dedalus Limited, 24-26, St Judith's Lane, Sawtry, Cambridgeshire PE28 5XE. Usually responds within one to three months. No feedback usually offered with rejections, unless the writer has come very close to acceptance. Authors are paid an advance/fee plus royalties.

WE SAY: We looked at *Ink in the Blood* by Stéphanie Hochet (translated by Mike Mitchell): a slim, perfect-bound 76-page publication, with a glossy cover and quality cream paper. The cover design is based on the tattoos that play a central part in the story, and looks appropriately dark and arcane. The blurb is well written and the formatting professional, but the shiny cover makes this book feel a little cheap. Dedalus are dedicated to literary fiction, and welcome translated work.

DIAMOND TWIG

SHORT STORY COLLECTIONS
9 Eversley Place,
Newcastle-upon-Tyne NE6 5AL
0191 276 3770
diamond.twig@virgin.net
Editor: Ellen Phethean
Established 1992. Predominantly publishes poetry (see p13), but also publishes short story collections. Publications available direct from publisher website; and by post and email order.
Diamond Twig title *The Ropes: poems to hold on to*, an anthology of poems for teenagers, was shortlisted for the 2009 CLPE Poetry Award (Centre for Literacy in Primary Education) (www.clpe.co.uk).
SUBMISSIONS: Submissions for book publication are by invitation only. Usually responds within one to three months. Rejection may include occasional unsolicited feedback. Authors are paid a flat fee and receive free copies of the book.
See also: *Diamond Twig* **(poetry e-zine) p183 and poetry publisher p25**

DIRT PIE PRESS

SHORT STORY ANTHOLOGIES
editors@riptidejournal.co.uk
www.riptidejournal.co.uk
Editors: Dr Virginia Baily, Dr Sally Flint
Established 2006. Mainly fiction, but also some poetry (see p13). Publications available direct from publisher website; by post and email order; from independent bookshops; and at local literary events. All stockists are listed on the website.
GENRES: Children's fiction; drama and criticism; erotica; fantasy/sci-fi; graphic/comics; horror; romance.
SUBMISSIONS: Open to all, guidelines on the website. Submit by email to editors@riptidejournal.co.uk. Usually responds within four to six months. No feedback offered with rejections. Authors receive a flat fee.
For a fuller description of this press see *Riptide Journal* (mixed-form literary magazine) p166. See also poetry publishers p13

DOG HORN PUBLISHING ☆

E-BOOKS / NOVELS / SHORT STORY COLLECTIONS AND ANTHOLOGIES / NON-FICTION
45 Monk Ings, Birstall, Batley WF17 9HU
01924 466853
editor@doghornpublishing.com
www.doghornpublishing.com
Editor: Adam Lowe

Established 2005. Also publishes poetry, see p13. Publications available direct from publisher website; by post and email order; from chain bookshops nationwide; from independent bookshops; at national and local literary events; and from Amazon and other bookshop websites, including lulu.com.

Titles from Dog Horn have won the *Guardian* First Book Award (reader nomination); the Noble (*not* Nobel) Book Prize; and have had multiple honourable mentions in the Year's Best Horror.

GENRES: Drama and criticism; fantasy/sci-fi; horror; literary fiction; YA; food and drink; health and lifestyle; humour; music, stage and screen; society, education and politics; spirituality and beliefs; sports and leisure; travel.

SUBMISSIONS: Submissions by invitation only. On invitation, submit by email to editor@doghornpublishing.com. Guidelines at www.doghornpublishing.com/wordpress/about. Usually responds in over six months. Rejections may occasionally include unsolicited feedback. Authors are paid royalties only and receive free copies of the book.

For a fuller description of this press see poetry publishers p13

DOIRE PRESS

E-BOOKS / SHORT STORY COLLECTIONS AND ANTHOLOGIES
Aille, Inverin, County Galway, Ireland
+353 091 593290
www.doirepress.com
Editor: John Walsh

Established 2007. Publishes poetry and short stories equally (see p13). Publications available direct from publisher website; from independent bookshops; at national literary events; from Amazon; and from kennys.ie. Doire Press title *Waiting for the Bullet* by Madeleine D'Arcy won the 2015 Edge Hill Readers' Prize.

SUBMISSIONS: Only open to writers living in Ireland, and not actively seeking submissions (though open to being approached by writers familiar with Doire's books who are sure their work will be a good fit. Submit by post (Aille, Inverin, County Galway, Ireland) or by email (doirepress@gmail.com).Guidelines at www.doirepress.com/submissions/. Usually responds within one to three months. No feedback offered with rejections. Book deals vary: authors may be paid royalties only; may be paid an advance/fee plus royalties; and/or may receive free copies of book – the deal depends on grant funding received.

For a fuller description of this press see poetry publishers p13

DREADFUL PRESS, THE ☆

E-BOOKS / NOVELS
Clonmoyle House, Coachford, Cork
the.p.dreadful@gmail.com
www.thepennydreadful.org
Editors: Marc O'Connell, John Keating

Mixed form: also publishes poetry (see p13). Publications available direct from publisher website; from selected/local chain bookshops; from independent bookshops; and at local literary events.

GENRES: Drama and criticism; graphic/comics; literary fiction.

SUBMISSIONS: Open to all – see guidelines at thepennydreadful.org/index.php/submit/. Usually responds within four weeks. Rejections may occasionally include unsolicited feedback. Authors are currently unpaid. **For a fuller description of this press see *The Penny Dreadful* (mixed-form literary magazine) p164. See also poetry publishers p13**

EMMA PRESS, THE
E-BOOKS / SHORT STORY COLLECTIONS / NON-FICTION
Spectacle Works, 16-24 Hylton Street, Jewellery Quarter, Birmingham
B18 6HN
queries@theemmapress.com
www.theemmapress.com
Editors: Emma Wright, Rachel Piercey
Established 2012. Primarily publishes poetry, but also some short story collections and non-fiction (see p13).
Publications available direct from publisher website; from chain bookshops and independent bookshops nationwide; at national and local literary events; and from Amazon and other bookshop websites.
The Emma Press was shortlisted for the 2014 Michael Marks Award for Poetry Pamphlet Publishers (organised by the Wordsworth Trust and the British Library, with the support of the Michael Marks Charitable Trust, in association with the TLS).
GENRES: Children's fiction; literary fiction; biography and true stories; humour; travel.
SUBMISSIONS: Open to all, during submissions windows. Submitters required to show proof of purchase from the press. Submit by email – a different address for each call. Please see guidelines at theemmapress. com/about/submissions. Usually responds within four to six months. Rejections may occasionally

include unsolicited feedback. Authors are paid royalties only, and receive free copies of the book. **For a fuller description of this press, including what They Say, see poetry publishers p28**

ESC ZINE
SHORT FICTION AND POETRY ANTHOLOGIES
escpeople@gmail.com
esczine.com
Editors: Jessica Maybury, Aine Belton
Established 2011. Mixed form: fiction and poetry (see p13). Publications available direct from publisher website; and at national and local literary events.
GENRES: Literary fiction; slipstream; experimental; art, fashion and photography.
SUBMISSIONS: During submissions windows, submit by email to escpeople@gmail.com. Guidelines at esczine.com/submissions/. Usually responds within four weeks. Rejections may occasionally include unsolicited feedback. Authors receive free copies of the book.
See also: poetry publishers p13

EYEWEAR PUBLISHING LIMITED ☆
E-BOOKS / NOVELS / NON-FICTION
info@eyewearpublishing.com
www.eyewearpublishing.com
Editors: Dr Todd Swift, Kelly Davio
Established 2012. Mainly publishes poetry (see p13), but does extend to non-fiction and fiction, including the new Squint series of non-fiction. Publications available direct from publisher website; by post and email order; at chain bookshops nationwide; at independent bookshops; at local literary events; and from Amazon and other

bookshop websites.
Eyewear won The Pegasus Award for Poetry Criticism, 2015 (from the Poetry Foundation).
GENRES: Crime/thriller/mystery; drama and criticism; literary fiction; YA; biography and true stories; humour; society, education and politics; spirituality and beliefs.
SUBMISSIONS: Open to all. Submit by email to info@eyewearpublishing.com. Sometimes charges a readers' fee – check guidelines at www.eyewearpublishing.com/about-us/submission-guidelines/. Usually responds within one to three months. No feedback offered with rejections. Authors are paid royalties only.
For a fuller description of this press see poetry publishers p13

FAHRENHEIT PRESS
NOVELS
chris@fahrenheit-press.com
www.fahrenheit-press.com
Fiction (crime and thrillers) with a punk ethos. Founded by editors with over 25 years of experience in the publishing industry.

FAIR ACRE PRESS ☆
E-BOOKS / NOVELS / SHORT STORY COLLECTIONS AND ANTHOLOGIES / NON-FICTION
fairacrepress@gmail.com
www.fairacrepress.co.uk
Editor: Nadia Kingsley
Established 2011. Predominantly publishes poetry (see p13), but with increasing focus on prose. Publications available direct from publisher website; and at national and local literary events. Represented by Signature Books and expects books to be more widely available soon.
GENRES: Some focus on art,

photography, popular science and nature.
SUBMISSIONS: Solicited work only, unless submissions made through competitions or other opportunities are announced on the website. Usually responds within one to three months. Rejections may occasionally include unsolicited feedback. Authors are paid royalties only and receive free copies of the book.
WE SAY: We looked at *Sitting Ducks*, by Lisa Blower. Fair Acre Press give the impression of being quietly political, and this book fits that impression well. Perfect bound and 240 pages long, this is a funny but angry novel with clear political alliances. It's a novel for the working class (and a strong indicator of just how small presses take risks that larger publishers wouldn't). The layout is clean; the book is quite weighty. The occasional image and the use of 'rounds' instead of chapters tick the box towards experimental literature. All round, the impression is that Fair Acre Press is one to keep an eye on.
See also: poetry publishers p13

FICTION DESK, THE
E-BOOKS / SHORT STORY ANTHOLOGIES
Suite 1, First Floor, 41 Chalton Street, London NW1 1JD
info@thefictiondesk.com
www.thefictiondesk.com
Fiction: short stories anthologies pulled together from open submissions. Resulting book themes depend entirely on what the press has been sent.

FITZCARRALDO EDITIONS ☆
243 KNIGHTSBRIDGE, LONDON SW7 1DN

info@fitzcarraldoeditions.com
www.fitzcarraldoeditions.com
Editor: Jacques Testard
Established 2014. Mixed-form publisher: primarily publishes literary fiction and non-fiction/ essays, but also some poetry (see p13). Publications available direct from publisher website; by post and email order; from chain bookshops and independent bookshops nationwide; at national and local literary events; and from Amazon. Offers a books subscription: £70 for eight books, £35 for four. Fitzcarraldo title *My Documents,* by Alejandro Zambra, was shortlisted for the 2015 Frank O'Connor Short Story Award.
SUBMISSIONS: Open to all.

FISH PUBLISHING ☆
E-BOOKS / NOVELS / SHORT STORY COLLECTIONS AND ANTHOLOGIES
Durrus, Bantry, Co. Cork, Ireland
info@fishpublishing.com
www.fishpublishing.com
Editors: Clem Cairns, Jula Walton, Mary-Jane Holmes

Fish Anthology 2015

Established 1995. Mixed form: anthologies include short fiction, poetry (see p13) and memoir. Publications available direct from publisher website; by post and email order; from chain bookshops nationwide; from independent bookshops; and from Amazon.
GENRES: Literary fiction; YA; biography and true stories.
SUBMISSIONS: Open to all, during submissions windows. Submit by post to Fish Publishing, Durrus, Bantry, Co Cork, Ireland or by email to info@fishpublishing.com. See guidelines at www.fishpublishing. com. Usually responds within four weeks. Rejections may occasionally include unsolicited feedback. Authors are paid a flat fee or royalties only, depending on the publication, and free copies of the book.

WE SAY: The *Fish Anthology* is a perfect-bound 248-page publication with a gloss laminate cover. We looked at the 2015 edition, which features the prizewinners from its many writing competitions (including memoir, flash, short fiction and poetry) – a must-read for any writer preparing submissions for a Fish Prize.

See also: poetry publishers p13

Usually responds within one to three months. Rejections may occasionally include unsolicited feedback. Authors are paid an advance/fee plus royalties.

WE SAY: Fitzcarraldo publications are instantly recognisable and top quality. We looked at *Pond* by Claire Louise-Bennett: an 184-page book of essays; paperback, with French flaps. The cover is plain: Fitzcarraldo's signature Royal blue, with white text. (The fiction titles invert the colours.) The inner formatting, on high-grade white paper, is clean and uncluttered, and the press uses its own serif typeface called Fitzcarraldo.

See also: poetry publishers p13

FIVE LEAVES PUBLICATIONS

E-BOOKS / SHORT STORY ANTHOLOGIES / NON-FICTION
Five Leaves Bookshop, 14a Long Row, Nottingham NG1 2DH
info@fiveleaves.co.uk
www.fiveleaves.co.uk
Editor: Ross Bradshaw

Established 1995. Primarily non-fiction, but also publishes fiction and poetry (see p13). Publications available direct from publisher website; by post and email order; from selected/local chain bookshops; from independent bookshops; at local literary events; from Amazon and other bookshop websites; and from Inpress.com.

GENRES: Literary fiction; history; society, education and politics; Jewish interest.

SUBMISSIONS: Solicited work only. Authors are paid an advance/fee plus royalties. Any unsolicited submissions receive a standard rejection.

For a fuller description of this press see poetry publishers p13

FLEDGLING PRESS

E-BOOKS / NOVELS / SHORT STORY COLLECTIONS / NON-FICTION
39 Argyle Crescent, Edinburgh EH15 2QE
0131 6572 8188
clare@fledglingpress.co.uk
www.fledglingpress.co.uk
Editor: Clare Cain

Mainly publishes fiction. Publications available direct from publisher website; from chain bookshops nationwide; from independent bookshops; and from Amazon and other bookshop websites.

Fledging Press title *The Incomers* by Moira McPartlin was shortlisted for the 2012 Saltire First Book Prize.

GENRES: Crime/thriller/mystery; historical fiction; YA; biography and true stories.

SUBMISSIONS: Open to all. Submit by email to submissions@fledglingpress.co.uk. Guidelines at www.fledglingpress.co.uk/submissions/. Usually responds within four to six months. Rejections may occasionally include unsolicited feedback; confirmed feedback only if requested. Authors are paid an advance/fee plus royalties.

WE SAY: We looked at the e-book version of *Board* by David C Flanagan. It's hard to convey quality in an e-book, but Fledgling have managed it, with a striking blue-and-green illustrated cover, and a quirky simple line-drawing at the start of every chapter, as well as a differently formatted first paragraph. Looks great as an e-book; presumably even better in print.

FLIGHT PRESS

SHORT STORY ANTHOLOGIES
Spread the Word
www.spreadtheword.org.uk
The publishing imprint of Spread
the Word, the London writer's
development agency, which
identifies and supports talented
writers from a diversity of
backgrounds. Publications include
anthologies featuring Toby Litt, KJ
Orr and Bidisha.
See also: *Flight Journal* **(prose
e-zine) p202**

FLIPPED EYE PUBLISHING

FICTION
Free Word Centre, 60 Farringdon
Road, London EC1R 3GA
books@flippedeye.net
www.flippedeye.net
Established 2001. Predominantly
publishes poetry, but also some
fiction.
**For a fuller description of this press
see poetry publishers p13**

FOR BOOKS' SAKE

SHORT STORY ANTHOLOGIES
www.forbookssake.net
Mixed-form publisher. Publishes
fiction and non-fiction prose,
but also some poetry (see p13).
Publications available direct from
publisher website; from selected/
local chain bookshops; from
independent bookshops; and at
national and local literary events.
For Book's Sake title *Furies: A
poetry anthology of women
warriors* was runner-up for the
Best Anthology prize at the 2015
Saboteur Awards.
GENRES: Literary fiction; YA;
biography and true stories;
music, stage and screen; society,
education and politics.
SUBMISSIONS: Open to self-

identifying women, and especially
encouraged from women of colour,
disabled women, queer women,
trans women and women from
low-income backgrounds. Submit,
during submissions windows only,
via Submittable (forbookssake.
submittable.com/submit –
guidelines at same address).
Usually responds within four weeks.
**For a fuller description of this press
see poetry publishers p13. See also:**
For Books' Sake **mixed-form e-zine
p143**

FOX SPIRIT

SHORT STORY ANTHOLOGIES
adele@foxspirit.co.uk
www.foxspirit.co.uk
Winner of the British Fantasy
Society's Best Small Press 2015.
Anthology fiction, in e-book and
print-on-demand formats, with calls
for submissions defined by theme
or anthology title.

FREIGHT BOOKS

E-BOOKS / NOVELS / SHORT STORY
COLLECTIONS AND ANTHOLOGIES
/ NON-FICTION
49 Virginia Street, Glasgow G1 1TS
info@freightbooks.co.uk
www.freightbooks.co.uk
Editor: Henry Bell
Established 2011. Mainly publishes
fiction, but also some non-fiction
and poetry (see p13). Publications
available direct from publisher
website; from chain bookshops
nationwide; from independent
bookshops; at national and local
literary events; and from Amazon
and other bookshop websites.
Shortlisted for the Saltire Society's
Scottish Publisher of the Year
Award 2013 and 2014.
GENRES: Crime/thriller/mystery;
historical fiction; literary fiction;

86

YA; art, fashion and photography; food and drink; humour; sports and leisure; travel. No children's fiction. **SUBMISSIONS:** Open to all. Guidelines on the website. Usually responds in over six months, with feedback only if requested. Authors are paid an advance/fee plus royalties.

For a fuller description of this press see *Gutter Magazine* (mixed-form literary magazine) p145. See also poetry publishers p13

GALLEY BEGGAR PRESS ☆

E-BOOKS / NOVELS / SHORT STORY COLLECTIONS / NON-FICTION
info@galleybeggar.co.uk
www.galleybeggar.co.uk
Editors: Eloise Millar, Sam Jordison
Established 2012. Mainly publishes fiction, including Galley Beggar singles – long short stories available as downloads. Publications available direct from publisher website; by post and email order; from chain bookshops nationwide; from independent bookshops; at national and local literary events; and from bookshop websites.
Won the Baileys Prize for Fiction 2014 with Eimear McBride's *A Girl is a Half-Formed Thing*.
GENRES: Literary fiction; biography and true stories.
SUBMISSIONS: Open to all. Submit by email to info@galleybeggar.co.uk. Guidelines at galleybeggar.co.uk/blog/201402/submissions. Usually responds within four to six months. Rejections may occasionally include unsolicited feedback. Authors are paid an advance/fee plus royalties.
WE SAY: We looked at one of Galley Beggar's 'singles': the novella *Rabbits* by Ruby Cowling.

We were offered three different file formats for this e-book; all equally plain and no-nonsense. E-books of full-length novels are somewhat fancier, but stick with the Galley Beggar aesthetic of plain cover and good formatting. The editors have an eye for experimental fiction, and received an influx of submissions after the success of *A Girl is a Half-formed Thing*. We commend their short story and singles publication options for emerging writers.

GATEHOUSE PRESS ☆

SHORT STORY COLLECTIONS / NOVELLAS
90 Earlham Road, Norwich, Norfolk NR2 3HA
admin@gatehousepress.com
www.gatehousepress.com
Editors: Meirion Jordan, Andrew McDonnell, Julia Webb, Philip Langeskov, Anna de Vaul, Jo Surzyn, Angus Sinclair, Scott Dahlie, Iain Robinson, Zoe Kingsley
Established 2006. Mainly publishes poetry (see p13), but also some fiction. Publications available direct from publisher website; from selected/local chain bookshops; from independent bookshops; at national and local literary events; and from bookshop websites.
GENRES: Literary fiction.
SUBMISSIONS: Submit during submissions windows. Usually responds within one to three months. No feedback offered with rejections. Writer payment/remuneration varies according to publication.
For a fuller description of this press see *Lighthouse* (mixed-form literary magazine) p151. See also poetry publishers p13

GEMSTONE ROMANCE
E-BOOKS / NOVELS / NOVELLAS
contact@gemstoneromance.com
gemstoneromance.com
Editor: Charlotte Courtney
Established 2015. Publications available direct from publisher website; and Amazon.
GENRES: Romance.
SUBMISSIONS: During submissions windows. Submit by email to submissions@gemstoneromance.com. Guidelines at gemstoneromance.com/?page_id=4. Usually responds within one to three months. All rejections include some feedback. Authors are paid an advance/fee plus royalties.
WE SAY: Romance publishers, and proud of it. Gemstone design and publish according to what romance fans expect: the painted portrait-type cover images, windswept landscapes, and pink banding are reminiscent of Mills & Boon.

GHASTLING PRESS, THE
SHORT STORY ANTHOLOGIES, ARTWORK AND ILLUSTRATION
editor@theghastling.com
www.theghastling.com
Editor: Rebecca Parfitt
Established 2014. Primarily publishes fiction. Publications available from Amazon.
GENRES: Graphic/comics; horror; literary fiction.
SUBMISSIONS: During submissions windows, submit by email to editor@theghastling.com. Usually responds within one to three months.
For a fuller description of this press, including what They Say, see *The Ghastling* (prose magazine) p203

GRANTA BOOKS
NOVELS / SHORT STORY COLLECTIONS AND ANTHOLOGIES / NON-FICTION
12 Addison Avenue, London W11 4QR
020 7605 1360
info@grantabooks.com
www.grantabooks.com
Editors: Sigrid Rausing, Laura Barber, Bella Lacey, Max Porter, Anne Meadows, Ka Bradley
Established 1989. Publications available from chain bookshops nationwide; from independent bookshops; at national and local literary events; and from Amazon and other bookshop websites. Shortlisted for the 2014 Independent Publisher of the Year Award.
GENRES: Literary fiction; history; popular science and nature; technology; medicine; society, education and politics; travel.
SUBMISSIONS: Agented submissions only. Usually responds within four weeks. Rejections may occasionally include unsolicited feedback. Writers are paid an advance/fee plus royalties.
WE SAY: One of the most well-heeled presses in this Guide, Granta's titles are of very high quality. *A Ghost's Story* by Lorna Gibb is a literary love story published as a chunky hardback (clothbound, with dust jacket). The cover has a slightly 80s romance aesthetic. Clear formatting and good blurb.
See also: *Granta Magazine* (mixed-form literary magazine) p144 and Portobello Books p105

GRAY FRIAR PRESS
NOVELS
www.grayfriarpress.com
Editor: Gary Fry

Well-regarded horror fiction publisher, with a bevy of established writers on its list.

GYLPHI LIMITED
E-BOOKS / NON-FICTION (ACADEMIC)
PO Box 993, Canterbury CT1 9EP
info@gylphi.co.uk
www.gylphi.co.uk
Established 2007. Academic non-fiction. Publications available direct from publisher website; from chain bookshops nationwide; from independent bookshops; and from Amazon.
GENRES: Academic books on twentieth- and twenty-first-century arts and humanities subjects for university-level study and research.
SUBMISSIONS: Usually from writers holding a university doctorate. Submit by post (Submissions, Gylphi Limited, PO Box 993, CT1 9EP) or by email (info@gylphi.co.uk). Usually responds within one to three months, with feedback. Authors receive free copies of the book.

HAFAN BOOKS (REFUGEES WRITING IN WALES)
SHORT STORY ANTHOLOGIES
c/o Tom Cheesman, Dept of Languages, Swansea University SA2 8PP
t.cheesman@swansea.ac.uk
lulu.com/hafan
sbassg.wordpress.com
Editors: Tom Cheesman, Jeni Williams
Established 2003. Mixed form: publishes poetry (see p13) and prose, and various refugee-related books and booklets. Publications available direct from publisher website; by post and email order; at local literary events; and from Amazon.

SUBMISSIONS: Open to all, by invitation only. Author contributions needed. Submit by email to t.cheesman@swansea. ac.uk. Usually responds within four weeks. Rejections may occasionally include unsolicited feedback. Authors receive free copies of the book; no fee or royalties.
WE SAY: Hafan Books is part of local community efforts to support asylum seekers and refugees. All proceeds from sales go to Swansea Bay Asylum Seekers Support Group.
See also: poetry publishers p13

HEAD OF ZEUS
E-BOOKS / NOVELS / SHORT STORY COLLECTIONS AND ANTHOLOGIES / NON-FICTION
020 7253 5557
hello@headofzeus.com
www.headofzeus.com
Editors: Anthony Cheetham, Amanda Ridout, Nicolas Cheetham, Laura Palmer, Rosie de Courcy, Neil Belton, Richard Milbank, Madeleine O'Shea
Established 2011. Mixed form. Publications available from chain bookshops nationwide; from independent bookshops; at national and local literary events; and from Amazon and other bookshop websites.
Winner: Digital Business of the Year at The Bookseller Awards 2015.
GENRES: Crime/thriller/mystery; fantasy/sci-fi; historical fiction; literary fiction; romance; biography and true stories; history; popular science and nature; society, education and politics.
SUBMISSIONS: Submit through the online form at www.headofzeus. com.
WE SAY: One of the largest and most established indie presses

that are still open to unsolicited submissions. Titles are available in print and digital formats. The paperback we checked out, *The Washington Stratagem* by Adam LeBor, is an adult thriller with a striking cover but slightly flimsy page quality. A slick website, elegant catalogue and active social media presence complete the polished HoZ package.

HONNO WELSH WOMEN'S PRESS

E-BOOKS / NOVELS / SHORT STORY ANTHOLOGIES / NON-FICTION
14 Creative Units, Aberystwyth Arts Centre, Aberystwyth, Ceredigion SY23 3GL
01970 623150
post@honno.co.uk
www.honno.co.uk
Editors: Caroline Oakley, Janet Thomas

Established 1986. Mainly fiction, including classics. Publications available direct from publisher website; from chain bookshops nationwide; from independent bookshops; at national and local literary events; and from Amazon and other bookshop websites. Winner of the Bread and Roses Award for Radical Publishing 2015 with *Here We Stand: women changing the world*.
GENRES: Crime/thriller/mystery; historical fiction; literary fiction; biography and true stories.
SUBMISSIONS: Submissions only open to women who are Welsh or living in Wales or have a significant Welsh connection. Submit by post to Commissioning Editor, 14 Creative Units, Aberystwyth Arts Centre, Aberystwyth, Ceredigion SY23 3GL. Guidelines at www.honno.co.uk/infowriters.php. Usually responds within four

THEY SAY

Great books, great writing, great women! Honno publishes vibrant new fiction, autobiography, short story anthologies, and classics from great Welsh women writers. Established in 1986, Honno is an independent co-operative press run by women and committed to bringing you the best in Welsh women's writing.

to six months. Rejections may occasionally include unsolicited feedback. Writers receive a flat fee or an advance/fee plus royalties, as well as free copies of their book.
WE SAY: We looked at *All Shall be Well*, a perfect-bound 356-page anthology that is professionally designed with a smart matt cover. Printed on quality paper, each item in the anthology is heralded by an image and, interestingly, it includes fiction and non-fiction pieces. This publication is full of wit and demonstrates the talent of Welsh women writers.

HOGS BACK BOOKS LTD
CHILDREN'S BOOKS
The Stables, Down Place, Hogs Back, Guildford GU3 1DE
enquiries@hogsbackbooks.com
www.hogsbackbooks.com
Bright and beautiful children's fiction and picture books up to age 10.

HOLLAND HOUSE BOOKS
E-BOOKS / NOVELS / SHORT STORY COLLECTIONS / NOVELLAS
Holland House, 47 Greenham Road, Newbury, Berkshire RG14 7HY
01635 36527
contact@hhousebooks.com
www.hhousebooks.com
Editors: Robert Peett, Bustles Lloyd, Natasha Robson
Established 2012. Fiction.
GENRES: Crime/thriller/mystery; historical fiction; literary fiction. No non-fiction.
SUBMISSIONS: Open to all. Submit via www.hhousebooks.com/submissions/ (guidelines at the same address). Usually responds within four weeks. Rejections may occasionally include unsolicited feedback. Authors are paid royalties only, and receive free copies of their book.
WE SAY: We looked at several e-books from Holland House. The cover images were simple and striking, and the books had working contents pages and a healthy amount of information about the authors. What struck us, though, was the lack of branding – no logos or prelims – which seemed odd. Reassuringly, though, the quality of design, materials and branding in the print versions are much higher, and the books would not look out of place in Waterstones.

HONEST PUBLISHING
NOVELS / NON-FICTION
Clapham North Arts Centre, 26-32 Voltaire Road, London SW4 6DH
info@honestpublishing.com
www.honestpublishing.com
Fiction and non-fiction. Looks for unique authors with alternative, original voices that have been neglected by the mainstream.

HORRIFIC TALES PUBLISHING
E-BOOKS / NOVELS
admin@horrifictales.co.uk
www.horrifictales.co.uk
Editors: Lisa Jenkins, Simon Marshall Jones, Kerri Patterson
Established 2011. Fiction. Publications available from chain bookshops nationwide; and from Amazon and other bookshop websites.
Horrific Tales Titles *High Moor*, *High Moor 2: Moonstruck*, *Whispers* and *Angel Manor* were all semi-finalists in the Bram Stoker awards (2011, 2012, 2013, 2014).
GENRES: Horror.
SUBMISSIONS: Open to all, during submissions windows. Submit by email to submissions@horrifictales.co.uk. Guidelines at www.horrifictales.co.uk/submissions. Usually responds within one to three months. Rejections may occasionally include unsolicited feedback. Authors are paid an advance/fee plus royalties and receive free copies of the book.
WE SAY: We saw PDF copies of *Lucky's Girl* by William Holloway and *Bottled Abyss* by Benjamin Kane Ethridge – both available as print and e-books. Horrific Tales' titles sport classic horror covers – *Lucky's Girl* is a doozy – a cross between the old Pan Horror anthologies and *Goosebumps*. The

inner pages are well formatted, with the occasional illustrative decoration between chapters. It's worth noting that Horrific Tales' website includes a merchandising section, where cover images are reprised as t-shirts etc. An ingenious bit of marketing.

IGNITE BOOKS
NOVELS / NON-FICTION
hello@ignitebooks.co.uk
www.ignitebooks.co.uk
Described by one reviewer as 'an act of defiance', Ignite works to prove that unmarketable books can be marketed. Bold, genre-defying writing in all forms.

INFINITY PLUS
NOVELS / SHORT STORY COLLECTIONS / NON-FICTION
kbrooke@infinityplus.co.uk
www.infinityplus.co.uk
Editor: Keith Brooke
Established 2010. Publications available in print and as e-books from Amazon and other bookshop websites, and orderable by bookshops.
GENRES: Fantasy/sci-fi; horror; biography and true stories.
SUBMISSIONS: Submissions by invitation or query only. Usually responds within four weeks. Rejections may occasionally include unsolicited feedback. Authors are paid royalties and receive free copies of the book.
WE SAY: We looked at the catalogue of e-books by Infinity Plus: another small press doing right by the genres it represents. The sci-fi in particular stands out: dreamy other-worldly covers replete with futuristic technology and chrome text. We weren't able to assess the print quality, but the blurbs are professional and the formatting flawless, so we feel confident that IP titles can easily hold their own against Orbit or any other large sci-fi publishing house.

INFLUX PRESS
E-BOOKS / NOVELS / SHORT STORY COLLECTIONS AND ANTHOLOGIES / NON-FICTION
Unit 3a, Mill Co Project,
3 Gaunson House, Markfield Road,
London N15 4QQ
www.influxpress.com
Editors: Kit Caless, Gary Budden
Established 2012. Mixed form: fiction, non-fiction and also poetry (p13). Publications available direct from publisher website; from chain bookshops nationwide; from independent bookshops; at local literary events; and from Amazon and other bookshop websites. Influx title *Above Sugar Hill* by Linda Mannheim was nominated for the Edge Hill Short Story Prize.
GENRES: Literary fiction; weird fiction; London writing; city literature; biography and true stories; history; society, education and politics; travel.
SUBMISSIONS: During submissions windows only, otherwise agented submissions or submissions by invitation only. Submit by email to submissions@influxpress.com. Guidelines at www.influxpress.com/submissions/. Usually responds within four to six months. No feedback offered with rejections. Authors are paid royalties only or an advance/fee plus royalties, and receive free copies of the book.
WE SAY: It's worth noting Influx Press are in the forefront of the drive to increase diversity in writing and publishing. They look for brave work that traditional publishers

wouldn't take risks on. We looked at digital versions of *Above Sugar Hill* by Linda Mannheim and *Imaginary Cities* by Darran Anderson. Although *Sugar Hill* is a short story collection and *Cities* is creative non-fiction, both are distinctly urban in feel. *Sugar Hill* includes an afterword explaining how the book came about, which indicates how closely Influx work with their authors. The covers are bright painted illustrations. Print versions appear to be on quality materials.

See also: poetry publishers p13

IRON PRESS

COLLECTIONS AND ANTHOLOGIES
5 Marden Terrace, Cullercoats,
North Shields NE30 4PD
0191 253 1901
ironpress@blueyonder.co.uk
www.ironpress.co.uk
Editor: Peter Mortimer
Established 1973. Primarily publishes poetry (see p13), but also releases some prose (fiction, drama, etc). Publications available direct from publisher website; by post and email order; from selected/local chain bookshops; from independent bookshops; and via Inpress Ltd.
Iron Press's 2014 Iron Age Literary Festival won Best Event: Tyneside in The Journal Culture Awards.
GENRES: Literary.
SUBMISSIONS: Contact the press before submitting work: see the website for guidelines. Submit by post (5 Marden Terrace, Cullercoats, North Shields NE30 4PD) or by email (ironpress@blueyonder.co.uk). Usually responds within one to three months. Rejections may occasionally include unsolicited feedback. Authors are paid a flat fee.
For a fuller description of this press, see poetry publishers p13

ISTROS BOOKS

E-BOOKS / NOVELS / SHORT STORY COLLECTIONS / NON-FICTION
Conway Hall, 25 Red Lion Square, London WC1R 4RL
0207 388 8886
info@istrosbooks.com
www.istrosbooks.com
Editor: Susan Curtis-Kojakovic
Established 2010. Primarily publishes fiction. Publications available direct from publisher website; from chain bookshops nationwide; from independent bookshops; and from Amazon and other bookshop websites.
GENRES: Literary fiction; history; society, education and politics.
SUBMISSIONS: Publication history required, as submissions are by invitation only. Submit by email to contact@istrosbooks.com. Usually responds within four weeks. Rejections may occasionally include unsolicited feedback. Authors are paid royalties and receive free copies of the book.
WE SAY: Specialising in translated work from Eastern Europe, Istros is on a mission to change the image of that region from 'grey tower blocks and cabbage' to the vibrant culture they are familiar with. A glance through their catalogue reveals designs that reflect this ethos: original illustrated covers with grey backgrounds and technicolour images. With their signature bright stripe of colour running down the edge of each cover, Istros books are instantly recognisable.

IVY PRESS

ILLUSTRATED NON-FICTION
210 High Street, Lewes BN7 2NS
www.ivypress.co.uk
Integrated, illustrated non-fiction
books for the international market,
released under three imprints.
Subject areas include popular
culture; art and design; crafts;
general reference; health and
parenting; mind, body, spirit;
humour and novelty. Unsolicited
proposals welcome (synopses, not
manuscripts) by email (ivyauthors@
quarto.com) or post.

KATABASIS

NON-FICTION
10 St Martin's Close, London
NW1 0HR
0207 485 3830
katabasis@katabasis.co.uk
www.katabasis.co.uk
Publishes both poetry and prose
– including essays and personal
accounts.
See also: poetry publishers p13

LAGAN PRESS

NOVELS / NON-FICTION
Verbal Arts Centre, Stable Lane
& Mall Wall, Bishop Street Within,
Derry-Londonderry BT48 6PU
028 7126 6946
info@laganpress.co
www.laganpress.co
Mixed form: also publishes poetry
collections. Looks for work of
'literary, artistic, social and cultural
importance to the north of Ireland'.
Irish and Ulster-Scots language
work also welcomed.
See also: prose publishers p65

LIBERTIES PRESS

NOVELS / NON-FICTION /
COLLECTIONS / ANTHOLOGIES /
E-BOOKS

140 Terenure Road North,
Dublin 6W, Ireland
+353 1905 6072
info@libertiespress.com
www.libertiespress.com
Founded in 2003 and billed as
Ireland's leading independent
publisher. Publishes non-fiction,
fiction and some poetry (see p13).
GENRES: Fiction; non-fiction;
business; memoir; health; history;
sport; short stories; essay.
See also: poetry publishers p13

LINEN PRESS

NOVELS / NON-FICTION
lynn@linen-press.com
linen-press.com
Run by women, for women.
Looks for literary fiction, top-
end contemporary fiction, and
memoir. Also considers non-fiction
that's relevant to women's lives
and experiences. Particularly
welcoming submissions from
established and emergent writers,
writers from minority groups and
translated work.

LITRO MAGAZINE LTD

SHORT STORIES COLLECTIONS
1- 15 Cremer Street, 21.3, Hoxton,
London E2 8HD
020 3371 9971
info@litro.com
www.litro.com
Editors: Eric Akoto, Precious Williams
Established 2005. Fiction. Litro also
runs a literary agency. Publications
available direct from publisher
website; from chain bookshops
nationwide; from independent
bookshops; at national and local
literary events; and at galleries and
public spaces across London.
GENRES: Crime/thriller/mystery;
drama and criticism; literary fiction;
art, fashion and photography; food

and drink; music, stage and screen; science, technology and medicine; society, education and politics; travel.

For a fuller description of this press, see *Litro Magazine* (mixed-form literary magazine and e-zine) p152

LITTLE TOLLER BOOKS

NON-FICTION
gracie@littletoller.co.uk
www.littletoller.co.uk
Editor: Adrian Cooper
Established 2008. Publications available direct from publisher website; by post and email order; from chain bookshops nationwide; from independent bookshops; at national and local literary events; and from Amazon and other bookshop websites.
Longlisted for the Thwaites Wainwright prize.
GENRES: Travel; natural landscape and place writing. No fiction.
SUBMISSIONS: Agent submissions only, by email to gracie@littletoller.co.uk. Usually responds within four to six months. Rejections may occasionally include unsolicited feedback. Authors are paid an advance/fee plus royalties.
WE SAY: High-quality non-fiction in paperback and hardback, Little Toller books include full-colour illustrations, beautiful layouts and informative reads. We particularly loved *Mermaids* by Sophia Kingshill, which charts the history of mermaid folklore through the ages, complete with images, anecdotes and tales. The limited edition Little Toller hardbacks, with clothbound covers, are also worth checking out.

LOOSE CHIPPINGS

NON-FICTION
The Paddocks, Back Ends, Chipping Campden, Gloucestershire GL55 6AU
01386 840435
contact@loosechippings.org
www.loosechippings.org
Editor: Arthur Cunynghame
Largely publishes non-fiction, including travel and memoir – but open to fiction submissions.

MAGIC OXYGEN

E-BOOKS / NOVELS / SHORT STORY ANTHOLOGIES
01297 442824
www.magicoxygen.co.uk
Mainly publishes fiction. Eco-friendly publisher: plants a tree for every book published.

MANDRAKE OF OXFORD

NON-FICTION / FICTION
mandrake@mandrake.uk.net
mandrake.uk.net
Particular interests in occultism, myths, legends, horror and true crime.

MOTHER'S MILK BOOKS ☆

E-BOOKS / NOVELS / SHORT STORY COLLECTIONS AND ANTHOLOGIES / NON-FICTION
Based in Nottingham
0115 937 4592
www.mothersmilkbooks.com
Editor: Teika Bellamy
Established 2011. Mixed form: also publishes poetry (see p13). Publications available direct from publisher website; from independent bookshops; at local literary events; and from Amazon.
GENRES: Children's fiction; fantasy/sci-fi; literary fiction; YA; parenting.
SUBMISSIONS: Open to all. During submissions windows, submit by

email to teika@mothersmilkbooks.com. Submitters are required to show proof of purchase from the press. Usually responds within one to three months. The editors try to give as much useful feedback with rejections as is possible within time constraints. Authors are paid a flat fee; royalties only; or an advance/fee plus royalties. They also receive free copies of the book.

WE SAY: We looked at *The Forgotten and the Fantastical*, a 132-page anthology of 'modern fables and ancient tales', edited by Teika Bellamy: a collection of modern fairy tales for an adult audience. Cover features a simple ink drawing which would definitely appeal to the target audience. Each story has a title page, complete with small illustration, and all were beautifully descriptive and well-written. We particularly enjoyed the 'Notes on the Stories' section at the end, in which each writer explained the origin of the story they'd written. Mother's Milk is essentially a one-woman operation, and the quality is admirable.

For a cover image example and further information, see poetry publishers p13

MUDFOG PRESS

SHORT STORY COLLECTIONS
c/o Beacon Guest, Chop Gate, Stokesley TS9 7JS
contact@mudfog.co.uk
www.mudfog.co.uk
Editors: Pauline Plummer, Jo Heather
Established 1993. Mixed form: also publishes poetry (see p13). Publications available direct from the publisher website.
GENRES: Environmental writing.
SUBMISSIONS: Favours writers

in the Tees Valley, stretching from Whitby to Sunderland, West to Darlington. However also occasionally publishes writers outside this area. Submit by post (Beacon Guest, Chop Gate, Stokesley TS9 7JS) or by email (contact@mudfog.co.uk). Guidelines at www.mudfog.co.uk/submissions/. Usually responds within one to three months. Rejections may occasionally include unsolicited feedback. Authors are able to buy a number of their books at cost-price and sell them at sales price.

WE SAY: *Invisible Sun* by Jan Hunter is a short story chapbook, A5 and 47 pages long, with a cardboard cover and staple spine. The materials used are high quality. The matt laminate cover has a simple photographic design, and the inner pages are satisfyingly thick. It contains just three stories, which are slice-of-life tales written with pathos and humour, and the final page includes a biography and colour photo of the writer.
See also: poetry publishers p13

MURDER SLIM PRESS

NOVELS
22 Bridge Meadow, Hemsby, Norfolk NR29 4NE
moonshine@murderslim.com
www.murderslim.com
Despite the name, not strictly crime fiction. Established in 2004, Murder Slim looks for 'writing at the razor's edge'.

MYRIAD EDITIONS ☆

GRAPHIC NOVELS / E-BOOKS / NOVELS / NON-FICTION
59 Lansdowne Place,
Brighton BN3 1FL
01273 720000

MYRMIDON BOOKS LTD

E-BOOKS / NOVELS / NON-FICTION
Rotterdam House, 116 Quayside,
Newcastle upon Tyne NE1 3DY
0191 206 4005
ed@myrmidonbooks.com
www.myrmidonbooks.com
Editor: Ed Handyside

Established 2006. Mainly publishes
fiction. Publications available
by post and email order; from
chain bookshops nationwide;
from independent bookshops;
at national and local literary
events; and from Amazon and
other bookshop websites. Awards
include winning the 2013 Man
Asian Literary Prize and Walter
Scott Prize for Best Historical
Fiction.

GENRES: Crime/thriller/mystery;
fantasy/sci-fi; historical fiction;
literary fiction; romance; biography
and true stories; history; humour.

SUBMISSIONS: Open to all. Submit
by post (Myrmidon, Rotterdam
House, 116 Quayside, Newcastle
upon Tyne NE1 3DY) or by email
(ed@myrmidonbooks.com).
Guidelines on the website. Usually
responds in over six months. No
feedback offered with rejections.
Authors are paid royalties only, or
an advance/fee plus royalties.

WE SAY: Big Five publications from
a small press. Myrmidon books
come complete with the blurb,
the marketing, the formatting
and the materials to be at home
in any bookshop. We particularly
loved the cover of *Angel* by Jon
Grahame, with its bolted-iron title
and action-filled, yet ethereal,
images.

THEY SAY

Myrmidon are always on the
look out for the following:
literary fiction of exceptional
quality with strong, timeless
stories that deal with big
themes and travel well
internationally – our focus
is always on titles we think
capable of winning major
literary awards; well-written,
page-turning thrillers, crime
novels and other stories with
serious commercial potential;
captivating non-fiction
works with popular appeal –
especially biography, history,
current affairs and TV drama
'tie-ins'.

info@myriadeditions.com
www.myriadeditions.com
Editors: Candida Lacey, Corinne
Pearlman, Vicky Blunden, Holly Ainley
Established 1993. Predominantly
publishes graphic novels.
Publications available direct
from publisher website; from
chain bookshops nationwide;
from independent bookshops; at
national and local literary events;
and from Amazon and other
bookshop websites.
Myriad Editions title *London
Triptych* by Jonathan Kemp won
the Authors' Club Best First Novel
Award 2010.
GENRES: Crime/thriller/mystery;
graphic/comics; historical fiction;
literary fiction; graphic memoir;
graphic medicine.
SUBMISSIONS: Open to all.
Submit by email to submissions@
myriadeditions.com. Guidelines at
www.myriadeditions.com/about/
submissions/. Usually responds
within one to three months.
Gives email feedback on every
submission, and offers more
detailed feedback and consultation
for a fee. Authors are paid an
advance/fee plus royalties, and
receive free copies of the book.
WE SAY: We looked at *Naming
Monsters* by Hannah Eaton, a
massive 176-page graphic novel.
It's beautifully designed, with a full
colour gloss cover and mono inner
pages. Eaton employs different
styles according to the part of the
story being told. Described in the
blurb as 'an adult *Where the Wild
Things Are*', *Naming Monsters* has
been shortlisted for two awards,
and is a reminder of how good
graphic novels can be, while
Myriad's quality act is a reminder of
how well they can be published.

NEGATIVE PRESS
SHORT STORY COLLECTIONS AND
ANTHOLOGIES
info@neg-press.com
www.neg-press.com
Publishes both prose and poetry
books. Visual and verbal creations
and photobooks.
See also: poetry publishers p13

NEON BOOKS
E-BOOKS / SHORT STORY
COLLECTIONS AND ANTHOLOGIES
info@neonmagazine.co.uk
www.neonmagazine.co.uk
Editor: Krishan Coupland
Established 2006. Mixed form:
also publishes poetry (see p13).
Publications available direct
from publisher website; from
independent bookshops; at local
literary events; and from Amazon.
All online content is freely available
to all.
GENRES: Horror; literary fiction. No
non-fiction.
SUBMISSIONS: Open to all. Submit
by email to subs@neonmagazine.
co.uk. Usually responds within one
to three months. Feedback given
to donors to/subscribers of *Neon*.
Authors are paid royalties only and
receive free copies of the book.
**For a fuller description of the
press, see *Neon Literary Magazine*
(mixed form) p158. See also poetry
publishers p13**

NEWCON PRESS
E-BOOKS / NOVELS / SHORT STORY
COLLECTIONS AND ANTHOLOGIES
www.newconpress.co.uk
Editor: Ian Whates
Multi-award-winning publisher
specialising in fantasy, sci-fi, horror
and dark fantasy.

NEW CURIOSITY SHOP, THE ☆

E-BOOKS / SHORT STORY
COLLECTIONS AND ANTHOLOGIES
/ NOVELLAS / NON-FICTION
editor@shorelineofinfinity.com
www.newcurioshop.com
Editor: Noel Chidwick
Established 2003. Publications
available direct from publisher
website; by post and email order;
from independent bookshops;
at local literary events; and from
Amazon.
GENRES: Fantasy/sci-fi; graphic/
comics; narrative non-fiction.
SUBMISSIONS: Open to all. Submit
through the online form at www.
newcurioshop.com/write-for-us/.
Guidelines at the same address.
Usually responds within one to
three months. Rejections may
occasionally include unsolicited
feedback. Writers are paid an
advance/fee plus royalties.
**For a fuller description of this press,
see also *Shoreline of Infinity* (prose
magazine) p207**

NEW ISLAND

NOVELS / NON-FICTION
16 Priory Office Park, Stillorgan,
County Dublin
+ 353 1 278 42 25
info@newisland.ie
www.newisland.ie
Drama, fiction and Irish-focused
non-fiction. Mixed form: also
publishes poetry collections
See also: poetry publishers p13

NIGHTJAR PRESS

SHORT STORY CHAPBOOKS
63 Ballbrook Court, Wilmslow Road,
Manchester M20 3GT
nightjarpress@gmail.com
nightjarpress.weebly.com
Editor: Nicholas Royle
Established 2009. Single-story

chapbooks. Publications available
direct from publisher website;
by post and email order; from
selected/local chain bookshops;
from independent bookshops; and
at local literary events,
GENRES: Fantasy/sci-fi; horror;
literary fiction; uncanny/gothic.
SUBMISSIONS: Open to all – but
strongly encourages writers to
research what the press does
before submitting. Submit by post
(63 Ballbrook Court, Wilmslow
Road, Manchester M20 3GT) or by
email (nightjarpress@gmail.com).
Guidelines at nightjarpress.weebly.
com/about.html. Usually responds
within one to three months.
Rejections may occasionally
include unsolicited feedback.
Authors are paid a flat fee.
WE SAY: Limited edition, single
short story chapbooks of between
12–16 pages, the stories are
published individually and
designed to a consistent house
style of textbook-ish covers and
simple, well-formatted inner pages.
The stories published are distinctly
odd and uncanny – take a good
look before you submit. Each
chapbook is signed by the author,
giving an exclusive, intimate feel.
We liked the succinct author bios
on the back covers.

NOSY CROW

NOVELS / PICTURE BOOKS /
NON-FICTION
The Crow's Nest, 10a Lant Street,
London SE1 1QR
020 7953 7677
submissions@nosycrow.com
www.nosycrow.com
Established 2011. Publisher of
parent-friendly children's books for
ages 0-14 yrs, both commercial
fiction and non-fiction (YA or New

NOTTING HILL EDITIONS ☆
E-BOOKS / NON-FICTION ESSAYS
The Old Vicarage, Broadhembury,
Devon EX14 3ND
contact@nottinghilleditions.com
www.nottinghilleditions.com
Editor: Kim Kremer

Established 2011. Only publishes essays, but on any subject. Publications available direct from publisher website; by post and email order; from chain bookshops nationwide; from independent bookshops; at national and local literary events; and from Amazon and other bookshop websites, including the *Guardian* bookshop. Notting Hill Editions won the 2011 Red Dot Design Award.
GENRES: Essays on art, fashion and photography; biography and true stories; history; science, technology and medicine; society, education and politics. No fiction.
SUBMISSIONS: Open to all. Submit by email to contact@nottinghilleditions.com. Usually responds within one to three months. Rejections may occasionally include unsolicited feedback. Authors are paid a flat fee or royalties only, and receive free copies of the book.
WE SAY: Hardback cloth-bound books with bright bold covers and thick high-quality paper, Notting Hill editions look fantastic on a shelf. These are books that readers collect for decoration as much as for content – which is not to belittle the intelligent, thoughtful writing within.

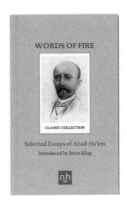

THEY SAY

Welcome to Notting Hill Editions – home of the essay. Notting Hill Editions is an independent publisher devoted to restoring the essay in literary and commercial form.

The unique purpose of the essay is to try out ideas and see where they lead. Hailed as 'the shape of things to come', the Notting Hill Editions brand represents intelligence and imagination, brevity, soul and wit.

Our beautifully produced pocket-sized hardbacks cover a wide range of subjects by some of the most prominent authors and thinkers of our time, as well as introducing new writers and works in translation.

Adult), and creates interactive multimedia apps.
Multi-award-winning publishers, including the 2016 IPG Independent Publisher of the Year Award and Children's Publisher of the Year Award.
SUBMISSIONS: Open to all, preferably by email. Guidelines at nosycrow.com/contact/submission-guidelines/. Tries to respond to all submissions within six months.

NOT BAD BOOKS

NOVELS / NON-FICTION
Port 57, 57 Albert Road, Portsmouth PO5 2SF
ben@notbadbooks.co.uk
www.notbadbooks.co.uk
Editor: Ben Aitken
Fiction and non-fiction.
Very new publishers.

NOTTINGHAM REVIEW, THE

E-BOOKS / SHORT STORY ANTHOLOGIES
thenottinghamreview@gmail.com
www.thenottinghamreview.com
Editor: Spencer Chou
Established 2015.
GENRES: Literary fiction.
SUBMISSIONS: Open to all. Submit by email to thenottinghamreview@gmail.com. Usually responds within four weeks. Rejections may occasionally include unsolicited feedback.
For a fuller description of this press, see *The Nottingham Review* (mixed-form literary magazine) p162

OLD STREET PUBLISHING

E-BOOKS / NOVELS / NON-FICTION
c/o Parallel.net, 8 Hurlingham Business Park, Sulivan Road, London SW6 3DU
020 8787 5812
info@oldstreetpublishing.co.uk
oldstreetpublishing.co.uk
Award-winning publisher: won the IMPAC with Rawi Hage's *De Niro's Game*, and the BBC National Short Story Award.

OXYGEN BOOKS

NOVELS / SHORT STORY COLLECTIONS / NON-FICTION
www.oxygenbooks.co.uk
Literary travel books, including the City-lit series.

PANKHEARST

E-BOOKS / NOVELS / SHORT STORY COLLECTIONS AND ANTHOLOGIES
editor@pankhearst.com
www.pankhearst.com
Editors: Evangeline Jennings, Lucy Middlesmass, Kate Garrett
Established 2012. Mixed form: also publishes poetry collections, anthologies and chapbooks (see p13). Publications available in independent bookshops; at local literary events; and from Amazon and other bookshop websites. Also publishes one poem and one short story a week online.
Pankhearst was shortlisted for the 2015 Saboteur Award for Excellence in Independent Publishing: Best Novella.
GENRES: Crime/thriller/mystery; fantasy/sci-fi; YA.
SUBMISSIONS: Open to all. Guidelines at pankhearst.wordpress.com/general-information/ (the submission process varies, project to project). Usually responds within four weeks. Rejections may occasionally include unsolicited feedback. Author payment varies by project, but writers are never asked to pay anything.
For a fuller description of this press see poetry publishers p13

PARTHIAN BOOKS
E-BOOKS / NOVELS / SHORT STORY
COLLECTIONS AND ANTHOLOGIES
/ NON-FICTION
426 Grove Building, Swansea
University, Singleton Park SA2 8PP
01792 606605
susieparthian@gmail.com;
c.houguez@gmail.com
www.parthianbooks.com
Editors: Susie Wild, Claire Houguez
Established 1993. Mixed form:
also publishes poetry (see p13).
Publications available direct from
publisher website; from chain
bookshops nationwide; from

PATRICIAN PRESS
E-BOOKS / NOVELS / SHORT
STORY COLLECTIONS
51 Free Rodwell House,
School Lane, Mistley,
Manningtree CO11 1HW
07968 288651
patricia@patricianpress.com
www.patricianpress.com
Editor: Patricia Borlenghi

Killing
Hapless Ally
Anna Vought

Established 2012. Mainly
publishes fiction, but also
some poetry books (see p13).
Publications available direct from
publisher website; from selected/
local chain bookshops; from
independent bookshops; at local
literary events; and from Amazon
and other bookshop websites,
including The Great British
Bookshop website.
GENRES: Children's fiction;
historical fiction; literary fiction;
art, fashion and photography;
biography and true stories;
children and teenagers; food
and drink; society, education and
politics.
SUBMISSIONS: Open to new
and unpublished writers
without agents. Submit during
submissions windows, by
email (patricia@patricianpress.
com) or via the form at www.
patricianpress.com/submissions/
(guidelines at the same address).
Usually responds within one to
three months. Rejections may
occasionally include unsolicited
feedback. Author contributions
are needed for publications.
Authors are paid royalties only.
WE SAY: We looked at the
e-book version of Patricia
Borlenghi's *Dorek: Deaf
and Unheard*, a novel that
incorporates poetry at the
beginning of each chapter and
includes an Afterword to set
the novel in context. The cover
design is abstract and well-
balanced.
See also: poetry publishers p13

independent bookshops; at local literary events; and from Amazon and other bookshop websites. Parthian Books' title *Forgotten Footprints* by John Harrison won the British Guild of Travel Writers' Best Narrative Award, 2014, and *Rhys Davies: A Writer's Life* by Meic Stephens won Wales Book of the Year 2014. Jemma King's *The Shape of a Forest* was shortlisted for the Dylan Thomas Prize in 2014. **GENRES:** Crime/thriller/mystery; drama and criticism; historical fiction; literary fiction; art, fashion and photography; biography and true stories; music, stage and screen; popular science and nature. **SUBMISSIONS:** Open to all. Submit by post to 426 Grove Building, Swansea University, Singleton Park, Swansea SA2 8PP. Guidelines at www.parthianbooks.com/contact. Usually responds within one to three months. Rejections may occasionally include unsolicited feedback. Authors are paid an advance/fee plus royalties. **WE SAY:** One of the larger 'small' presses, Parthian has an international reach and produces high-quality books.
See also: poetry publishers p13

PEEPAL TREE PRESS
NOVELS / SHORT STORY COLLECTIONS AND ANTHOLOGIES
contact@peepaltreepress.com
www.peepaltreepress.com
Editors: Jeremy Poynting, Kwame Dawes, Jacob Ross, Kadija Sesay
Established 1986. Mixed form: also publishes poetry (see p13). Specialises in Caribbean and Black British writing. Publications available direct from publisher website; by post and email order; from chain bookshops and independent bookshops nationwide; at national and local literary events; and from Amazon and other bookshop websites. Peepal Tree title *Sounding Ground* by Vladimir Lucien was overall winner for The OCM Bocas Prize for Caribbean Literature 2015. **GENRES:** Drama and criticism; literary fiction; historical fiction; biography and true stories; history; music, stage and screen. **SUBMISSIONS:** Open to all, specialising in Caribbean and Black British writing. Submit through Submittable at peepaltreepress. submittable.com (guidelines at same address). Usually responds within four to six months. Rejections may occasionally include unsolicited feedback, and some manuscripts by UK-based authors are offered a (free) in-depth reader report through the press's Inscribe Writer Development Programme. Authors are paid royalties only. **For a fuller description of this press see poetry publishers p13**

PEIRENE PRESS
NOVELLAS
17 Cheverton Road, London N19 3BB
020 7686 1941
www.peirenepress.com
Award-winning boutique publishing house with a focus on European literature in translation.

PENDRAGON PRESS
NOVELS / SHORT STORY COLLECTIONS AND ANTHOLOGIES / NOVELLAS
chris@pendragonpress.co.uk
www.pendragonpress.co.uk
Horror, fantasy and sci-fi, widely distributed, specialising in novella-length work.

PENNED IN THE MARGINS

E-BOOKS / NOVELS / NON-FICTION / NOVELLAS
Toynbee Studios, 28 Commercial Street, London E1 6AB
020 7375 0121
info@pennedinthemargins.co.uk
www.pennedinthemargins.co.uk
Editor: Tom Chivers

Established 2006. Mixed form: also publishes poetry (see p13). Publications available direct from publisher website; by post and email order; from selected/local chain bookshops; from independent bookshops; at local literary events; and from Amazon.
Penned in the Margins won

PENNYSHORTS ☆

SHORT FICTION SINGLE E-BOOKS
editor@pennyshorts.com
www.pennyshorts.com
Editor: Catherine Horlick

Established 2015. Short fiction of all genres. Digital publications available by post and email order – accessible by purchase only.
GENRES: Crime/thriller/mystery; fantasy/sci-fi; horror; historical fiction; romance; biography and true stories.
SUBMISSIONS: Open to all. Submit by email to editor@pennyshorts.com. Usually responds within four weeks. Rejections may occasionally include unsolicited feedback.
WE SAY: Lovely e-book nuggets to dip in and out of – we were impressed by the marketing strategy behind pennyshorts, ensuring authors are paid. The e-books/pdfs are very simple – the illustrations for the stories that appear on the website don't carry over to the epubs we looked at. Tightly written and edited fiction straight to your device. Highly recommended.

THEY SAY

pennyshorts sells original short stories of all genres (except children's) online, splitting the proceeds with authors. All stories are professionally proofread and edited and only the very best make the cut. Purchasers are emailed a PDF, a MOBI and an EPUB file for each story. Readers can browse by genre, author, word count or date of publication. Single stories are available on a pay-per-click basis, as are discounted story bundles. Authors can showcase their writing and get paid, and readers can rate and review stories. A subscription makes an ideal Christmas present! Submissions welcome.

Most Innovative Publisher at the Saboteur Awards 2015.
GENRES: Drama and criticism; fantasy/sci-fi; literary fiction and non-fiction.
SUBMISSIONS: Publication history required. Submit by email to submissions@pennedinthemargins. co.uk. Usually responds within one to three months. Rejections may occasionally include unsolicited feedback. Authors are paid royalties only.
For a fuller description of this press see poetry publishers p13

PENNILESS PRESS PUBLICATIONS
NOVELS / SHORT STORY COLLECTIONS
10 Albert Road, Grappenhall, Warrington WA4 2PG
editor@pennilesspress.co.uk
www.pennilesspress.co.uk
Editors: Alan Dent, Ken Clay
Established 2010. Mainly fiction, with some literary criticism. Publications available direct from publisher website; by post and email order; from independent bookshops; and from Amazon and

PERISCOPE
E-BOOKS / NOVELS / NON-FICTION
www.periscopebooks.co.uk
Publisher and commissioning editor: Mitchell Albert

Established 2015. Mixed form: fiction and non-fiction. Publications available by post and email order; from chain bookshops nationwide; from independent bookshops; at national and local literary events; and from Amazon and other bookshop websites.
Periscope title *The Moor's Account* by Laila Lalami was long-listed for the 2015 Man Booker Prize.
GENRES: Crime/thriller/mystery; historical fiction; literary fiction; biography and true stories; food and drink; history; popular science and nature; society, education and politics.
SUBMISSIONS: Open to all.

Submit by email to mitch@ periscopebooks.co.uk. Usually responds within four to six months. Rejections may occasionally include unsolicited feedback. Authors are paid an advance/fee plus royalties and receive free copies of the book.
WE SAY: Periscope publishes books from around the world: top-quality productions on heavy paper; cover designs and formatting are beautiful.

other bookshop websites.
GENRES: Drama and criticism;
literary fiction; literary criticism.
See also: *Penniless Press Magazine*
(mixed-form digital magazine) p164

PETER OWEN PUBLISHERS
E-BOOKS / NOVELS
81 Ridge Road, London N8 9NP
020 8350 1775
info@peterowen.com
www.peterowenpublishers.com
One of the longest-established
small presses. Fiction and non-
fiction. Authors include seven
Nobel Prize winners. A very highly
regarded press.

PHOENIX YARD BOOKS
CHILDREN'S BOOKS
Phoenix Yard, 65 King's Cross Road,
London, WC1X 9LW
020 7239 4968
info@phoenixyardbookscom
www.phoenixyardbooks.com
Children's fiction. Publications
available from chain bookshops
nationwide and from independent
bookshops.
Phoenix Yard books was a winner
in the IPG Independent Publishing
Awards 2013.
GENRES: Children's fiction; YA.
No non-fiction.
SUBMISSIONS: Agented
submissions only.

PILRIG PRESS
NOVELS / E-BOOKS / NON-FICTION
32 Pilrig Street, Edinburgh EH6 5AL
0131 554 1857
enquiries@pilrigpress.co.uk
www.pilrigpress.co.uk
Literary fiction, new crime fiction,
as well as historical fiction and
non-fiction with a focus on
Scotland.

PLATYPUS PRESS
E-BOOKS / SHORT STORY
COLLECTIONS
enquiries@platypuspress.co.uk
www.platypuspress.co.uk
Editors: Michelle Tudor,
Peter Barnfather
Established 2015. Mainly publishes
poetry – see p13. Publications
available from Amazon and other
bookshop websites.
SUBMISSIONS: Open to all.
Submit by email to submissions@
platypuspress.co.uk. Usually
responds within four weeks. No
feedback offered with rejections.
Authors are paid royalties only and
receive free copies of the book.
For a fuller description of this press,
see poetry publishers p13

PLUTO PRESS
E-BOOKS / NON-FICTION
345 Archway Road, London N6 5AA
020 8348 2724
www.plutobooks.com
Editors: David Castle, David Shulman,
Anne Beech
Active for over 40 years, and
independent since 1979. One
of the world's leading radical
publishers, specialising in
progressive, critical perspectives
in politics and the social sciences.
Known for working very closely
with authors and open to
proposals.
SUBMISSIONS: See the extensive
submission information available
at www.plutobooks.com/page/
authors.

PORTOBELLO BOOKS
NOVELS / SHORT STORY
COLLECTIONS / NON-FICTION
12 Addison Avenue, London W11 4QR
020 7605 1360
info@portobellobooks.com;

publicity@portobellobooks.com
www.portobellobooks.com
Editors: Sigrid Rausing, Laura Barber,
Bella Lacey, Max Porter, Anne
Meadows, Ka Bradley
Established 2005. Mixed form:
publishes both fiction and non-
fiction equally. Publications
available from chain bookshops
nationwide; from independent
bookshops; at national and local
literary events; and from Amazon
and other bookshop websites.
Portobello Books was shortlisted
for the 2009 Independent Publisher
of the Year Award.
GENRES: Literary fiction; history;
popular science and nature;
technology and medicine; society,
education and politics; travel.
SUBMISSIONS: Agented
submissions only. Usually responds
within four weeks. Rejections may
occasionally include unsolicited
feedback. Authors are paid an
advance/fee plus royalties.
WE SAY: An imprint within Granta,
Portobello exhibits the same high
standards of publication, but with a
touch more elegance, worldliness
and experimentation. We looked
at *The End of Days* by Jenny
Erpenbeck: a 192-page paperback
available in print and digital
format, and comprising a number
of short stories documenting the
possible lives of the same woman.
We loved the 1920s-inspired cover.
Extremely engaging and highly
recommended.
**See also: Granta Books p87 and
Granta Magazine (mixed-form
literary magazine) p144**

PS PUBLISHING
E-BOOKS / NOVELS / SHORT STORY
COLLECTIONS AND ANTHOLOGIES
/ NON-FICTION

Grosvenor House, 1 New Road,
Hornsea, East Yorkshire
01964 537575
nickycrowther@pspublishing.co.uk
www.pspublishing.co.uk
Editor: Nicky Crowther
Established 1991. Mainly publishes
fiction, but also some poetry
(see p13). Publications available
direct from publisher website;
from Amazon and other bookshop
websites; and at the British Science
Fiction Convention and British
Fantasy Convention.
PS Publishing won The Karl
Wagner Award at the British
Fantasy Awards 2012.
GENRES: Crime/thriller/mystery;
fantasy/sci-fi; horror; literary fiction;
biography and true stories.
SUBMISSIONS: Submissions
welcome by invitation only or
from agents, during submissions
windows. Submit by email to
nickycrowther@pspublishing.
co.uk. Usually responds within one
to three months. Rejections may
occasionally include unsolicited
feedback. Authors may be paid
a flat fee; royalties only; or an
advance/fee plus royalties; and/
or receive free copies of the book
(depending on agreement).
See also: poetry publishers p13

PUSHKIN PRESS
NOVELS / NON-FICTION
Pall Mall Deposit, Unit 43, 124-128
Barlby Road, London W10 6BL
020 3735 9078
books@pushkinpress.com
www.pushkinpress.com
Managing director: Adam
Freudenhaim
Established 1997. One of the
larger indie presses, with a wide
range across fiction and non-
fiction, including novels, essays,

memoirs and children's book. Styles range from timeless classic to urgent contemporary. Includes imprint One.

QUICK BROWN FOX PUBLICATIONS
E-BOOKS / NOVELS / NON-FICTION
adam@quickbrownfoxpublications
co.uk
www.quickbrownfoxpublications.co.uk
Editor: Adam Kirkman
Mainly publishes fiction, but also non-fiction, including cookbooks.

RACK PRESS
NON-FICTION
The Rack, Kinnerton, Presteigne, Powys LD8 2PF
07817 424560
rackpress@nicholasmurray.co.uk
www.rackpress.blogspot.com
Editor: Nicholas Murray
Established 2015. Primarily publishes poetry (see p13). Publications available direct from publisher website; by post and email order; from chain bookshops and independent bookshops nationwide; at national and local literary events; and from bookshop websites.
Rack Press won the 2014 Michael Marks Award for Publisher of the Year.
GENRES: Poetry criticism.
SUBMISSIONS: Open to all. Submit by post (The Rack, Kinnerton, Presteigne, Powys, Wales LD8 2PF) or by email (rackpress@ nicholasmurray.co.uk). Guidelines at www.nicholasmurray.co.uk/ About_Rack_Press.html. Usually responds within four weeks. Rejections may occasionally include unsolicited feedback. Authors receive free copies of the book., plus other copies at discount price

for sale at readings etc.
For a fuller description of this press, see poetry publishers p13

RED SQUIRREL PRESS
E-BOOKS / NOVELS / SHORT STORY COLLECTIONS / NON-FICTION
Briery Hill Cottage, Stannington, Morpeth NE61 6ES
info@redsquirrelpress.com
www.redsquirrelpress.com
Editors: Sheila Wakefield
Established 2006. Mainly publishes poetry (see p13). Publications available direct from publisher website; by post and email order; from chain bookshops nationwide; from independent bookshops; at national and local literary events; and from Amazon and other bookshop websites; and from Inpress.com.
Red Squirrel was shortlisted for the Callum Macdonald Memorial Award 2015.
GENRES: Crime/thriller/mystery; wildlife (non-fiction).
SUBMISSIONS: Open to all. Submit by post to Briery Hill Cottage, Stannington, Morpeth NE61 6ES. Guidelines at www. redsquirrelpress.com/submissions. Usually responds in over six months. No feedback offered with rejections. Authors receive free copies of the book.
For a fuller description of this press, see poetry publishers p13

ROASTBOOKS
SHORT STORY COLLECTIONS AND ANTHOLOGIES
No 31 Peninsula Heights, 93 Albert Embankment, London SE1 7TY
0207 300 7293
info@roastbooks.co.uk
www.roastbooks.co.uk
Specialist short story and flash

fiction publisher, with modern and beautiful designs.

ROUTE PUBLISHING LTD
E-BOOKS / NOVELS / SHORT STORY COLLECTIONS AND ANTHOLOGIES / NON-FICTION
34 Banks Avenue, Pontefract WF8 4DR
01977 793442
info@route-online.com
www.route-online.com
Editor: Ian Daley
Established 2000. Primarily publishes non-fiction above other prose and poetry (see p13). Publications available direct from publisher website; by post and email order; from chain bookshops nationwide; from independent bookshops; at national and local literary events; and from Amazon and other bookshop websites. Route has been shortlisted for the Pen/Ackerley Prize (2008); the James Tait Black Memorial Prize for Fiction (2011); NME Book of the Year (2015); and the Penderyn Prize (Music Book of the Year) (2015).
GENRES: Literary fiction; biography and true stories; music, stage and screen; and sports and leisure.
SUBMISSIONS: Submit during submissions windows. Guidelines at www.route-online.com/submissions. Usually responds within four to six months, with feedback only if an SAE is provided. No feedback offered with rejections. Authors are paid a flat fee, or royalties only, or an advance/fee plus royalties.
WE SAY: *Rites* by Sophie Coulombeau is a contemporary thriller, looking at the false memories of childhood. A well-written and professionally presented 192-page publication that we saw in hardback, with a dust-jacket. A simple effective cover, the title made up of embroidered letters, with threads stretched taut across the page. High-quality materials, professionally formatted.
See also: poetry publishers p13

RUFUS STONE LIMITED EDITIONS
NON-FICTION
07789 220956
mark@rufuspublications.com
www.rufuspublications.com
Editor: Mark Smith
Established 2011. Publications available direct from publisher website.
GENRES: Art, fashion and photography; music, stage and screen.
SUBMISSIONS: Open to all. Submit by email to mark@rufuspublications.com. Usually responds within four weeks. Rejections may occasionally include unsolicited feedback. Authors are paid an advance/fee plus royalties.
WE SAY: We saw the marketing video for a hardback photographic history of Led Zeppelin's *Five Glorious Nights Earls Court 1975*: a coffee-table book on high quality paper, containing 230 photographs of the band, plus articles, with beautiful layout. We liked the unique approach of a YouTube video advertising the book.

SACRISTY PRESS
NOVELS / NON-FICTION
PO Box 612, Durham DH1 9HT
0191 303 8313
enquiries@sacristy.co.uk
www.sacristy.co.uk
Editor: Thomas Ball
Established 2011. Primarily

publishes non-fiction, but also some novels and poetry (see p13). Publications available direct from publisher website; from selected/local chain bookshops; from independent bookshops; at local literary events; and from Amazon and other bookshop websites.

GENRES: Historical fiction; history; spirituality and beliefs.

SUBMISSIONS: Open to all. All submission information at www.sacristy.co.uk/info/authors. Author contributions needed. Usually responds within one to three months. Rejections may occasionally include unsolicited feedback. Authors are paid royalties only.

See also: poetry publishers p13

SALT PUBLISHING LTD

E-BOOKS / NOVELS / SHORT STORY COLLECTIONS AND ANTHOLOGIES
12 Norwich Rd, Cromer NR27 0AX
01263 511011
jen@saltpublishing.com
www.saltpublishing.com
Editors: Jen Hamilton-Emery, Nicholas Royle

Established 1999. Primarily publishes fiction. Publications available direct from publisher website; by post and email order; from chain bookshops nationwide; from independent bookshops; at national and local literary events; and from Amazon and other bookshop websites.

Salt title *The Redemption of Galen Pike* by Carys Davies won the International Frank O'Connor Short Story Prize.

GENRES: Crime/thriller/mystery; literary fiction; YA.

SUBMISSIONS: Agent submissions only. Guidelines at www.saltpublishing.com/pages/

submissions. Usually responds within four to six months, with feedback only if requested. Authors are paid royalties only, or an advance/fee plus royalties, and receive free copies of the book.

WE SAY: A major player in the indie publishing world, Salt's perfect-bound paperbacks are of an exceedingly high quality: cool crisp cover designs, big-name blurb quotes and beautifully edited stories on cream paper. The sleek website, stellar reputation and faultless social media presence (150,000 Twitter followers) put Salt in the same league as the heavy hitters of the industry.

SANDSTONE PRESS

NOVELS / NON-FICTION
Dochcarty Road, Dingwall, Ross-shire IV15 9UG
01349 865 484
info@sandstonepress.com
www.sandstonepress.com

Established 2002. Publishes high-quality literary fiction and non-fiction, particularly crime/thriller/mystery. Publications from Sandstone Press have won or been shortlisted for literary prizes including the Man Booker, Commonwealth, Arthur C Clarke and many many more. A very full publishing schedule, but open to submissions.

SUBMISSIONS: Open to all, via email. Submitters must complete the form at sandstonepress.com/contact/submissions to accompany their query. May take several months to respond.

SARABAND

E-BOOKS / NOVELS
Suite 202, 98 Woodlands Road, Scotland G3 6HB

0141 339 5030
hermes@saraband.net
www.saraband.net

Memoir, history, arts and environment titles. Particularly welcomes fiction from Scottish and women writers.

SCRIBE

E-BOOKS / NOVELS / NON-FICTION
2 John Street, London WC1N 2ES
020 3405 4218
scribepublications.co.uk

Operating for nearly 40 years, and spanning the globe despite still being 'small', Scribe publishes local, international and translated fiction, and serious narrative and literary non-fiction.

SEIN UND WERDEN BOOKS

E-BOOKS / SHORT STORIES / NOVELLAS
9 Dorris Street, Manchester M19 2TP
seinundwerden@gmail.com
www.kissthewitch.co.uk/
seinundwerden/sein.html
Editor: Rachel Kendall

Established 2004. Mixed form: also publishes poetry (see p13). Publications available from website.
GENRES: Crime/thriller/mystery; fantasy/sci-fi; horror; literary fiction; surreal; art, fashion and photography; music, stage and screen; travel.
SUBMISSIONS: Open to all. Submit by email to seinundwerden@gmail.com. Guidelines at www.kissthewitch.co.uk/seinundwerden/submissions.html. Usually responds within one to three months. Rejections may occasionally include unsolicited feedback.
For a fuller description of this press see *Sein und Werden* (mixed-form e-zine) p167. See also poetry publishers p13

SEREN BOOKS ☆

E-BOOKS / NOVELS / SHORT STORY COLLECTIONS AND ANTHOLOGIES / NON-FICTION
57 Nolton Street, Cardiff, Wales CF31 3AE
01656 663018
seren@serenbooks.com
serenbooks.com
Editor: Amy Wack

Established 1963. Mixed form: also publishes poetry (see p13). Publications available direct from publisher website; by post and email order; from chain bookshops nationwide; from independent bookshops; at national and local literary events; and from Amazon.
GENRES: Drama and criticism; literary fiction; poetry; art, fashion and photography; biography and true stories; history; travel; books about Wales.
SUBMISSIONS: Open to all. Submit by post to 57 Nolton Street, Bridgend CF31 3AE. Guidelines at www.serenbooks.com/seren/submissions-policy. Usually responds within one to three months. Rejections may occasionally include unsolicited feedback. Authors are paid an advance/fee plus royalties and receive free copies of the book, as well as other copies at a discount price.
For a fuller description of this press, see poetry publishers p13 and *Poetry Wales* (poetry magazine) p190

SHOESTRING PRESS

NOVELS / SHORT STORY COLLECTIONS / NON-FICTION
19 Devonshire Avenue, Beeston, Nottingham NG9 1BS
0115 925 1827
info@shoestringpress.co.uk

SPECTRAL PRESS

E-BOOKS / SHORT STORY
COLLECTIONS AND
ANTHOLOGIES / NON-FICTION /
NOVELLAS AND CHAPBOOKS
spectralpress@gmail.com
spectralpress.wordpress.com
Editor: Simon Marshall-Jones

Established 2011, and
includes Theatrum Mundi
and rEvolution SF. Primarily
publishes fiction. Chapbook
subscriptions available
(£16UK/£23.50EU/$45US &
RoW). Publications available
direct from publisher website;
from independent bookshops;
at Amazon; and at conventions
and book launches.
Spectral Press won the 2015
Shirley Jackson Award for Best
Short Fiction (Shirley Jackson
Awards Committee).
GENRES: Fantasy/sci-fi; horror;
ghosts; the surreal; TV and film
non-fiction.
SUBMISSIONS: Submissions by
invitation only. Usually responds
within one to three months.
Rejections may occasionally
include unsolicited feedback.
Authors are paid royalties only
and receive free copies of the
book.
WE SAY: The books and
chapbooks produced by
Spectral are high quality and
limited edition, with compelling
cover designs, clear formatting
and thick paper. The press went
into temporary abeyance last

THEY SAY

British Fantasy Award,
Aurealis Award, and Shirley
Jackson Award-winning
Spectral Press, along with
offshoots Theatrum Mundi
(contemporary fantasy,
surrealist, and magical realist)
and rEvolution SF (cutting-
edge science fiction), aims to
provide discerning readers
with highly literate and
high-quality genre literature,
professionally packaged and
presented. Chapbook, novellas,
collections, and anthologies.

year, but as we go to print we
understand it's getting back on its
feet, with new releases due soon
and produced to the same high
standard as before.

www.shoestring-press.com
Editor: John Lucas
Mainly publishes poetry (see p13), but also some prose. Publications available direct from publisher website; by post and email order; from independent bookshops; at national and local literary events; and from Amazon.
Shoestring titles have been shortlisted for Vondel Prize for Translation and for the Cricket Club Writers' Book of the Year.
GENRES: Historical fiction; literary fiction; biography and true stories.
SUBMISSIONS: Submit by invitation only. Usually responds within four weeks. No feedback offered with rejections. Authors are paid royalties only and receive free copies of the book.
For a fuller description of this press see poetry publishers p13

SILHOUETTE PRESS
E-BOOKS / NOVELS / NOVELLAS / GRAPHIC FICTION / NON-FICTION
ICE, Parkside, Coventry, CV1 2NE
adam.steiner@silhouettepress.co.uk
www.silhouettepress.co.uk
Editor: Gary Sykes-Blythe
Established 2012. Publishes fiction and poetry (see p13). Publications available direct from publisher website; by post and email order; from independent bookshops; and at various bookshop websites.
GENRES: No fixed genre.
SUBMISSIONS: Open to all. Submit through Submittable to silhouettepress.submittable.com/submit/40008. Guidelines at same address. Usually responds within four to six months. Rejections may occasionally include unsolicited feedback. Authors are paid royalties only.
For a fuller description of this press,

see *Here Comes Everyone* (mixed-form literary magazine) p146. See also poetry publishers p13

SIREN PRESS, THE
E-BOOKS / NOVELS / SHORT STORY COLLECTIONS AND ANTHOLOGIES
King William House IV, Mickleham, Surrey RH5 6EL
lucy@thesiren.co.uk
www.thesiren.co.uk
Editor: Lucy Carroll
Established 2014. Mainly publishes fiction. Publications available direct from the publisher website; from independent bookshops; at local literary events; and from Amazon.
GENRES: Crime/thriller/mystery; fantasy/sci-fi; horror; literary fiction; art, fashion and photography.
SUBMISSIONS: Open to all. Submit by email (lucy@thesiren.co.uk) or via the online submissions form (thesiren.co.uk/submit). Guidelines at the same address. Usually responds within one to three months. Rejections may occasionally include unsolicited feedback. Authors are paid royalties only.
WE SAY: Siren Press's anthology *Fugue*, the press's first publication, features 14 short stories, selected from open submissions. The book is well packaged – matt cover, perfect-bound, professional design, quality materials. The stories, as promised in the blurb, are contemporary and original. A good beginning for a press clearly going from strength to strength.

SNOWBOOKS LTD
E-BOOKS / NOVELS / SHORT STORY ANTHOLOGIES / NON-FICTION
Chiltern House, Thame Road, Haddenham HP17 8BY

020 7837 6482
info@snowbooks.com
www.snowbooks.com
Established 2003. Mainly publishes fiction. Publications available direct from publisher website; by post and email order; from chain bookshops nationwide; from independent bookshops; at national and local literary events; and from Amazon and other bookshop websites.
Snowbooks won Futurebook Best Innovation of the Year 2013.
GENRES: Fantasy/sci-fi; horror; sports and leisure.
SUBMISSIONS: Open to all. Submit by email to manuscripts@ snowbooks.com. Guidelines at snowbooks.com/pages/ submissions. Usually responds within four to six months or more. No feedback offered with rejections. Authors are paid royalties only, and receive free copies of the book.
WE SAY: Snowbooks publishes a wide range of books – up to and including colouring books and choose-your-own-adventure – and in a number of formats, including hardback, paperback, clothbound and e-book (though not every book is available in all formats). We were particularly impressed with the production values of *Alice's Nightmare in Wonderland* by Jonathan Green, which includes beautiful illustrations and an Afterword by the author.

SOARING PENGUIN PRESS
E-BOOKS / GRAPHIC NOVELS AND COMICS
4 Florence Terrace, London SW15 3RU
07985 201621
submissions@soaringpenguinpress. com
www.soaringpenguinpress.com
Editors: John Anderson, Ruth O'Callaghan
Established 2012. Mainly publishes fiction, but also poetry (see p13). Publications available direct from publisher website; by post and email order; from selected/ local chain bookshops; from independent bookshops; national literary events; and from Amazon and other bookshop websites.
Title *To End All Wars* was nominated for two Eisner Awards: Best Anthology and Best Non-fiction Title.
GENRES: Fantasy/sci-fi; graphic/ comics; horror.
SUBMISSIONS: Open to all. Submit by post (4 Florence Terrace, London SW15 3RU) or by email (submissions@ soaringpenguinpress.com). Guidelines at www.soaringpenguinpress.com/ submissions/. Usually responds within four to six months or more. Rejections may occasionally include unsolicited feedback. Authors are paid royalties only, and receive free copies of the books and a discount purchase price on future copies.
See also: *Meanwhile* (mixed-form literary magazine) p155 and poetry publishers p13

STINGING FLY PRESS, THE ☆
SHORT STORY ANTHOLOGIES AND COLLECTIONS
PO Box 6016, Dublin 1, Ireland
stingingfly@gmail.com
www.stingingfly.org
Editors: Thomas Morris, Declan Meade
Established 1997. Mainly fiction. Publications available direct from publisher website; from selected/

local chain bookshops; from independent bookshops; and at national and local literary events. Stinging Fly title *Young Skins* by Colin Barrett won the 2014 Guardian First Book Award and the 2014 Frank O'Connor Short Story Award.

GENRES: Irish literary fiction.
SUBMISSIONS: By invitation.
For a fuller description of this press see *The Stinging Fly* (mixed-form literary magazine) p170

STONEWOOD PRESS

SHORT STORY COLLECTIONS
97 Benefield Road, Oundle,
Peterborough PE8 4EU
0845 456 4838
stonewoodpress@gmail.com
www.stonewoodpress.co.uk
Editor: Martin Parker
Established 2011. Also publishes poetry (see p13). Publications available direct from publisher website; from chain bookshops and independent bookshops nationwide; and from Amazon and other bookshop websites.

GENRES: Fantasy/sci-fi; literary fiction.
SUBMISSIONS: Open to all. Submit by post to 97 Benefield Road, Oundle, Peterborough PE8 4EU. See guidelines at www. stonewoodpress.co.uk/about/ submissions/. Usually responds within one to three months. Rejections may occasionally include unsolicited feedback. Authors are paid royalties only and receive free copies of the book.
For a fuller description of this press, see poetry publishers p13

STORGY ☆

E-BOOKS / SHORT STORY
ANTHOLOGIES

59 Montague Road, Hanwell,
London W7 3PG
07792 411560
storgy@outlook.com
www.storgy.com
Editors: Tomek Dzido, Anthony Self, Sally-Anne Wilkinson, A Suiter Clarke
Established 2013. Anthologies printed as part of the e-zine and competitions.

GENRES: Literary fiction.
SUBMISSIONS: Open to all. Submit by email to storgy@outlook.com. Guidelines on website. Usually responds within one to three months. No feedback offered with rejections. Authors receive free copies of the book. No fee or royalties paid.
WE SAY: We looked at Storgy's *2014 Short Story Competition Anthology*, 173 pages of short stories. The design has a contemporary aesthetic with full-colour illustrations. Interviews with the winner and runners up provide information on their writing process. A nice touch.
See also: *Storgy Magazine* (prose magazine) p209

STRANGE ATTRACTOR PRESS

E-BOOKS / NOVELS / SHORT STORY
COLLECTIONS AND ANTHOLOGIES
/ NON-FICTION
458 Hackney Rd, London E2 9EG
07939 862 684
mark@strangeattractor.co.uk
www.strangeattractor.co.uk
Editors: Mark Pilkington,
Jamie Sutcliffe
Established 2004. Primarily publishes non-fiction. Publications available direct from publisher website; from chain bookshops nationwide; at national and local literary events; and from Amazon and other bookshop websites.

GENRES: Fantasy/sci-fi; horror; art, fashion and photography; history; popular science and nature; science, technology and medicine; and spirituality and beliefs.

SUBMISSIONS: Open to all. Submit by post (BM SAP, London WC1N 3XX) or by email (proposals@strangeattractor.co.uk). Usually responds in up to six months. Rejections may occasionally include unsolicited feedback. Authors are paid royalties only and receive free copies of their book.

STRUCTO PRESS

FICTION CHAPBOOKS
editor@structomagazine.co.uk
www.structomagazine.co.uk
Editor: Euan Monaghan
Established 2008. Mixed form: also publishes poetry chapbooks (see p13). Publications available direct from publisher website; from independent bookshops; and from bookshop websites.

GENRES: Slipstream.

SUBMISSIONS: Open to all, during submissions windows. See guidelines at structomagazine.co.uk/submissions/.

For a fuller description of this press, see *Structo* (mixed output e-zine) p171. See also poetry publishers p13

SWAN RIVER PRESS

NOVELS / SHORT STORY COLLECTIONS AND ANTHOLOGIES
swanriverpress.ie
Editor: Brian Showers
Established 2003. Publications available direct from publisher website; by post and email order; from independent bookshops; at national and local literary events; and from independent online retailers.

Swan River Press title *Dreams of Shadow and Smoke: Stories for J.S. Le Fanu* won the Ghost Story Award for best book.

GENRES: Fantasy/sci-fi; horror; literary fiction; history; literary criticism.

SUBMISSIONS: By invitation only. See guidelines at swanriverpress.ie/contact.html. Usually responds within four weeks. Rejections may occasionally include unsolicited feedback. Authors are paid a flat fee.

WE SAY: We saw the hardcover (with dust-jacket) edition of Joel Lane's posthumous short story collection, *The Anniversary of Never*. A handsome book, with a textured, striking cover image.

See also: *The Green Book* (prose magazine) p202

SYLPH EDITIONS

NOVELS / SHORT STORY COLLECTIONS / NON-FICTION
020 7625 3223
info@sylpheditions.com
www.sylpheditions.com
Established 2006. Primarily publishes fiction. Publications available direct from publisher website and from independent bookshops.

GENRES: Literary fiction; art, design, photography and culture.

SUBMISSIONS: Open to all. Submit by email to info@sylpheditions.com. Usually responds within four weeks. Authors receive free copies of the book. No fee or royalties paid.

WE SAY: We looked at the *Cahiers* series, a staple-spine, folded paper series of essay pamphlets. Around 40 pages long, with dust jackets over the thick textured paper covers. The essays are thoughtful and accessible, and illustrated with full-colour images.

SYNCHRONISE WITCHES PRESS

SHORT STORY ANTHOLOGIES
16 Mayfield Road,
Manchester M16 8FT
07876 410543
www.cherrystyles.co.uk
Editor: Cherry Styles
Established 2012. Mixed form: also publishes poetry (see p13). Publications available direct from publisher website; by post and email order; from independent bookshops; at national and local literary events; at zine fairs; and in art bookshops.
The press was shortlisted for the Turn The Page artists' book award, 2015.
GENRES: Literary fiction; poetry; art, fashion and photography; biography and true stories; music, stage and screen; society, education and politics.
SUBMISSIONS: Open to women writers only. Submit by email (thechapess@gmail.com) or via online form (cherrystyles.co.uk/the-chapess/). Usually responds within one to three months. Rejections may occasionally include unsolicited feedback.
For a fuller description of this press, see *The Chapess* **(mixed-form magazine) p137. See also poetry publishers p13**

TANGENT BOOKS

NOVELS / NON-FICTION / SHORT STORY ANTHOLOGIES
Unit 5.16, Paintworks
Bristol BS4 3EH
0117 972 0645
richard@tangentbooks.co.uk
www.tangentbooks.co.uk

Founded in 2004, Tangent's mission statement is 'to publish interesting stuff' and provide 'quality books for the discerning punter' – their range is extensive. Resolutely independent and supportive of local businesses.
See also: poetry publishers p13

TANGERINE PRESS

NOVELS / NON-FICTION
18 Riverside Road, Garratt Business Park, London SW17 0BA
michael@eatmytangerine.com
www.eatmytangerine.com
Mixed form, including photography, poetry (see p13) and fiction.
See also: poetry publishers p13

TARTARUS PRESS

NOVELS / E-BOOKS
Coverley House, Carlton, Leyburn, North Yorkshire DL8 4AY
tartarus@pavilion.co.uk
www.tartaruspress.com
Collectable hardback limited editions of literary supernatural/strange/horror fiction, as well as paperbacks and e-books.

TEAM ANGELICA PUBLISHING

E-BOOKS / NOVELS / SHORT STORY COLLECTIONS AND ANTHOLOGIES
51 Coningham Road, London W12 8BS
john@teamangelica.com
www.teamangelica.com
Editor: John R Gordon
Established 2011. Predominantly publishes fiction. Also produces film and theatre projects. Publications available from independent bookshops; and from Amazon and other bookshop websites.
Team Angelica title *Fairytales for Lost Children* by Diriye Osman won

the Polari Prize for Best First Book (2014).
GENRES: Self-help/inspirational; graphic/comics; literary fiction; biography and true stories; health and lifestyle.

TIRGEARR PUBLISHING

E-BOOKS / NOVELS /
SHORT STORY COLLECTIONS
AND ANTHOLOGIES / NOVELLAS
info@tirgearrpublishing.com
www.tirgearrpublishing.com

Established 2012. Commercial adult and cross-genre fiction. Publications available by post and email order, and from Amazon and other bookshop websites, and by request from most bookshops.
GENRES: Commercial adult genre and cross genre fiction: mystery; horror; thrillers; suspense; detective/PI; police procedurals; romance; romantic suspense; erotic romance; historical fiction; historical romance; sci-fi/fantasy.
SUBMISSIONS: Open to all. Submit via online form at www.tirgearrpublishing.com/submissions (guidelines at the same address). Usually responds within one to three months, and provides feedback with all rejections. Authors are paid royalties only and receive free copies of book.
WE SAY: E-book-only publisher, Tirgearr has an extensive list of genre fiction. The cover designs echo those of big commercial print publishers (passionate gazing-into-the-distance for romance; chrome and planets for sci-fi, etc). The stories are well edited and entertaining.

THEY SAY

Tirgearr Publishing is a small independently-owned publishing company of commercial adult genre fiction. We offer full-circle services, working with authors on a one-on-one basis through editing and cover design states, to ensure each book we publish is of the highest quality. Using our expertise from nearly twenty years in the publishing business, we work side-by-side with our authors to develop effective marketing plans and promotional programs, advising on career choices and forward career planning, and assist in setting up the author's overall image.

SUBMISSIONS: Submissions by invitation only. Email contact john@teamangelica.com. Usually responds within four weeks. No feedback offered with rejections, but they may occasionally include unsolicited feedback. Writers are paid an advance/fee plus royalties.
WE SAY: We looked at the award-winning *Fairytales for Lost Children* by Diriye Osman. A black-and-white image of the author in an Elizabethan gown adorns the cover, which has a slightly rubbery matt laminate feel, and there are ornate drop-cap letters at the beginning of each story, as befits the fairytale title. Set in Kenya, Somalia and South London, the stories explore identity in terms of gender, sexuality, family and country. A prime example of the important work Team Angelica is publishing.

TRAMP PRESS

E-BOOKS / NOVELS / SHORT STORY COLLECTIONS AND ANTHOLOGIES
info@tramppress.com
www.tramppress.com
Editors: Sarah Davis-Goff, Lisa Coen
Established 2014. Publications available direct from publisher website; at chain and independent bookshops nationwide; at national and local literary events; and from Amazon and other bookshop websites. Some online content freely available to all.
Tramp Press's 2015 title *Spill Simmer Falter Wither* was nominated for the *Guardian* First Book Award, and the press, its authors and individual titles have been nominated, shortlisted and won a variety of other awards and prizes.
GENRES: Crime/thriller/mystery;

fantasy/sci-fi; horror; literary fiction; YA.
SUBMISSIONS: Open to all. Submit by email to submissions@tramppress.com. Guidelines at www.tramppress.com/submissions/. Usually responds within four weeks. Rejections may occasionally include unsolicited feedback. Authors are paid an advance/fee plus royalties.
WE SAY: Tramp Press hit headlines in 2015 with an article in the *Irish Times* about sexism in publishing. Their books are equally bold and outspoken. We were unable to access a print copy, but as their list includes the incredible *Spill Simmer Falter Wither* by Sara Baume we know they have great taste in fiction (their cover designs are lush too).

TTA PRESS

E-BOOKS / NOVELS / SHORT STORY COLLECTIONS AND ANTHOLOGIES / NOVELLAS
5 Martins Lane, Witcham, Ely, Cambridgeshire CB6 2LB
www.ttapress.com
Editor: Andy Cox
Established 1994. Fiction. Publications available direct from publisher website; by post and email order; from chain bookshops nationwide; from independent bookshops; at national and local literary events; and from Amazon and other bookshop websites. All online content available to all.
GENRES: Crime/thriller/mystery; fantasy/sci-fi; horror; literary fiction.
SUBMISSIONS: Open to all. Submit via tta.submittable.com/submit. Usually responds within four weeks. Rejections may occasionally include unsolicited feedback. Authors are paid a flat fee and

receive free copies of the book. **For fuller descriptions of this press, see also *Interzone* (sci-fi prose magazine) p204, *Black Static* (horror prose magazine) p199, and *CrimeWave* (crime prose magazine) p200**

TWO RIVERS PRESS
NON-FICTION
7 Denmark Road, Reading RG1 5PA
tworiverspress@gmail.com
www.tworiverspress.com
Editor: Sally Mortimore
Established 1994. Publishes mainly non-fiction and some poetry (see p13). Publications available direct from publisher website; by post and email order; from selected/ local chain bookshops; from independent bookshops; at local literary events; and from Amazon and other bookshop websites.
GENRES: Books about Reading and the Thames Valley; art books.

UKAUTHORS/UKAPRESS
NOVELS / SHORT STORY ANTHOLOGIES / NON-FICTION
ukauthors@ukauthors.com
www.ukapress.com
Fiction and non-fiction unrestricted by genre of style. Looking for quality writing with 'originality, sparkle and the promise of something unexpected'.

UNBOUND
E-BOOKS / NOVELS / SHORT STORY COLLECTIONS AND ANTHOLOGIES / NON-FICTION
2nd Floor, 19 Buckingham Gate, London SW1E 6LB
020 7802 5413
www.unbound.co.uk
Established 2011. Mixed form: also publishes poetry (see p13). Publications available direct from publisher website; by post and email order; at chain and independent bookshops nationwide; at national and local literary events; and through Amazon and other bookshop websites. Publications are subsidised by crowdfunding. Multi-award-winning: Unbound title *The Wake* won Book of the Year at the 2015 Bookseller Industry Awards and the 2014 Gordon Burn Prize; was shortlisted for the 2014 Goldsmiths Prize; and longlisted for the Man Booker Prize 2014, the Desmond Elliott Prize 2014, and the Folio Prize 2014. Unbound won Best Publisher Website 2014 at the FutureBook Innovation Awards and British Book Design and Production Awards, and Best Start-Up at the 2011 FutureBook Innovation Awards. Also won the Literature Award 2013, for *26 Treasures*, at the British Book Design and Production Awards.
GENRES: Crime/thriller/mystery; fantasy/sci-fi; graphic/comics; historical fiction; literary fiction; biography and true stories; food and drink; history; popular science and nature; society, education and politics.
SUBMISSIONS: Open to all. Submit via the online form at unbound. co.uk/authors/work-with-us. Guidelines at the same address. Usually responds within one to three months. Rejections may occasionally include unsolicited feedback. Authors are paid royalties: a 50/50 profit share from crowdfunding.
WE SAY: We looked at *The Wake* by Paul Kingsnorth: a prime example of an indie taking a punt on a risky book. *The Wake* is a post-apocalyptic novel, set

in 1066, and written in a version of Old English. The production values on this book are impressive, from the textured cover to the wonderfully thick paper. Unbound's crowdfunding approach to publishing means it can afford to get the best materials possible, knowing future readers have already covered the cost. And with *The Wake* already a modern classic, the editors clearly have an eye for the market.
See also: poetry publishers p13

UNTHANK BOOKS
E-BOOKS / NOVELS / SHORT STORIES COLLECTIONS AND ANTHOLOGIES / NON-FICTION
PO Box 3506, Norwich NR7 7QP
information@unthankbooks.com
www.unthankbooks.com
Editors: Robin Jones, Ashley Stokes
Established publishers of adult literary fiction and non-fiction, with imprints including Unthank Cameo, which is behind Unthank's Words & Women anthology series. Unthank is supportive of first-timers and authors 'of any profile, age, gener, religious, sexual or political orientation'.
SUBMISSIONS: Open to all. Submit by mail to Unthank Submissions, PO Box 3506, Norwich NR7 7QP. Guidelines at www.unthankbooks. com/contacts.html.
See also: *Unthology* (prose magazine) p209

VALLEY PRESS
E-BOOKS / NOVELS / SHORT STORY COLLECTIONS AND ANTHOLOGIES / NON-FICTION
Woodend, The Crescent, Scarborough YO11 2PW
www.valleypressuk.com
jamie@valleypressuk.com

Editor: Jamie McGarry
Established 2008. Mixed form: also publishes poetry (see p13). Publications available direct from publisher website; by post and email order; from chain bookshops nationwide; from independent bookshops; at national and local literary events; and from Amazon and other bookshop websites. *Love and Eskimo Snow* by Sarah Holt was shortlisted for the People's Book Prize 2014.
GENRES: Children's fiction; drama and criticism; historical fiction; literary fiction; biography and true stories; humour; music, stage and screen; and travel.
SUBMISSIONS: During submissions windows, submit by post to Valley Press, Woodend, The Crescent, Scarborough YO11 2PW. Submitters are required to show proof of purchase from press. Usually responds within four to six months. Rejections may occasionally include unsolicited feedback. Authors are paid royalties only and receive free copies of book.
For a fuller description of this press see poetry publishers p13

VANE WOMEN PRESS
SHORT STORY COLLECTIONS AND ANTHOLOGIES
vane.women@ntlworld.com
www.vanewomen.co.uk
Editors: SJ Litherland, Marilyn Longstaff (assistant editor), Pat Maycroft (art editor)
Established 1993. Mainly publishes poetry (see p13). Publications available direct from publisher website; by post and email order; at local literary events; and at Vane Women events and workshops. Vane Women title *The Spar Box* by

Pippa Little was the 2006 Poetry Book Society Pamphlet choice. **SUBMISSIONS:** Open to previously unpublished women in North East England. Contact by email (submissions@vanewomen.co.uk) in the first instance, and a postal address to send poems and short stories to will be provided if appropriate. Full submission guidelines at www.vanewomen. co.uk/submissions.html. Usually responds in up to six months. Rejections may occasionally include unsolicited feedback. Authors receive free copies of their book.

For a fuller description of this press see poetry publishers p13

WARD WOOD PUBLISHING

NOVELS / ANTHOLOGIES / E-BOOKS / PLAYS / NOVELLAS / SHORT FICTION
6 The Drive, Golders Green, London NW11 9SR
adele@wardwoodpublishing.co.uk
www.wardwoodpublishing.co.uk
Mixed form publisher, established in 2010. Looking for 'innovative good reads of a high literary standard'. Submissions preferred by invitation only.
See also: poetry publishers p13

WAYWISER PRESS ☆

E-BOOKS / NOVELS / SHORT STORY COLLECTIONS / NON-FICTION / ILLUSTRATED WORKS
Christmas Cottage, Church Enstone, West Oxfordshire OX7 4NN
01608 677492
waywiserpress@aol.com
www.waywiser-press.com
Editors: Philip Hoy, Joseph Harrison, Dora Malech, V Penelope Pelizzon, Eric McHenry, Greg Williamson, Clive Watkins, Matthew Yorke

Established 2001. Mainly publishes poetry (see p13). Publications available direct from publisher website; by post and email order; at chain bookshops and independent bookshops nationwide; and via Amazon and other bookshop websites, including Inpress Books.
GENRES: Fantasy/sci-fi; graphic/comics; horror; biography and true stories; literary criticism; literary history.
SUBMISSIONS: Prose can be submitted year round. Submit by post to Christmas Cottage, Church Enstone, Chipping Norton OX7 4NN. Guidelines at waywiser-press.com/authors.html. Usually responds within one to three months, no feedback offered if rejected. Authors receive royalties and receive free copies of the book.
For a fuller description of this press see poetry publishers p13

WRECKING BALL PRESS ☆

E-BOOKS / NOVELS / SHORT STORY COLLECTIONS AND ANTHOLOGIES / NON-FICTION
44-46 High Street, Danish Buildings, Hull HU1 1PS
01482 211499
editor@wreckingballpress.com
www.wreckingballpress.com
Editors: Shane Rhodes, Russ Litten
Established 1997. Mainly publishes poetry (see p13). Publications available direct from publisher website; by post and email order; at chain and independent bookshops nationwide; at literary events; and on Amazon. Some online content available to all. Wrecking Ball Press title *The Scene of My Former Triumph* by Matthew Caley was nominated for Best

First Collection, The Forward Prize 2005.

GENRES: Drama and criticism; fantasy/sci-fi; literary fiction; biography and true stories.

SUBMISSIONS: Open to all. Submit by post (Wrecking Ball Press, 44-46 High Street, Danish Buildings, Hull HU1 1PS) or by email (editor@ wreckingballpress.com). Guidelines on the website. Usually responds within one to three months. Rejection may occasionally include unsolicited feedback. Authors are paid royalties and receive free copies of the book.

For a fuller description of this press see poetry publishers p13

Y LOLFA

E-BOOKS / NOVELS / NON-FICTION
Talybont, Ceredigion, Wales SY24 5HE
01970 832304
ylolfa@ylolfa.com
www.ylolfa.com
Editors: Lefi Gruffudd, Eirian Jones
Established 1967. Mainly publishes non-fiction. Publications available direct from publisher website; by post and email order; at chain and independent bookshops; at local literary events; and through bookshop websites.

Titles from Y Lolfa have been shortlisted for British Sports Book of the Year and won Welsh Book of the Year.

GENRES: Welsh interest; biography and true stories; history; sports and leisure; travel.

SUBMISSIONS: Open to all. Submit by post (Y Lolfa, Talybont, Ceredigion, SY24 5HE) or email (edit@ylolfa.com). Guidelines at www.ylolfa.com/en/cyhoeddi.php. Usually responds within four weeks. Rejection may occasionally include unsolicited feedback. Authors

are paid royalties or an advance/ fee plus royalties. Some titles may require crowdfunding or author contribution.

WE SAY: We looked at *The Shadow of Nanteos* by Jane Blank, a weighty perfect-bound paperback publication that connects the matt finish of the professional design to the dark plot within the novel. The quality continues within with high-quality cream paper. This dark historic novel provides a gripping gothic chill and oozes Welsh history: a great read for anyone who wants to find more about Welsh heritage.

ZED BOOKS

NON-FICTION
The Foundry, 17 Oval Way, London
SE11 5RR
editorial@zedbooks.net
zedbooks.co.uk
Editors: Ken Barlow, Kim Walker, Kika Sroka-Miller

Non-fiction only. An independent, scholarly publishing house, Zed Books caters to academics and students, and more widely, activists and policy-makers. It promotes diversity, alternative voices and progressive social change through critical and dynamic publishing.

GENRES: Politics and international; relations; economics; development studies; gender studies; area studies (Africa, the Middle East, Asia and Latin America); environment.

SUBMISSIONS: Open to all. Extensive guidelines are available at zedbooks.co.uk/for-authors.

Part 2:
Literary magazines
and e-zines

The precarious lives of literary magazines

The world of small presses and literary magazines is a precarious one. With magazines and e-zines in particular, new titles bob up to the surface and then drown again in the space of a few months, and more than once we started tracing contact details for an editor only to find that the press had recently shut up shop or was just about to do so.

On the surface, running a magazine seems like fun: a way to print work you believe deserves to be read. And with the advent of e-zines (magazine-like websites) and digital magazines, the overheads can be kept to an absolute minimum. All very appealing. Indeed, some well-known print magazines, such as *Southward*, have recently gone over to digital only publication.

But though most literary magazines launch with great enthusiasm and passion, these labours of love take time. Editors find their evenings and weekends are spent sifting through submissions, laying out pages, untangling code, talking to printers, marketing – and editing, of course. Factor in the day job, getting their own writing done (the majority of editors are writers too), and trying to spend time with family and friends, and many editors eventually become ground down and burnt out. This, combined with disappointing sales, can be rather disheartening. Some presses and magazines are supported by the various Arts Councils and local government; others are paid for by their founders, or their founders' generous benefactor/s. In a few rare cases, such as *Granta*, a wealthy sponsor has stepped in. Very few are able to survive on income from subscription and single sales alone.

It's fascinating to read the farewell statement 'Memoirs of a Dying Swan' (available at medium.com/@megapad) by the editors of the recently defunct illustrated literary magazine *The Alarmist*, which details their early idealism and the daunting challenges they faced. Because those literary magazines that survive do so against the odds.

Having said that, the growth of online magazines means that more readers are able to stumble on your hard-won words, and a real sense of community does build up between people submitting to and being published in both the print and screen magazines. Once you start reading them, you'll notice that certain names tend to crop up repeatedly here and there. Keep reading, and you'll find that some of those names will eventually be announced as the debut author of a a new book – quite possibly published by the press who also publishes one of the magazines they've appeared in.

So bear this in mind when submitting to magazines. The editors love good writing, and want to share it with the world – but they are almost certainly working for nothing, can afford to pay very little (if at all) for the writing they publish, and are scrabbling for the time to get the work into the world. They rarely have time to tailor individual rejection letters – don't underestimate just how many submissions even the smallest publication receives.

As a writer you can help by sticking to submission guidelines, ensuring your work matches their aesthetic, and being patient as you wait for a reply (see p12 for where we've laid all of this out in more detail!). If you do receive a rejection, take it on the chin (or go and have a little cry), but don't lash out at the poor editor.

As a reader, you can help by actually reading the magazines you are submitting to. Buy a single copy, at least; if you love it, take out a subscription. If it's an online-only publication, share the love. Spread the word about particular items you've enjoyed and alert people when there's a new issue out. In particular try to share beyond your immediate circle, and help break the cycle of writers who only read in order to be published. There are some amazing stories, heart-stopping poems and beautiful, accessible e-zines and magazines out there, and they deserve to be read by everyone.

Mixed-form literary magazines

By 'mixed form', we mean magazines that publish both poetry and prose (fiction and/or non-fiction), as opposed to focusing exclusively on either poetry or prose, as in the later sections of this Guide. Some magazines may have a bias towards one form, such as poetry, but also mix in a few short stories and/or reviews – or vice versa. And some feature poetry and prose in a particular genre, such as fantasy or science fiction. Whatever you write, you're sure to find a place to submit here.

Mixed-form literary magazines

AFRICAN WRITING
PRINT AND E-ZINE
398-400 Holdenhurst Road BH7 7JQ
editor@african-writing.com
www.african-writing.com
Editor: Chuma Nwokolo
Mixed form, including poetry, essays, fiction, memoir and other prose. Its 'natural constituency of writers and material are African or Diasporan' but any writer who publishes into the African Condition will be considered.

ALLITERATI
DIGITAL AND E-ZINE
editor@alliteratmagazine.com
alliteratimagazine.com
Senior Editor: Adam Thompson
With roots and an editorial team based at Newcastle University, this magazine has grown to international popularity since moving online in 2010. Accepts poetry, fiction, and visual creative work and other media (art, music and film).

AMBIT MAGAZINE ☆
PRINT AND DIGITAL
Staithe House, Main Road, Brancaster Staithe, Norfolk PE31 8BP
07503 633 601
contact@ambitmagazine.co.uk
www.ambitmagazine.co.uk
Editors: Briony Bax, Kate Pemberton, Declan Ryan
Established 1959. Mixed form. Subscription £29.99 per annum. Available direct from publisher website; by post and email order; from selected/local chain bookshops; from independent bookshops; and at local literary events. Only subscribers/purchasers can access online content.
GENRES: Drama and criticism; literary fiction; poetry.
SUBMISSIONS: Open to all, during submissions windows. Submit by post (Staithe House, Main Road, Brancaster Staithe, Norfolk PE31 8BP) or through Submittable (ambit.submittable.com/submit). Guidelines available at www.ambitmagazine.co.uk/submit. Usually responds within one to three months. Rejections may include occasional unsolicited feedback. Contributors can choose between receiving payment (set rate), a discount subscription, or print copy/ies.
WE SAY: At 96 pages and slightly larger than A5, *Ambit*'s contents are entirely selected from unsolicited submissions. The magazine's plain white cover is wrapped with a funky jacket sleeve. Each full-colour issue has a different atmosphere – the one we read (Issue 221) combined writing from established names like Carolyn Jess-Cooke with newer artistic talents in photography, illustration and graphics. We loved the way the various mediums were creatively interspersed throughout.

A NEW ULSTER
PRINT AND DIGITAL
sites.google.com/site/anewulster/our-company
Editor: Amos Greig
Established 2012. Poetry focus,

with some stories. Available direct from publisher website, and by post and email order. Some digital content available to all. Nominated for the 2013 Saboteur Awards.

GENRES: Literary and poetry. No non-fiction.
SUBMISSIONS: Submit during submissions windows, by email to g.greig3@gmail.com. See guidelines at sites.google.com/

A3 REVIEW, THE ☆
PRINT
PO Box 65016, London N5 9BD
020 7193 7642
a3@writingmaps.com
writingmaps.com
Editor: Shaun Levin

Established 2014. Mixed form, including comics/graphics.
GENRES: Graphic / comics; literary fiction; biography and true stories.
SUBMISSIONS: Open to all, during submission windows. Submit via Submittable at writingmaps.submittable.com/ submit (guidelines at the same address); a reading fee is charged for submissions. Usually responds in one to three months. No feedback offered with rejections. Contributors receive a print copy of the magazine, and the top three contributors per issue receive cash prizes.
WE SAY: Microfiction, poetry and illustrations printed on both sides of one piece of thick, coloured A3 paper, with the creases acting as page dividers. The illustrations pull the page as a whole together. It's an ingenious design idea; the fiction and poetry are nuggets of strong writing, whole narratives in just a few words.

THEY SAY

The A3 Review comes out every six months, with 12 contributions sourced from our monthly themed contest. We're a magazine that behaves like a map and are published by Writing Maps. We believe in words and images, and love a combination of the two. We're looking for prose, poetry, graphic stories, photography, paintings, drawings, and other visual and word-based creations and various combinations of the above. Three overall winners are chosen per issue to win cash prizes. 1st = £150, 2nd = £75, 3rd = £50 (approx $220, $110, $75).

site/anewulster/contact-us-1.
Usually responds within four
weeks and may offer occasional
unsolicited feedback with a
rejection. Contributors receive a
digital copy of the magazine.
WE SAY: We looked at a digital
version of *A New Ulster* (Issue
34), which champions the work
of Northern Irish writers, as well
as welcoming global writers. It
has a neatly presented design –
plain, with minimal artwork – and
includes biographies of its featured
writers. It also showcases their
work well, allowing for a good
number of poems for each poet,
interspersed with stories. Clearly
dedicated and filling the gaps
left by *The Honest Ulsterman* and
Fortnight magazines.

ARCHIPELAGO
PRINT
PO Box 154, Thame OX9 3RQ
info@clutagpress.com
www.clutagpress.com/archipelago/
Non-fiction prose and verse.
Occasional magazine – no fixed
publication dates.
**See also: Clutag Press (poetry
publisher) p22**

ARETÉ MAGAZINE
PRINT
8 New College Lane, Oxford OX1 3BN
01865 289194
aretebooks@gmail.com
www.aretemagazine.com
Editor: Craig Raine
Established 1999. Mixed form.
Annual subscription costs: £27
UK individual; £30 library; $65
overseas; $85 overseas library.
Issues available direct from the
publisher website; in selected/local
chain bookshops; in independent
bookshops; and on Amazon. Some

online content available to all.
GENRES: Drama and criticism;
literary fiction; poetry; art, fashion
and photography; biography and
true stories; music, stage and
screen.
SUBMISSIONS: Open to all.
Submit by post to Areté, 8 New
College Lane, Oxford, OX1 3BN.
Guidelines at www.aretemagazine.
co.uk/about-arete/. Usually
responds within one to three
months. Rejections may include
occasional unsolicited feedback.
Contributors receive a print copy of
the magazine.
WE SAY: We looked at Issue 43,
which is a beautifully produced
perfect-bound paperback: 157
thick, bright white pages contained
in a dark-gray matt, French flap
cover with a smart wraparound
design and a pink cardboard inner
cover. The bright coloured titles
look appropriately sophisticated
and scholarly. The sheer quantity
of closely-typed text inside is
rather daunting, but the reviews,
poetry and fiction are actually very
accessible.
**See also: Areté Books (poetry
publisher) p18**

BANIPAL
PRINT
1 Gough Square, London EC4A 3DE
020 7832 1350
editor@banipal.co.uk
www.banipal.co.uk
Editor: Margaret Obank
Primarily translated literature,
exclusively featuring authors from
the modern Arab world.

BANSHEE
PRINT AND DIGITAL
bansheelit@gmail.com
www.bansheelit.com

Editors: Laura Jane Cassidy, Claire Hennessy, Eimear Ryan Established 2014. Mixed form.

Issues available direct from publisher website and at independent bookshops and local

BARE FICTION MAGAZINE ☆

PRINT AND DIGITAL
177 Copthorne Road, Shrewsbury
SY3 8NA
info@barefiction.co.uk
www.barefictionmagazine.co.uk
Editor: Robert Harper

Established 2013. Mixed form. Annual subscriptions cost £20 print/£12 digital (both include digital access to all back issues). Issues available direct from publisher website; by post and email order; and from independent bookshops. Most online content is only accessible to subscribers/purchasers, with some available to all. Shortlisted for Best Magazine in Saboteur Awards 2014; runner-up for Best Magazine in Saboteur Awards 2015.
GENRES: Drama and criticism; literary fiction; poetry.
SUBMISSIONS: Open to all, during submissions windows. Submit through Submittable at www.barefictionmagazine.co.uk/submissions/. Usually responds within one to six months. No feedback offered with rejections. Contributors receive a print copy of the magazine.
WE SAY: A4 and perfect bound on quality paper, *Bare Fiction* uses a two-column layout, with effective chunky design quirks that reflect the logo. The cover images vary within the banded blue and white

THEY SAY

The only reason for publishing a literary magazine is for the love of words and what they can do to a reader. *Bare Fiction* publishes poetry, fiction and theatre, with every single submission we receive being read blind because we feel it's the words that are the only important and deciding factor in whether we include your work. Whatever stage you are at in your literary career, we judge your work on its merits in isolation from your competition wins or publishing history. At *Bare Fiction* we're proud to publish newcomers and old hands side by side.

framing: sometimes cool and futuristic, sometimes busy black-and-white. It's a contemporary, recognisable brand that has rapidly built a name for itself.
See also: Bare Fiction (poetry publisher) p18

literary events. Some online content available to all.

GENRES: Literary fiction; memoir and personal essays.

SUBMISSIONS: Open to all, during submissions windows. Submit by email to bansheelit@gmail.com. See guidelines at bansheelit.tumblr.com/submissionsguidelines. Usually responds within one to three months. Rejections may occasionally include unsolicited feedback. Contributors are paid a set rate and receive a print copy of the magazine.

WE SAY: Issue 1 of *Banshee* scores points for its design. It's a 98-page A5 magazine, with a photo image cover – Issues 1 and 2 feature depictions of figures dwarfed within natural spaces. We looked at a PDF, so can't comment on the print production, but the design is clean and neatly presented, alternating stories with poems. The writing is bold and engaging – we recognised several emerging names in the contributors list.

BELLEVILLE PARK PAGES

PRINT AND E-ZINE
words@bellevilleparkpages.com
www.bellevilleparkpages.com
Bi-monthly, mixed form: a folded A3 page of microfiction and poetry on cream paper with a classic, stylish look.

BIBLIOPHILIA MAGAZINE

DIGITAL (WITH PLANS FOR PRINT)
bibilophilia@outlook.com
bibliophiliamag.wordpress.com
Editor: Natasha McGregor
Established 2014. Mixed form. All content available to read on Issuu.

GENRES: Crime/thriller/mystery; fantasy/sci-fi; horror; literary fiction; poetry; reviews.

SUBMISSIONS: Open to all, but please pay attention to theme deadlines. Guidelines at bibliophiliamag.wordpress.com/submission-guidelines/. Submit by email to bibliophilia@outlook.com. Usually responds within four weeks, Rejections may include occasional unsolicited feedback. Contributors are unpaid.

WE SAY: Self-described as 'by writers, for writers', *Bibliophilia*'s rather plain and clunky cover gives the impression that the editors are still experimenting with design. The inner pages are better, with a slick layout of fiction and poetry interspersed with writing exercises, prompts, reviews and interviews. With a different theme for each issue, what shines through is respect for the written word and support for the writers featured. One to watch.

BLACK & BLUE

PRINT
33 Cheval Court, 335 Upper Richmond Road, London SW15 6UA
07983 529329
info@blackbluewriting.com
www.blackbluewriting.com
Editors: Dane Weatherman, Miriam Tobin, Beckie Stewart, Harriet Hill-Payne, Alice Popplewell, Peter Masheter
Established 2012. Mainly poetry, but also art, prose, typography and graphic stories. Available direct from publisher website; by post and email order; at selected/local chain bookshops and independent bookshops; and at local literary events. Online articles are available to all.

GENRES: Drama and criticism; fantasy/sci-fi; graphic/comics;

literary fiction; poetry; interpretation (non-fiction); and other fiction.
SUBMISSIONS: Open to all, during submissions windows. Submit by email to submissions@blackbluewriting.com. Guidelines at www.blackbluewriting.com/memory. Usually responds within four to six months. Rejection emails include free feedback. Contributors receive a print copy of the magazine.
WE SAY: *Black & BLUE* publications are perfect-bound journals, with a wealth of experimental, angry, strong writing inside. The cover designs wouldn't be out of place in a modern art gallery; we particularly loved *#3 City*, with its white-on-black cityscape line art and *#4 Revolution*'s black-on-green prose poem, with the title picked out in white. *Black & BLUE* is looking for work with 'authenticity, voice and bite' – titles of featured pieces include 'Fuckers', 'Wolves libertines monsters' and 'No places'.
See also: Black & BLUE (poetry publisher) p19

BLACK MARKET RE-VIEW
DIGITAL
Edge Hill University, Lancashire
blackmarketreview@googlemail.com
blackmarketre-view.weebly.com
Editors: Luke Thurogood,
Sarah Billington (poetry),
Laura Tickle (fiction)
Mixed-form magazine in PDF format. Short stories, flash fiction, poetry, and art and photography.

BOHEMYTH, THE
E-ZINE
thebohemytheditor@gmail.com
www.thebohemyth.com
Editor: Michael Shanks
Established 2012. Mixed form. All online content available to all.

Nominated for the Blog Awards Ireland 2015.
GENRES: Crime/thriller/mystery; fantasy/sci-fi; horror; literary fiction; poetry; art, fashion and photography; biography and true stories; humour; music, stage and screen; travel.
SUBMISSIONS: During submissions windows, submit by email to thebohemytheditor@gmail.com. Usually responds within three months. Rejection may include occasional unsolicited feedback. Contributors are unpaid.
WE SAY: *Bohemyth*'s home page displays the contents of the latest issue in a chart of green circles with the writers' names in them. There's no clue as to whether you'll be clicking through to poetry or prose, but this means readers have the opportunity to discover writing they might otherwise not have been drawn to. It's a striking, unique and tidy design, free of adverts and images apart from the *Bohemyth* logo (a bear silhouette). The poetry and prose is evocative, thoughtful and very, very good.

BRITISH JOURNALISM REVIEW
PRINT AND E-ZINE
SAGE Publications, 1 Oliver's Yard, 55 City Road, London EC1Y 1SP
020 7324 8500
editor@bjr.org.uk
www.bjr.org.uk
Editor: Kim Fletcher
Non-fiction magazine with a focus on society, education and politics.

BRITTLE STAR ☆
PRINT AND DIGITAL
97 Benefield Road, Oundle, Peterborough PE8 4EU
0845 456 4838
brittlestarmag@gmail.com

www.brittlestar.org.uk
Editors: Martin Parker,
Jacqueline Gabbitas
Established 2000. Poetry and short
stories, articles and reviews of first
full collections. Subscription £12
(UK) or £20 (world) for two issues.
Available direct from publisher
website, and by post and email
order. Digital edition available at
www.0s-1s.com/brittle-star. Some
online content available to non-
subscribers.
GENRES: Literary fiction; poetry.
SUBMISSIONS: Open to all new and
emerging writers (no established
writers from major presses, please).
Submit by post to 97 Benefield
Road, Oundle, Peterborough PE8
4EU. Guidelines at www.brittlestar.
org.uk/submissions/. Usually
responds within one to six months,
no feedback offered on rejections.
Contributors receive a print copy
and a discount purchase price.
WE SAY: *Brittle Star* is a bit smaller
than A5 and perfect bound. The
PDF issue we looked at (Issue 37)
was 86 pages long. The cover is
striking – *Brittle Star* seems to go
for images with texture, in this case
a repeated pattern of grey cells
(or are they pebbles?). Detailed
line drawings are placed at the
start of each story. The writing is
punchy and in some cases rather
experimental, blurring the line
between poetry and prose.

BUNBURY MAGAZINE
DIGITAL AND E-ZINE
5 Chester Street, Bury, Lancashire
BL9 6EU
07446 025630
admin@bunburymagazine.com
www.bunburymagazine.com
Editors: Christopher Moriarty,
Keri-Ann Edwards

Established 2013. Mixed form.
All content available to all.
GENRES: Crime/thriller/mystery;
fantasy/sci-fi; horror; literary
fiction; poetry; art, fashion and
photography; biography and true
stories; humour; music, stage and
screen; society, education and
politics.
SUBMISSIONS: Open to all.
Submit by email to submissions@
bunburymagazine.com. Guidelines
at bunburymagazine.com/submit-
to-us/. Usually responds within
one to three months. Rejections
may include occasional unsolicited
feedback. Contributors receive a
digital copy.
WE SAY: *Bunbury* makes the
most of being a digital magazine:
full-colour and plenty of design,
including page backgrounds (faded
wallpaper for poems; lined paper
for stories). The cover is an image
taken from featured illustrator Iñaki
Oñate's work. There's a warning to
readers about any violence, sexual
content or explicit language in the
work published. Poems come first,
are center justified and given plenty
of space. Interviews follow (with
plenty of photos); then flash fiction
(single column) and short stories
(two columns). The stories run
straight on from each other rather
than starting on new pages, which
can feel slightly relentless. A busy,
bright publication.
**See also: Bunbury Publishing Ltd
(poetry publisher p21 and prose
publisher p73)**

CADAVERINE
E-ZINE
thecadaverine@hotmail.com
www.thecadaverine.com
Under 30s only. Poetry, prose,
and non-fiction. 'Showcasing

contemporary, innovative and original new writing from the next generation of talent.'

CAKE MAGAZINE
PRINT
English and Creative Writing Department, County Main, Lancaster University, Lancashire LA1 4YD
themixingbowl@hotmail.co.uk
www.cake-magazine.co.uk
Short fiction, poetry, comment/ essays, reviews and artwork. Set up by students at Lancaster University in 2009. Every issue named for a type of bake.

CAMBRIDGE LITERARY REVIEW
PRINT
Trinity Hall, Cambridge CB2 1TJ
cambridgeliteraryreview@gmail.com
www.cambridgeliteraryreview.org
Editors: Lydia Wilson, Rosie Snajdr
Established 2009. Mixed form. Subscription £20/€30/$50. Available direct from publisher website and in independent bookshops.
GENRES: Drama and criticism; literary fiction; poetry; history; and essays on a variety of subjects but mostly in the humanities, and mostly on some aspect of literature.
SUBMISSIONS: Open to all. Submit by post (Trinity Hall, Cambridge CB2 1TJ) or by email (cambridgeliteraryreview@googlemail.com). Usually responds within four to six months. Rejections may include occasional unsolicited feedback. Contributors receive a print copy of the magazine.
WE SAY: *Cambridge Literary Review* is a perfect-bound print magazine, with a clean design (black and white imagery with red accents); a fairly intellectual, high-brow affair, that warrants attention from *TLS*. We looked at the available online content (the website reflects the print design and is easy to navigate), which includes poetry, short fiction, essays and criticism. The creative work is contemporary and accessible; the essays and criticism weighted with theoretical knowledge, but not so intellectual as to be alienating.

CARILLON MAGAZINE
PRINT
19 Godric Drive, Brinsworth, Rotherham, South Yorkshire S60 3JB
grippon@carillonmag.org.uk
www.carillonmag.org.uk
Editor: Graham Rippon
Mixed form. A long-established magazine, with a great reputation. UK residents must submit by post (overseas may use email). Subscribers are given preference.

CATERPILLAR, THE ☆
PRINT
Ardan Grange, Belturbet, Co. Cavan, Ireland
editor@thecaterpillarmagazine.com
www.thecaterpillarmagazine.com
Editor: Will Govan
Sibling magazine to *The Moth* (see p156). Mixed form: poetry, stories and art aimed at children between the ages of 11 and 17. Annual subscription €24.
SUBMISSIONS: Open to all. See guidelines at www. thecaterpillarmagazine.com/a1-page.asp?ID=4150&page=5.
See also: *The Moth* (mixed-form literary magazine) p156

CHAPESS, THE
PRINT
Flat 5, 16 Mayfield Road,
Manchester M16 8FT
cherrystyles@hotmail.co.uk
www.cherrystyles.co.uk
Editor: Cherry Styles
Established 2012. Mixed form.
Available direct from publisher
website; by post and email order;
and at zine fairs and art bookshops.
Shortlisted for the 'Turn The Page'
artists' book award 2015.

GENRES: Literary fiction; poetry;
art, fashion and photography;
biography and true stories;
music, stage and screen; society,
education and politics.
SUBMISSIONS: Open to women
writers and artists only. Submit by
email (thechapess@gmail.com) or
through the online submissions
manager at cherrystyles.co.uk/
the-chapess/ (guidelines at
same address). Usually responds
within one to three months.

CŌNFINGŌ
PRINT AND DIGITAL
2 Stonecraft, Parkfield Road South,
Didsbury, Manchester M20 6DA
0161 445 0546
www.confingopublishing.uk/
Editors: Tim Shearer, Zoe McLean

Established 2014. Fiction and
poetry focus. Subscription £15.00
per annum. Available direct from
publisher website; from selected/
local chain bookshops; from
independent bookshops; and at
local literary events. Some online
content available to all.
GENRES: Literary fiction; poetry;
art.
SUBMISSIONS: Open to all, during
submissions windows. Submit by
email to tim@confingopublishing.
uk. Guidelines at www.
confingopublishing.uk/#!form/cry1.
Usually responds within one to
three months. Rejections may
occasionally include unsolicited
feedback. Contributors are paid a
set rate and receive a print copy of
the magazine.

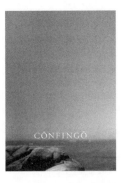

WE SAY: Perfect bound, A4
and featuring full-colour
bright, contemporary images,
Cōnfingō gives an impression of
spaciousness, with cutting-edge
art and writing framed in plenty
of white space, printed on thick
matt paper and interspersed with
contemporary poetry and fiction.
Online readers can also access
well-considered interviews and
comments on literature and art.
The website, too, is clean and
bright.

Rejection may occasionally include unsolicited feedback. Contributors receive digital copies.

WE SAY: A 44-page quarterly magazine with a controversial artistic design. Black and white images punctuate the articles and poetry. A magazine with a spontaneous feel and urban edge.

See also: Synchronise Witches Press (poetry publisher p58 and prose publishers p116)

CORK LITERARY REVIEW
PRINT
info@bradshawbooks.com
www.bradshawbooks.com
Editor: Eugene O Connell
Established 1985, a high-end journal featuring poetry and writing from both established and emerging writers.

For a slightly fuller description of this press, see also Bradshaw Books (prose publisher p73 and poetry publisher p20)

CRO MAGNON, THE ☆
E-ZINE
51 Wakefield House, Goldsmith Road, Peckham, London SE15 5SU
www.thecromagnon.com
Editor: Henry Tobias Jones
Established 2015. Mixed form. All online content available to all.
GENRES: Drama and criticism; historical fiction; literary fiction; poetry; art, fashion and photography; history; music, stage and screen; popular science and nature; society, education and politics.
SUBMISSIONS: Open to all. Submit by email to editors@thecromagnon.com. Guidelines at thecromagnon.com/about/contribute/. Sometimes charges a reading fee. Usually responds

within one to three months. Offers feedback on submissions only if requested. Contributors receive a digital copy. Otherwise unpaid.
WE SAY: *The Cro Magnon* describes itself as a 'multiplatform hub for creatives and thinkers'. The home page is image-heavy – you click to see where the pictures lead. The contents pages are blocky with plenty of teaser text. The text is grey, which can make it tiring to read, but well worth the effort – it's been carefully curated and published.
See also poetry publisher p24 and prose publisher p77

CRYSTAL MAGAZINE
PRINT
3 Bowness Avenue, Prenton, Birkenhead CH43 0SD
0151 608 9736
christinecrystal@hotmail.com
www.christinecrystal.blogspot.com
Editor: Christine Carr
Established 2001. Mixed form, including articles. Subscription £18 UK/£20 overseas for six issues. Available direct from publisher website.
GENRES: Literary fiction; poetry; articles; popular science and nature; travel; pets.
SUBMISSIONS: Open to subscribers only. Submit by post to 3 Bowness Avenue, Prenton, Birkenhead CH43 0SD or by email to christinecrystal@hotmail.com. Usually responds within four weeks. No feedback offered with rejection. The writer of the most popular piece in each issue receives £10.
WE SAY: A 42-page A4 wiro-bound monthly magazine, with a warm informal community aesthetic. Editor Christine Carr addresses subscribers as 'Crystallites'

and her Editor's Letter includes personal news as well as the usual introduction to the issue's contents. It publishes (mostly rhyming) poetry, short stories, comment, prose poems and personal anecdotes, with occasional colour photographic and clip-art illustrations. The subject matter is mainly autobiographical. A three-page Readers' Letters section comments on the contents of the previous magazine ('kind comments or none at all').

CUCKOO CHRONICLE ☆

PRINT AND E-ZINE
3 Ellison Terrace, University of Northumbria, Newcastle upon Tyne NE1 2AS
0191 204 8850
cuckoo@newwritingnorth.co.uk
chronicle.cuckoowriters.com
Editors: a committee of young people
Presented by Cuckoo Writers and established in 2012. Primarily fiction focus. Available in independent bookshops, at local literary events and distributed with NARC magazine. All online content openly available to all.
GENRES: Literary fiction; poetry; YA; art, fashion and photography; children and teenagers; music, stage and screen; society, education and politics.
SUBMISSIONS: Open to young writers aged 15-21, during submissions windows. Submit by email to cuckoochroniclenwn@gmail.com. Guidelines at chronicle.cuckoowriters.com/submit/. Usually responds within one to three months. Rejections may occasionally include unsolicited feedback. Contributors are paid a set rate and receive a print copy of the magazine.

WE SAY: A literary magazine written and edited by young writers of the North East. We looked at the e-zine. With a bold orange and cream pallette and an art-deco font logo, *Cuckoo Chronicle* has an uncluttered contemporary design that is easy to navigate. Clicking on an issue link takes you to the editors' letter and contents page (ordered poetry; shorts; theme; non-fiction; periodicals), where the link to each piece is highlighted with a cartoon of a cuckoo. This is for a younger audience, and the standard of writing is very high.

DACTYL ZINE STUB

PRINT AND DIGITAL
wearedactyl@gmail.com
www.dactylzine.com
Established 2013. A Scottish-based publication for poetry, prose, illustration and photography.

DAWNTREADER MAGAZINE, THE

PRINT
Indigo Dreams Press, 24 Forest Houses, Halwill, Beaworthy, Devon EX21 5UU
publishing@indigodreams.co.uk
www.indigodreams.co.uk
Editors: Ronnie Goodyer, Dawn Bauling
Established 2005 (ltd company since 2010). Mainly poetry, some stories and articles. Subscription £16/year for four issues. Available direct from publisher website; by post and email order; from nationwide chain bookshops; from independent bookshops; and on Amazon.
The Editors won the Ted Slade Award for Services to Poetry 2015

(organised by Poetry Kit).
GENRES: Myth; legend; in the landscape; nature; spirituality and love; the mystic, the environment.
SUBMISSIONS: Open to all. Submit by post (IDP, 24 Forest Houses, Halwill, Beaworthy, Devon EX21 5UU) or by email (dawnidp@ gmail.com). Guidelines at www. indigodreams.co.uk. Usually responds within four weeks. No feedback offered with rejection.
WE SAY: One of the Indigo Dreams' publications, *The Dawntreader* is an A5, 52-page monthly magazine, perfect bound with a (rare, these days) glossy full colour cover. IDP encourage comment on the included work, and welcome environmental, spiritual, folklorish etc work, which is described by one reader as 'poetry for the soul'. The magazine has an international readership and IDP foster a community of readers.
For what They Say, see Indigo Dreams Publishing Ltd (poetry publisher) p37. See also: *Sarasvati* (mixed-form literary magazine) p167 and *Reach Poetry* (poetry magazine) p191

DISSECTIONS
E-ZINE
CLT, University of Brighton, Falmer, Brighton BN1 9PH
01273 643115
www.simegen.com/writers/dissections/
Editors: Gina Wisker, Michelle Bernard
Established 2006. Mainly fiction. All online content available to all.
GENRES: Fantasy/sci-fi; horror; literary fiction; poetry; non-fiction (horror, literary criticism).
SUBMISSIONS: Open to all. Submit by post (CLT, University of Brighton, Falmer, Brighton BN1 9PH, to Gina Wisker) or by email

(ginwskr@aol.com / michelle. bernard2@ntlworld.com). Usually responds within four weeks. Rejections may occasionally include unsolicited feedback. Unpaid.
WE SAY: An occasionally updated e-zine that focuses on the horror genre. Line drawings illustrate each piece, and it has a dark palette. It's easy to navigate to poems, short stories and reviews, which are contemporary and have to have a fresh take on any horror tropes. The poetry we saw was mainly narrative and lyrical in style, and the prose was gripping. No writer biographies were offered.

DON'T DO IT
E-ZINE
editors@dontdoitmag.co.uk
dontdoitmag.co.uk
Quarterly publication accepting fiction, poetry, critical writing, reviews and art. 'Heartfelt critical enquiry with a GSOH'.

ELBOW ROOM ☆
PRINT
138 Erlanger Rd, London SE14 5TJ
ayupublishing@gmail.com
www.elbow-room.org
Editors: Rosie Sherwood, Zelda Chappel
Established 2012. Mixed form: short stories, poetry, visual arts. Annual subscription £25 including P&P (four issues). Available direct from publisher website; in selected/local chain bookshops and independent bookshops; and at local literary events including Artists' Book Fairs (national) and the Small Publishers Fair. Some tasters of content available online.
GENRES: Unrestrained by genre – work selected is what's liked by

the Editors, regardless of genre, medium or type of fiction/poetry.

SUBMISSIONS: Open to all during submissions windows. Submit by email to elbowroomsubmissions@gmail.com. Guidelines at www.elbow-room.org/submissions. Usually responds within one to three months, with feedback only if requested. Contributors receive a print copy of the magazine.

WE SAY: We looked at Volume 9, a sewn-spine, 14-page magazine with a chapbook aesthetic. The cover is dark green textured card hand-stamped with the logo and issue number. Inner pages are thick and cream; the ink is a rather lovely dark cyan. This is an artisan publication. The text is laid out with an eye to the space around the words, and interspersed with full-colour art images. There is a crowded biography page with lots of information about contributors. The final page is marked with a limited edition counter (26/50), and a confirmation that 'Submissions are (VERY) welcome'. The published writing is achingly lyrical, and redefines the ways in which we view the world.

See also: As Yet Untitled (prose publishers p70 and poetry publishers p18)

ESC ZINE

PRINT AND DIGITAL
escpeople@gmail.com
www.esczine.com
Editors: Jessica Maybury, Aine Belton
Established 2011. Mixed form, including 'pocket ESC', which are small poetry and micro-fiction digital anthologies and chapbooks. Print publications available direct from publisher website and at national and local literary events.

All online content is available to all.

GENRES: Literary fiction; poetry; slipstream; experimental; art, fashion and photography.

SUBMISSIONS: During submissions windows, submit by email to escpeople@gmail.com. Guidelines at esczine.com/submissions/. Usually responds within four weeks. Rejection may occasionally include unsolicited feedback. Contributors receive a print copy of the magazine; otherwise unpaid.

WE SAY: We looked at ESC online, but images of the print version show a lovingly handmade publication. The Pocket ESC mini-issues, which are free and digital, consist of single pieces of work, sometimes hand-written and scanned in, complete with ink illustrations. The titles are in Irish (with English translation), and the work punchy and well designed.

FAR OFF PLACES

PRINT, DIGITAL AND PODCAST
Flat 14, 24 East Parkside, Edinburgh EH16 5XN
words@faroffplaces.org
www.faroffplaces.org
Editor: Annie Rutherford
Established 2013. Mixed form. Available at local literary events and from the publication website. Only subscribers/purchasers can access all of the online content, though some of it is freely available to all.

GENRES: Children's fiction; drama and criticism; literary fiction; poetry; creative non-fiction.

SUBMISSIONS: Open to all during submissions windows. Submit by email to submissions@faroffplaces.org. Guidelines at faroffplaces.org/submissions. Usually responds within one to three months, and

regularly offers free feedback on submissions. Contributors receive a digital copy of the magazine and 'a drink, if we meet them'.
WE SAY: A 64-page themed

magazine – we looked at a PDF of Volume III, Issue 1, which contains poetry and short stories on the theme of 'The Second Breakfast.' It's a straightforward

FIREWORDS QUARTERLY

PRINT AND DIGITAL
info@firewords.co.uk
www.firewords.co.uk
Editor: Dan Burgess

Established 2014. Mainly fiction. Annual subscription £21 including postage. Publication available direct from publisher website and at independent bookshops.
GENRES: Short stories and poetry. No non-fiction.
SUBMISSIONS: Open to all during submissions windows. Submit via online submissions form at www.firewords.co.uk/submit (guidelines found at the same place). Responses take up to three months, with feedback only if requested. Contributors receive a copy of the magazine.
WE SAY: You'd never guess this perfect-bound, full-colour literary magazine wasn't produced by a full-time team. Smaller than A5 and full of bold design, it's an innovative 48-page affair printed on matt paper. The writing is thought-provoking, unique and contemporary, but it was the unexpected design quirks that had us hooked, from the striking illustrations to the contents laid out on the back cover like a rock album.

THEY SAY

Firewords is an independent literary magazine packed full of powerful fiction and poetry from the best emerging writers – brought to life by bold design. As well as actively publishing new writers from around the world, we also work with the best artists, illustrators, photographers, hand-letterers and designers to bring each piece of writing we publish to life. In this way, we hope *Firewords* makes for a unique literary experience. We are looking for work that surprises us and stories that stay with the reader long after they have read the last word.

mono design, the only illustration being a line-drawing on the cover. However the theme is strong: the editors provide a recipe rather than a letter, and a 'menu' rather than contents. Poetry and stories mingle, divided into 'Aperitif', 'All-Day Breakfasts', etc, and the writing is, literally, mouthwatering. This issue made us hungry. The biography pages at the end are funny and whimsical, albeit not professionally informative.

FIVE DIALS
DIGITAL
craig@fivedials.com
fivedials.com
Established 2008. Mixed form, including literary fiction; poetry; general essays and literary criticism. All online content is freely available to all.

FOR BOOKS' SAKE
E-ZINE
jane@forbookssake.net
www.forbookssake.net
Editor: Jane Bradley
Mainly fiction, reviews, interviews, articles. All online content available to all.
GENRES: Literary fiction; poetry; YA; biography and true stories; music, stage and screen; society, education and politics.
SUBMISSIONS: Submit during submissions windows. Open to self-identifying women and especially encouraged from women of colour, disabled women, queer women, trans women and women from low-income backgrounds. Submit through Submittable at forbookssake. submittable.com/submit. Pitches for reviews/features can be emailed to reviews@forbookssake.

net / features@forbookssake. net. Guidelines at forbookssake. submittable.com/submit. Usually responds within four weeks.
For a fuller description of this press, see poetry publisher p33, and also prose publisher p85

FUNHOUSE MAGAZINE
PRINT AND DIGITAL
info@funhousemagazine.com
fwww.funhousemagazine.com
Editor: Oliver Zarandi
A new perfect-bound colour-illustrated magazine, containing poems, short stories, essays and comics. Issue 1 sold out (but is still available digitally), and the press's ethos is to 'make reading fun again' and create a magazine for writers and artists who 'feel like outsiders' or who 'feel their work is too strange for other magazines'.

FUR-LINED GHETTOS
PRINT
85 Gertrude Road, Norwich NR3 4SG
editorsalopress@gmail.com
fur-linedghettos.weebly.com
Editor: Sophie Essex
Established 2012. Mainly poetry. Publication available direct from publisher website; and at local literary events.
GENRES: Literary fiction; poetry. No non-fiction.
SUBMISSIONS: Open to all. Submit by email to editorflg@gmail.com. Guidelines at fur-linedghettos. weebly.com/submit.html. Usually responds within one to three months, with feedback only if requested. Contributors receive a print copy of the magazine.
WE SAY: An A5, 58-page magazine with a beautifully illustrated cover. We looked at a PDF of Issue 6.

The inner pages are text only, in a faux-typewriter font that suits the magazine's edgy, experimental aesthetic. The contents alternate prose and poetry (and prose poetry). We were struck by the sad anger in the work.

GOLD DUST MAGAZINE
PRINT AND DIGITAL
55 Elmsdale Road, Walthamstow, London E17 6PN
mailtallulah@gmail.com
www.golddustmagazine.co.uk
Editors: Omma Velada,
David Gardiner
Established 2004. Mixed form. Also releases 'best of' anthologies containing the best short stories and poetry. Available direct from publisher website. All online content is freely available to all.
GENRES: Crime/thriller/mystery; drama and criticism; fantasy/sci-fi; literary fiction; romance; writing.
SUBMISSIONS: Open to all. Submit by email to sirat@davidgardiner.net or bramwith22@aol.com. Usually responds within one to three months. Includes feedback with rejection. Unpaid.
WE SAY: *Gold Dust* offers its 50-page magazine in three formats: as digital (free), black-and-white print (cheapish), and full-colour print (less cheap). We looked at the digital version of Issue 28 on issuu.com. Alternating features, reviews, stories and poems throughout, the magazine is liberally scattered with photo illustrations. Its layout is closer to a lifestyle magazine than your average literary magazine. The contents are well curated – we think most people would find something to enjoy here.

GORSE
PRINT AND E-ZINE
info@gorse.ie
gorse.ie
Established 2014. Mixed form. Subscription: two issues €35 (Ireland); €45 (rest of the world). Available direct from the publisher website; from independent bookshops; and at local literary events, with some online content available to all, updated on a rolling basis.
Gorse was shortlisted for the Association of Illustrators awards, Book Category, 2014.
GENRES: Literary fiction; poetry; essays; interviews.
SUBMISSIONS: During submissions windows, submit by email to info@gorse.ie. Usually responds within one to three months, with a standard rejection (no feedback). Contributors are paid a set rate, and receive a print copy and a discount purchase price on the magazine.
WE SAY: Thick enough to be an anthology, the most recent issue of *Gorse* is 200 pages in a beautiful matt cover with one of regular artist Niall McCormack's bold, textured paintings. Containing essays, poems and stories, this is a high-quality publication in every sense of the word. The writing is sharp, sometimes traditional, sometimes experimental (see the poems from Kimberly Campanello in Issue 4, available online).

GRANTA MAGAZINE
PRINT AND DIGITAL
12 Addison Avenue, London W11 4QR
020 7605 1360
info@granta.com
www.granta.com
Editor-in-Chief: Sigrid Rausing

Established 1979. Mixed form. Annual subscription £32 (print and digital); £12 (digital only). Available direct from publisher website; by post and email order; at chain bookshops nationwide; in independent bookshops; at national literary events; at local literary events; and from Amazon and other bookshop websites. Only subscribers/purchasers can access all of the online content, but some online content is freely available to all.

GENRES: Literary fiction; poetry; biography and true stories; history; popular science and nature; society, education and politics; travel.

SUBMISSIONS: During submissions windows, submit via Submittable to granta.submittable.com/submit (guidelines at the same address). Agented submissions also welcome. Usually responds within one to three months. A rejection may occasionally include unsolicited feedback. Contributors are paid a set rate.

WE SAY: A literary magazine available in print and online, *Granta* is one of the writing world's heavy weights: hard to get your work into, but worth the effort. Your work would be rubbing shoulders with some big names. The style of writing leans towards the literary, but is always entertaining and readable. Work tends to have an international slant as well.

See also: Granta Books p87 and Portobello Books p105 (prose publishers)

GRIND, THE
PRINT AND DIGITAL, E-ZINE, PODCASTS, SHORT FILMS
07714 735 500
thegrindjournal@gmail.com
the-grind.co.uk
Editor: Gordon Robert Johnstone
Established 2013. (Very) mixed form. Publication available direct from publisher website, and all online content isavailable to all.

GENRES: Crime/thriller/mystery; fantasy/sci-fi; horror; poetry; weird fiction; experimental fiction; Scots fiction.

SUBMISSIONS: Open to all. Submit by email to thegrindsubmissions@gmail.com. Guidelines at the-grind.co.uk/submission-guidelines. Usually responds within one to three months, with feedback only if requested. Contributors receive a digital copy.

WE SAY: The multimedia aspect of *The Grind*'s publications means it is much more than just the digital publication. The issue we looked at ('V') was published under the title 'Fuck the Grind' and announced a change of direction, so we are not sure exactly what's coming next. But we can say that *The Grind* is modern, angry, edgy and experimental. The design is packed with bright, hard images, moody photography and well laid out poetry and short stories. Text changes colour, layouts alter, but it all looks fantastic.

See also: The Grind (poetry publisher) p35

GUTTER MAGAZINE
PRINT AND DIGITAL
Freight Books, 49 Virginia Street, Glasgow G1 1TS
info@guttermag.co.uk
www.guttermag.co.uk
Editor: Henry Bell
Established 2011. Mainly fiction. Annual subscription £12. Available direct from publisher website;

from some chain and independent bookshops; and at literary events. Some online content is available to all.

GENRES: Crime/thriller/mystery; historical fiction; literary fiction; poetry; YA; art, fashion and photography; food and drink; humour; society, education and politics; travel.

SUBMISSIONS: Open to all. Submit by email to info@guttermag.co.uk. Guidelines at www.guttermag.co.uk/?page_id=20. Usually responds in over six months, with feedback only if requested. Contributors receive a print copy of the magazine.

WE SAY: Perfect-bound 184-page magazine with the feel of an anthology that highlights new Scottish writing. An eye-catching design on high quality cream paper. The magazine publishes literary poetry and prose, plus interviews and reviews.

See also: Freight Press (poetry publisher p33 and prose publisher p85)

HAND JOB ZINE
PRINT
handjobzine@gmail.com
handjobzine.com
Editors: Jim Gibson, Sophie Pitchford
Established 2012. Mixed-form magazine, branching out into books with an anthology of short stories and poetry coming soon. Available direct from publisher website; in independent bookshops; at local literary events; and from online shop Big Cartel.

GENRES: Literary fiction; poetic realism; humour; society, education and politics.

SUBMISSIONS: Open to all, during submissions windows. Submit by email to handjobzine@gmail.com. Guidelines at handjobzine.com/about/. Usually responds in between four weeks and three months. Rejections may occasionally include unsolicited feedback. Contributors receive a print copy of the magazine.

WE SAY: *Hand Job Zine* is, as the name cheekily implies, a seemingly hand-made affair. It reminded us of the original zines, before easy technology came along, when the production process revolved around typewriters, cardboard and photocopying. A certain neatness of layout implies that modern processes are being used to achieve a retro look. 66 pages long, with a red cardboard cover and stapled spine, *Hand Job* is crammed with photocopied artwork and adult stories – not erotica, but not shying away from sex and swearing. The issue we saw included an A4, thick paper, folded zine called *One O Clock Gun* (free), and a handwritten poem on an NHS evaluation form.

HAVERTHORN MAGAZINE
PRINT
haverthorn@gmail.com
www.hvtn.co.uk
Editors: Andrew Wells, A Leyla Hess
Established 2015. Mixed form - poetry, fiction (including flash fiction), non-fiction and art. Issues are available via the website, and from Amazon. The editors look for 'writing that affects us before we know why and how it does so... writing that is greater than the sum of its parts'.

HERE COMES EVERYONE
PRINT AND DIGITAL
ICE, Parkside, Coventry CV1 2NE

adam.steiner@silhouettepress.co.uk
herecomeseveryone.me
Editor: Gary Sykes-Blythe
Established 2012. Mixed form.
Publication available direct from
publisher website; by post and
email order; and from independent
bookshops and bookshop
websites.
GENRES: No fixed genres.
SUBMISSIONS: Open to all.
Submit through Submittable
at silhouettepress.submittable.
com/submit/40008. Usually
responds within four to six months.
Rejection may occasionally include
unsolicited feedback. Unpaid.
WE SAY: *Here Comes Everyone*
revels in its design. We looked
at the 'Kitsch' issue, in PDF format,
which has a cover very much
living up to the theme, and inner
pages drenched in acid yellows
and hot pinks. The layout alternated
between prose and poetry, all
illustrated with saturated photos
or bright and beautiful artwork.
The layout is colour-coded too –
yellow page corners for poetry,
pink for fiction, blue for non-fiction.
The writing is superb: contemporary
and self-aware with a touch of
humour.
**See also: Silhouette Press (poetry
publisher p54 and prose publisher
p112)**

HOAX

PRINT AND DIGITAL
hoaxpublication@gmail.com
www.hoaxpublication.co.uk
Editor: Lulu Nunn
Established 2012. Mixed form.
Print publications available by post
and email order; in independent
bookshops and art galleries
worldwide; and at national and
local literary events. All online
content is freely available to all.
GENRES: No non-fiction.
SUBMISSIONS: Open to all. Submit
by email to hoaxpublication@
gmail.com. Guidelines at www.
hoaxpublication.co.uk/p/
submissions-guidelines.html.
Usually responds within one to
three months, with feedback only
if requested. Contributors currently
unpaid.
WE SAY: A six-page A5 booklet,
with a DIY approach in the vein
of classic zines. Basically folded
paper, *Hoax* illustrates its brief
stories and poems with artwork in
colour and black-and-white, and
is cleanly laid out. The aesthetic is
unmistakeably modern; perfectly
judged for its market. This is a
publication for people passing
through, without much time on
their hands, who will slip it in their
bag and rediscover it in peace.

HOLDFAST MAGAZINE

DIGITAL
submissions@holdfastmagazine.com
www.holdfastmagazine.com
Editors: Laurel Sills, Lucy Smee
Established 2013. Mainly publishes
fiction. Available direct from the
publisher website. All online
content is available to all.
Winner of British Fantasy Award
for best magazine/periodical 2015
(organised by the British Fantasy
Society).
GENRES: Drama and criticism;
fantasy/sci-fi; horror; speculative;
humourous non-fiction; literary
criticism and interviews.
SUBMISSIONS: Open to
all. Submit by email to
submissions@holdfastmagazine.
com. Guidelines at www.
holdfastmagazine.com/submission-
guidelines/4582814806.

Usually responds within one to three months. Rejections may occasionally include unsolicited feedback. Contributors receive an equal cut of any profit made from fundraising throughout the year (the amount varies year on year). **WE SAY:** A quarterly digital magazine, that jumps straight into the issue on the homepage. *Holdfast* makes use of the multimedia possibilities of digital publication to include a playlist to listen to as you read, and stretches its non-fiction work into 'crossmedia', so essays explore TV, film etc., as well as literature. A thoroughly contemporary publication.

INKAPTURE

E-ZINE
inkapturemagazine@gmail.com
www.inkapturemagazine.co.uk
Editors: Conner Brown, Lily Peters
Established 2011. Mixed form, including poetry, fiction, non-fiction and observation. All online content is freely available to all.
GENRES: Literary.
SUBMISSIONS: Submit via the online form at www.inkapturemagazine.co.uk/submissions/. Guidelines available at the same address. Usually responds within one to three months, and offers feedback on all submissions. Unpaid.
WE SAY: A quarterly literary e-zine based in the North East of England. Rather confusing to navigate – the archive listings are easier to use. The site is otherwise well-structured and the writing includes lyrical poetry and engaging fiction: a pleasure to read.

INTERPRETER'S HOUSE, THE ☆

PRINT
36 College Bounds, Old Aberdeen, Aberdeen, Scotland AB24 3DS
01224 487094
theinterpretershouse@aol.com
www.theinterpretershouse.com
Editors: Martin Malone,
Charles Lauder Jnr (Deputy Editor)
Established 1984. Mainly poetry. Annual subscription £15. Available direct from publisher website; by post and email order; and at independent bookshops and local literary events.
GENRES: Poetry; short stories on all subjects; reviews.
SUBMISSIONS: Open to all, during submissions windows (though past contributors are asked to wait three issues after appearing in the magazine before submitting again). Submit by post (36 College Bounds, Old Aberdeen, Aberdeen, Scotland AB24 3DS) or by email (theinterpretershouse@aol.com). Guidelines at www.theinterpretershouse.com/submissions. Usually responds within one to three months. Rejections may include occasional unsolicited feedback. Contributors receive a print copy of the magazine.
WE SAY: A perfect-bound 108-page A5 publication, professionally designed and printed on high-quality cream paper. The work published has a confident contemporary literary aesthetic. The edition we looked at included the winning poems from the 2015 Open House Poetry Competition, followed by selected poetry submissions and a (very) few short stories, arranged in alphabetical order by author. The Editor's Letter is a bracing plea for 'poetry that is different', specifically poetry that

deviates from the autobiographical topics that 'zillions of other poets' are writing about.

IRISH LITERARY REVIEW
E-ZINE
editor@irishliteraryreview.com
www.irishliteraryreview.com

Editor: Catherine Higgins-Moore
Mixed form, including interviews. Welcomes submissions from Ireland and around the world
GENRES: Literary fiction; poetry.

INK, SWEAT & TEARS ☆
E-ZINE
www.inksweatandtears.co.uk
Editor: Helen Ivory

Established 2007. Primarily poetry. All online content available to all. Nominated for the 2015 Saboteur Award for Best Magazine.
GENRES: Poetry; word and image work; flash and short fiction (under 750 words); reviews of poetry books.
SUBMISSIONS: Open to all. Submit by email to www. inksweatandtears.co.uk/. Guidelines at www.inksweatandtears.co.uk/ pages/?page_id=23. Usually responds within one to three months. No feedback with rejection. Unpaid, but readers vote for Pick of the Month and the winning writer receives a £10 gift card.
WE SAY: Clearly signposted and publishing new content each day. The magazine focuses mainly on poetry and reviews and takes a contemporary approach to its content, with a fair amount of free verse and prose-poetry, but without stepping into the realms of the wildly experimental. There's a clear sense of curation and selection. Each piece of creative writing includes a brief biography

THEY SAY

Ink Sweat & Tears is a UK-based webzine run by Kate Birch and edited by Helen Ivory. We publish poetry, short prose, prose-poetry and experimental work that combines words and images, and everything in between. Our tastes are eclectic and magpie-like and we publish something new every day. We enjoy finding a spark of brilliance in work from newer writers and aim to nurture potential, as well as to showcase work from more established practitioners. We listen to our readers – you can follow us on Twitter and Facebook and vote for your pick of the month, every month.

of the contributor. Given that the site's set up makes it a satisfying read, this is a good site for a poet's CV, allowing easy access, a welcoming way for readers to discover your work.
See also: Ink Sweat & Tears books (poetry publishers) p36

IRISH PAGES: A JOURNAL OF CONTEMPORARY WRITING

PRINT

129 Ormeau Road, Belfast BT7 1SH

028 9043 4800

editor@irishpages.org

www.irishpages.org

'Ireland's premier literary journal'. A bi-annual, mixed-form publication. Postal submissions only.

ISLAND REVIEW, THE

E-ZINE

mail@theislandreview.com

www.theislandreview.com

Editors: Jordan Ogg, Malachy Tallack

Established 2013. Mixed form. All online content freely available to all.

GENRES: Crime/thriller/mystery; fantasy/sci-fi; historical fiction; literary fiction; poetry; art, fashion and photography; biography and true stories; history; popular science and nature; travel.

SUBMISSIONS: Open to all. Submit through Submittable at theislandreview.submittable. com/submit/ (guidelines at same address). Usually responds in up to six months. Usually no feedback if rejected, but may include occasional unsolicited feedback. Unpaid.

WE SAY: A clean, heavily illustrated website, featuring writing inspired by islands. It's a niche subject with great potential. One story we particularly liked imagines Glasgow as a city of islands. The site is updated regularly, with work well curated and presented.

JOTTERS UNITED LIT-ZINE ☆

E-ZINE

unitedjotters@gmail.com

jottersutd.wix.com/jotters-united

Editor: Nick Gerrard

Established 2014. Mainly fiction. Free access – all online content available to all.

GENRES: Literary fiction; poetry; biography and true stories; travel.

SUBMISSIONS: Open to all. Submit by email to unitedjotters@gmail. com. Guidelines at jottersutd.wix. com/ju-lit-zine#!submit/c24cc. Usually responds within four weeks. Rejections may occasionally include unsolicited feedback. Unpaid.

WE SAY: Bold and bright, *Jotters United* combines bright illustration and surreal artwork with videos, music, slideshows and, of course, writing. The menu starts at Issue 1, so it's a bit of a scroll to get to the most recent work, but once you find it, it's clearly laid out, with six writers per issue. The writing itself is in a clear large-ish font; the stories very much slices of life.

LABLIT.COM

E-ZINE

editorial@lablit.com

www.lablit.com

Editor: Dr Jennifer Rohn

Mixed lab-lit genre writing – fiction, non-fiction, reviews, interviews etc. Note: lab lit is *not* sci fi. Realistic science only, please. See website for definition.

LAMPETER REVIEW, THE

DIGITAL

The Journal of the Lampeter Creative Writing Centre

info@lampeter-review.com

lampeter-review.com

Mixed form: accepts submissions of prose, poetry and screenplays/plays. Contributors receive a hard copy of the magazine.

LETTERS PAGE, THE

DIGITAL
School of English, University of
Nottingham, Nottingham NG7 2RD
editor@theletterspage.ac.uk
www.theletterspage.ac.uk
Editor: Jon McGregor

Established 2013. Mixed form.
Available direct from publisher
website, with all online content
freely available to all.
GENRES: Literary and poetry
correspondence.
SUBMISSIONS: Open to all.
Submit by post to *The Letters
Page*, School of English, University
of Nottingham, Nottingham
NG7 2RD. Guidelines at www.
theletterspage.ac.uk/letterspage/
submissions.aspx. Usually responds
within one to three months. No
feedback is offered with rejections.
Contributors are paid a set rate.
WE SAY: The art of letter writing
turned into a lit-zine, *The Letters
Page* consists of handwritten letters
that have been transcribed into a
simple and effective layout. These
letters appear in the magazine
'illustrated' by scanned images of
the original letter. There's something
voyeuristic and satisfying about
the resulting reading experience.
The tone varies – sad, humourous,
matter-of-fact – and it's almost
impossible to distinguish between
memoir, essay and inventeion. An
unique idea, presented well.

LIARS' LEAGUE

E-ZINE WITH VIDEO AND PODCAST
07808 939535
liarsleague@yahoo.co.uk
www.liarsleague.com
Editor: Katy Darby

Established 2007. Fiction suitable
for performance. All online content
available to all. Liar's League won
the 2014 Saboteur Award for Best
Regular Spoken Word Event.
GENRES: Crime/thriller/mystery;
fantasy/sci-fi; horror; historical
fiction; literary fiction; romance.
No YA or children's fiction.
SUBMISSIONS: Open to all. Submit
by email to liars@liarsleague.com.
Guidelines at www.liarsleague.
com/liars_league/forthcoming-
events-themes.html. Usually
responds within four weeks. Offers
feedback only on shortlisted
stories. Contributors are offered
payment in kind (books, free ticket
and/or drinks).
WE SAY: Including *Liars' League*
in this Guide is somewhat of an
anomaly, as they are primarily
known for performances.
Submitted stories are chosen to
be performed by a professional
actor in front of an appreciative
audience; those same stories are
also published on the website in
an easy-to-browse archive, along
with the performances on videos
and audio (there are podcast and
youtube channels). The *League* is
noted for great taste in fiction and
looks for surprising, unique work
that fits themes that are announced
well in advance. A great way to get
your name known and your work
performed.

LIGHTHOUSE ☆

PRINT
90 Earlham Road, Norwich NR2 3HA
admin@gatehousepress.com
www.gatehousepress.com/lighthouse
Editors: Meirion Jordan,
Andrew McDonnell, Julia Webb,
Philip Langeskov, Anna de Vaul,
Jo Surzyn, Angus Sinclair,
Scott Dahlie, Iain Robinson,
Zoe Kingsley

Established 2006. Poetry and

short fiction. Subscription £22.50 per year (four issues). Available direct from publisher website; at selected/local chain bookshops and independent bookshops; at national and local literary events; and from other bookshop websites. Only subscribers/purchasers can access any online content. *Lighthouse* won the Saboteur Award for Best Magazine 2015.

GENRES: Literary fiction; poetry. No non-fiction.

SUBMISSIONS: Submit during submissions windows. Usually responds within one to three months. No feedback offered on submissions. Contributors receive a print copy of and a discount purchase price on the magazine.

WE SAY: We looked at a PDF of Issue 9, a 96-page A5 quarterly magazine is printed in a font that reminded us of old novels (in a good way). Stories are laid out as if in a standard book, without much white space, and both stories and poems are interspersed with artwork that looks like line drawings of slanted sunlight. Poetry, prose and prose poetry is gathered here, all very high quality. Features are saved for last, and are very in-depth.

See also: Gatehouse Press (poetry publisher p33 and prose publisher p86)

LITERATEUR, THE
E-ZINE
editor@literateur.com
www.literateur.com
Editors: Sadie Levy-Gale, James Marriott, Adam Crothers, Eleanor Carless
Established 2009. Mixed form. All online content freely available to all, frequent updates. Has plans to expand into print publication.

GENRES: Literary fiction; poetry; literary criticism; reviews.

SUBMISSIONS: Open to all. Submit by email to submissions@literateur. com. Guidelines at literateur. com/about/contribute/. Usually responds in up to three months. No feedback usually offered with rejections, unless requested; but editors will say if they'd like to look at other work. Unpaid, but publicises contributors' work and writing profile.

WE SAY: A very professional site layout, with judicious use of colour and images. *The Literateur* is easy to navigate, looks smart, and someone has put a lot of thought and effort into how best to display the work. The poems and stories we read looked at the world in a fresh way. The site also feature interviews and reviews, but appears to update only intermittently.

LITRO MAGAZINE
PRINT AND DIGITAL
1- 15 Cremer Street, Studio 213, Hoxton, London E2 8HD
020 3371 9971
info@litro.com
www.litro.com
Editors: Eric Akoto, Precious Williams
Established 2005. Mainly publishes fiction, in print, online and as a podcast. For subscription information see www.litro.co.uk/join/. Available direct from publisher website; at chain bookshops nationwide; at independent bookshops; and at national and local literary events. Only subscribers/purchasers can access all online content, although some is available as a preview. *Litro* has been shortlisted for awards.

GENRES: Crime/thriller/mystery; drama and criticism; literary fiction; poetry; art, fashion and photography; food and drink; music, stage and screen; science, technology and medicine; society, education and politics; travel.

SUBMISSIONS: Submit across all of *Litro*'s platforms via Submittable. Guidlines and link at www.litro.co.uk/submit/.

WE SAY: Perfect-bound 40-page magazine featuring fiction, essays, interviews and culture. Matt finish, striking cover design (we looked at Issue 144: 'Transgender'), and full-colour inside, printed on thick quality paper. *Litro* has its roots in the city, and this is reflected in its aesthetic, which is contemporary and edgy. The expansive website features a large number of articles, interviews, weekly flash fiction etc., as well as the contents of the print version of the magazine. The sheer scale of the site was somewhat difficult to navigate – there's a lot going on – but the content is unceasingly interesting and well-written.

See also: Litro Magazine Ltd (prose publisher) p93

LONDON MAGAZINE, THE ☆
PRINT AND DIGITAL
11 Queen's Gate, London SW7 5EL
020 7584 5977
admin@thelondonmagazine.org
www.thelondonmagazine.org
Editor: Steven O'Brien
Established 1732. Mixed form. Annual subscription £33. Available direct from publisher website; by post and email order; from chain bookshops; and from independent bookshops. Some online content is freely available to all.

GENRES: Literary fiction; poetry; art, fashion and photography; biography and true stories; history; music, stage and screen; society, education and politics; travel.

SUBMISSIONS: Open to all. Submit by post (to 11 Queen's Gate, London, SW7 5EL), by email (admin@thelondonmagazine.org) or through Submittable (thelondon magazine.submittable.com/submit). Sometimes charges a reading fee. Usually responds within one to three months. Rejections may occasionally include unsolicited feedback. Contributors are paid (rate by negotiation) and receive print copy/ies and a digital copy of the magazine.

WE SAY: A long-established perfect-bound 118-page magazine with a contemporary aesthetic. The cover design is eyecatching; the materials high quality. The publication takes an intellectual, literary approach in its critical essays and reviews, and is strict about the quality of the free verse it publishes – the poems must have a purpose and no word should be wasted. The creative writing is engaging and tightly written, somewhat traditional and often London-focused.

LONELY CROWD, THE
PRINT AND E-ZINE
johnlavin@thelonelycrowd.org
thelonelycrowd.org
Editor: John Lavin
Billed as 'the new home of the short story', but does also publish a small amount of poetry. Founded by *Wales Arts Review*'s Fiction Editor, Dr John Lavin. Also looks for artwork, and pays for print contributions.

LOSSLIT MAGAZINE

DIGITAL MAGAZINE / E-ZINE
losslituk@gmail.com
www.losslit.com
Editors: Kit Caless, Aki Schilz

Established 2014. Mixed form including, but not limited to, poetry, short stories and micro-fiction. All online content freely available to all. LossLit was shortlisted for the Saboteur Awards: Best Collaborative Work 2015.

GENRES: Crime/thriller/mystery; fantasy/sci-fi; historical fiction; literary fiction; poetry; memoir; psychogeography; creative non-fiction; essays.

SUBMISSIONS: Open to all. Submit by email to losslituk@gmail.com. Guidelines at losslit.com/submissions. Aims to respond within three months and will always get in touch if interested in seeing more work, or if they have feedback. However may not always be able to get back to everyone. Unpaid.

WE SAY: *LossLit* consists of an easily navigated website, the home page of which takes you straight to the most recent issue. It's a plain, almost austere site, appropriate for its content, which focuses on all forms of loss. In addition to the website, there is the collaborative *LossLit* Twitter project, on the first Wednesday night of the month. Writers share microfiction about loss (#LossLit) and respond to

THEY SAY

LossLit is an attempt by its creators, Kit Caless and Aki Schilz, to explore the various influences of loss in literature. Collating original fiction, poetry, audio and essays by contributing writers as well as building a canon of important existing LossLit titles, *LossLit Magazine* will produce a body of work that will look at loss from all angles, alongside its online micro-project, the #LossLit hashtag on Twitter. A Twitter writeclub is hosted every first Wednesday of the month between 9 and 11pm GMT. The writeclub is online and open to all, with updates and RTs on @LossLit.

each others' work. The result is archived to be read at leisure. *LossLit* is an interesting read, with a truly original use of social media.

MEANWHILE...

PRINT AND DIGITAL / E-BOOKS
4 Florence Terrace, London SW15 3RU
07985 201621
submissions@soaringpenguinpress.com
www.soaringpenguinpress.com
Editors: John Anderson,
Ruth O'Callaghan

Established 2012. Graphic fiction.
Annual subscription £20. Available
direct from publisher website; by
post and email order; at selected/
local chain and independent
bookshops; at national literary
events; and via Amazon and other
bookshop websites (including
Diamond Comics Distributors).
Only subscribers can access online
content.
GENRES: Fantasy/sci-fi;
graphic/comics; horror;
poetry.
SUBMISSIONS: Open to all.
Submit by post (4 Florence
Terrace, London SW15 3RU)
or by email (submissions@

MANCHESTER REVIEW, THE

E-ZINE
Centre for New Writing, Mansfield
Cooper Building, University of
Manchester M13 9PL
0161 2753167
manreviewsubmissions@gmail.com
www.themanchesterreview.co.uk
Editors: Ian McGuire, John McAuliffe,
Lucy Burns

Established 2007. Mixed form. Two
issues a year, plus rolling reviews. All
online content available for free.
GENRES: Literary fiction; poetry;
creative non-fiction.
SUBMISSIONS: Open to all during
submissions windows. Submit by
email to manreviewsubmissions@
gmail.com. Usually responds within
four to six months. Rejections may
occasionally include unsolicited
feedback. Contributors are paid (by
negotiation).
WE SAY: This e-zine has a clean and
simple design, with straightforward
navigation and easy access to the
archives. Each issue's contents are

THEY SAY

The Manchester Review is
published from the University
of Manchester's Centre
for New Writing and will
continue to host podcasts of
its readings and discussion
events, as well as publishing
new writing twice a year, in
Spring and Autumn: the site
is regularly updated with
reviews of books, art, film,
and music in the hopes of
documenting the constantly
evolving cultural landscape
of Manchester and across the
north.

tied together by simply using
the art from one artist, in
one style for each signpost
illustration – a different artist/
style for each Issue. Very
effective and adds a splash of
colour. The e-zine also has a
podcast.

soaringpenguinpress.com).
Usually responds within four to six
months or more. Rejections may
occasionally include unsolicited
feedback. Contributors are paid
(set rate or by negotiation), and
receive print copy/ies and a
discount purchase price on the
magazine.
See also: Soaring Penguin Press

(poetry publisher p56 and prose
publisher p113)

MECHANICS' INSTITUTE REVIEW, THE
E-ZINE
editorial@writershub.co.uk
mironline.org
Established 2010 (previously
Writers' Hub). Mixed form. All

MOTH, THE ☆
PRINT
Ardan Grange, Belturbet,
County Cavan, Ireland
editor@themothmagazine.com
www.themothmagazine.com
Editor: Rebecca O'Connor

Established 2010. Mixed form.
Annual subscription €24.
Available direct from publisher
website; by post and email
order; at independent
bookshops; and in Eason and
newsagents in Ireland.
The Moth has won a Dublin
Airport Authority Arts Award,
and a poem published in *The
Moth* was shortlisted for the
Forward Prize for Best Single
Poem.
GENRES: Children's fiction (see
The *Caterpillar* p136; literary
fiction; poetry; interviews.
SUBMISSIONS: Open to all.
Submit by post (The Moth,
Ardan Grange, Belturbet, Co.
Cavan, Ireland) or by email
(editor@themothmagazine.
com). Guidelines at www.
themothmagazine.com/a1-
page.asp?ID=1972&page=18.
Usually responds within four

to six months. Rejections may
occasionally include unsolicited
feedback. Contributors receive a
print copy of the magazine.
WE SAY: A 35-page magazine
featuring interviews, literature
and art. Professional design
with a matt-finish that continues
onto its back cover. Contents are
published on quality white paper
with coloured images of artworks.
Poems are well-written and
engaging. Short fiction reflects a
lyrical aesthetic.
See also: *The Caterpillar* (mixed-
form literary magazine) p136

online content available to all.
GENRES: Literary fiction; poetry; features; reviews; biography and true stories.
SUBMISSIONS: Open to all, during submissions windows. Submit by email to editor@mironline. org. Guidelines at mironline.org/ submissions/. Usually responds within four to six months.

MSLEXIA ☆
PRINT AND DIGITAL
PO Box 656, Newcastle upon Tyne
NE99 1PZ
0191 204 8860
postbag@mslexia.co.uk
www.mslexia.co.uk
Editor: Debbie Taylor

Established 1999. Mixed form. Subscription £34.75 (UK) a year for four issues. Available direct from publisher website; by post and email order; at selected chain bookshops and independent bookshops; and at national and local literary events. Only subscribers/purchasers can access all of the online content, although some content is available to read freely.
GENRES: Literary fiction; poetry; features; biography and true stories; history; society, education and politics.
SUBMISSIONS: Open to all. Submit by post (PO Box 656, Newcastle upon Tyne NE99 1PZ), by email (submissions@mslexia. com) or via online form. Guidelines at mslexia.co.uk/submit-your-work/. Usually responds within one to six months. Feedback overview of all entries offered with rejections (for creative work). Contributors are paid a set rate and may receive a copy of the magazine.

THEY SAY

No other magazine provides *Mslexia*'s unique mix of debate and analysis, advice and inspiration; news, reviews, interviews; competitions, events, courses, grants. All served up with a challenging selection of new poetry and prose. *Mslexia* is read by top authors and absolute beginners. A quarterly masterclass in the business and psychology of writing, it's the essential magazine for women who write. We are a vibrant, ambitious and growing organisation, and we aim to provide a high-profile platform for new and established voices with every copy of the magazine.

Rejections may include occasional unsolicited feedback. Unpaid.

WE SAY: *MIRonline* is the online publication from Birkbeck University, which also produces the high quality *MIR* print publication (which contains work only by Birkbeck students and well-known authors). The site is clean and easy to navigate – fiction, poetry, features and reviews are all separately signposted, so readers in the mood for a long read can just work their way down the backlist or easily search the archives. There's even some audio, if you prefer your poetry to go straight to the ear. It's a professional, organised, easy-on-the-eye site – and as the student editorial staff rotates annually, never a place to cross off as 'not for my work', because the tastes and design change with the staff.

MINOR LITERATURE[S]
E-ZINE
minorliteratures@gmail.com
minorliteratures.com
Innovative literature: essay and memoir; experimental prose; book reviews; interviews.

MOVING WORLDS: A JOURNAL OF TRANSCULTURAL WRITINGS
PRINT
School of English, University of Leeds, West Yorkshire LS2 9JT
0113 233 4792
mworlds@leeds.ac.uk
www.movingworlds.net
Editors: Professor Shirley Chew, Professor Stuart Murray
Established 2001. Mixed form.
GENRES: Literary fiction; poetry; society, education and politics; spirituality and beliefs.

MYTHS OF THE NEAR FUTURE (NAWE)
DIGITAL
www.nawe.co.uk/young-writers-hub/myths/about-myths.html
For writers aged between 16 and 25. 'Tread[s] the tightrope between demanding quality and encouraging talent.'

NEON LITERARY MAGAZINE
PRINT AND DIGITAL
info@neonmagazine.co.uk
www.neonmagazine.co.uk
Editor: Krishan Coupland
Established 2006. Mixed form. Subscription £12 plus P&P (four issues). Available direct from publisher website; from independent bookshops; at local literary events; and from Amazon. All online content is freely available to all.
GENRES: Horror; literary fiction; poetry. Strictly no non-fiction.
SUBMISSIONS: Open to all. Submit by email to subs@neonmagazine.co.uk. Usually responds within one to three months. Subscribers, donors and purchasers of the magazine are eligible for feedback on their submissions. Contributors are paid a set rate, and receive a print copy and a discount purchase price on the magazine.
WE SAY: A 70-page quarterly magazine. We looked at a digital issue. Despite the name, this mag is dark – dark in writing aesthetic and dark in presentation, with black and white images and spooky covers. The stories and poems are literary, experimental, edgy and usually have some solid narrative at the core.
See also: Neon Books (prose publisher p97 and poetry publisher p42)

NEW WALK MAGAZINE

PRINT

c/o Dr Rory Waterman, Department of English, Mary Ann Evans Building, Nottingham Trent University, Clifton Campus, Clifton Lane, Nottingham NG11 8NS

newwalkmagazine@gmail.com

newwalkmagazine.wordpress.com

Editors: Rory Waterman, Nick Everett, Libby Peake

Established 2010. Mixed form. 18-month subscription £19.95. Available direct from publisher website; from independent bookshops; and at national and local literary events.

GENRES: Drama and criticism; literary fiction; poetry; art, fashion and photography.

SUBMISSIONS: Open to all. Submit by email to newwalkmagazine@gmail.com. Guidelines at www.newwalkmagazine.wordpress.com/purchase-submit/. Usually responds within one to three months. A rejection may occasionally include unsolicited feedback. Contributors receive a print copy of the magazine.

WE SAY: With varying styles of cover (Issue 11 is particularly striking) *New Walk* has been on a learning curve with its design, but is looking good these days. It's a hotbed of known poetry names, plus some great non-fiction (including a feature in which experienced poets offer critiques of their own first collections).

NEW WELSH REVIEW ☆

E-ZINE

PO Box 170, Aberystwyth SY23 1WZ

01970 628410

admin@newwelshreview.com

www.newwelshreview.com

Editor: Gwen Davies

Established 1988. Mainly reviews, with previews of *New Welsh Reader* fiction and articles. Only subscribers/purchasers can access all content, although some content is available to read freely.

GENRES: Drama and criticism; literary fiction; poetry; art, fashion and photography; biography and true stories; history; popular science and nature; society, education and politics.

SUBMISSIONS: Open to all. Submit by post (Submissions, PO Box 170, Aberystwyth SY23 1WZ) or by email (editor@newwelshreview.com). Guidelines at www.newwelshreview.com/submissions.php. Usually responds within one to three months. No feedback offered with rejections. Contributors are paid a set rate and receive a discount purchase price on the magazine.

WE SAY: Previously a print magazine, *New Welsh Review* is now web-based only, on a bright and easy-to-navigate site packed with features, articles, commentary and reviews. The site also features video interviews. There's no indication, though, as to which content is free and which requires subscription. So we'd suggest you subscribe...

See also: *New Welsh Reader* (print mixed-form literary magazine), next page

NEW WRITING SCOTLAND

PRINT

ASLS, 7 University Gardens, Glasgow, G12 8QH

0141 330 5309

office@asls.org.uk

www.asls.org.uk

Editors: Gerry Cambridge, Diana Hendry

NEW WELSH READER ☆

FORMERLY NEW WELSH REVIEW
PRINT
PO Box 170, Aberystwyth SY23 1WZ
01970 628410
admin@newwelshreview.com
www.newwelshreview.com
Editor: Gwen Davies

Established 1988 as *New Welsh Review*, and was rebranded *New Welsh Reader* in 2015. Now contains creative content only, with all review content appearing online as part of the e-zine, which is still *New Welsh Review*. Subscription £16.99 a year. Available direct from publisher website; by post and email order; at chain bookshops nationwide and independent bookshops; at national and local literary events; and from Amazon. Only subscribers/purchasers can access all of the online content, although some content is available to read freely (see *New Welsh Review*).
GENRES: Drama and criticism; literary fiction; poetry; art, fashion and photography; biography and true stories; history; popular science and nature; society, education and politics.
SUBMISSIONS: Open to all. Submit by post (Submissions, PO Box 170, Aberystwyth SY23 1WZ) or by email (editor@newwelshreview.com). Guidelines at www.newwelshreview.com/submissions.php. Usually responds within one to three months. No feedback offered with rejections. Contributors are paid a set rate and receive a discount purchase price on the magazine.

THEY SAY

New Welsh Review was founded in 1988 and is Wales's foremost literary magazine in English, offering a vital outlet for the very best new fiction, creative non-fiction and poetry, a forum for critical debate, and a rigorous and engaged reviewing culture. The magazine's creative content was rebranded as *New Welsh Reader* in May 2015, with reviews moving entirely online. We also run the New Welsh Writing Awards and the New Welsh Rarebyte imprint, publishing the winning entry from the Awards.
www.newwelshreview.com

WE SAY: Perfect-bound 80-page magazine. A high-quality glossy design, with a mixture of greyscale and colour images. Contemporary writing, all connected to Wales, well presented to readers.
See also: *New Welsh Review* (mixed form e-zine) p159

Established 1970. Fiction, non-fiction and poetry. One of a number of publications (including academic journals and study guides) produced by ASLS. Subscription: £47 for a full membership package, which includes *New Writing Scotland* along with all other ASLS titles. (no subscription available for *New Writing Scotland* alone). Available direct from publisher website; by post and email order; at local/selected chain bookshops and independent bookshops; at national literary events and local literary events; and from Amazon and other bookshop websites. All online content is freely available to all.

GENRES: Any and all genres of short fiction; prose work on all topics, particular interest in Scottish literary and linguistic topics for e-zine *The Bottle Imp*.

SUBMISSIONS: open to works by writers resident in Scotland or Scots by birth, upbringing or inclination. During submissions windows, submit by post to *New Writing Scotland*, ASLS, 7 University Gardens, Glasgow G12 8QH. Guidelines at asls.arts.gla. ac.uk/NWSsubs.html. Usually responds within four to six months. No feedback offered with rejection. Contributors are paid a set rate and receive a print copy and a discount purchase price on the magazine.

WE SAY: We looked at Issue 33, 'The Rooftop Busker', a perfect-bound 182-page anthology-like publication, featuring poetry and short fiction from new and upcoming Scottish writers. A matt-laminate cover displaying a detail from Marc Chagall painting 'The Blue Fiddler' gives you a sense of what this publication is about: artistic, quality, but totally accessible. There are several poems in Scottish Gaelic and at least one story written in dialect. Poetry and stories alternate in a pleasant and well-curated read. The editorial letter includes a plea for submissions to be as polished as possible (what did we tell you?). **See also: ASLS (poetry publishers p18 and prose publishers p71)**

NEXT REVIEW, THE
PRINT
Basement Flat, 116 Offord Road, London N1 1PF
thenextreview@gmail.com
www.thenextreview.co.uk
Editor: Patrick Davidson Roberts
Established 2013. Mixed form. Annual subscription £25/£35. Publication available direct from publisher website; at chain bookshops nationwide; at independent bookshops; and at local literary events.

GENRES: Drama and criticism; literary fiction; poetry; book reviews, author profiles and interviews.

SUBMISSIONS: Open to all. Submit by post or by email to Basement Flat, 116 Offord Road, London N1 1PF or thenextreviewer@ gmail.com. Guidelines at www. thenextreview.co.uk/#!submissions/ cee5. Usually responds within four weeks. Rejection may occasionally include unsolicited feedback. Contributors receives a print copy of the magazine.

WE SAY: The font used and layout of *The Next Review* reminds us of a 70s photocopied zine – but on thicker paper and with a far better print quality. It varies the lettering colour on each issue cover, but sticks to bold and deep colours – orange, blue, green, purple. The impression is of serious text – slightly at odd with the editor's penchant for original essay topics and lyric poetry. There's usually a headlining conversation with a highly-regarded poet, followed by a stable of featured writers we would be proud to be published alongside.

See also: poetry publisher p42

NORTHWORDS NOW

PRINT AND DIGITAL
6 Kippendavie Lane, Dunblane, Perthshire FK15 0HL
editor@northwordsnow.co.uk
www.northwordsnow.co.uk
Editor: Chris Powici
Established 2005. Mixed form. Available by post and email order; from selected/local chain bookshops and independent bookshops; at national and local literary events; from other bookshop websites; and at libraries, galleries and other outlets in Scotland. All online content is freely available to all.
GENRES: Literary fiction; poetry; short stories (strictly no novel extracts); biography and true stories; travel; literary essays.
SUBMISSIONS: Open to all. Submit by post to The Editor, *Northwords Now*, 6 Kippendavie Lane, Dunblane, Perthshire, FK15 0HL. Guidelines at www.northwordsnow. co.uk/submissions.asp. Usually responds within four to six months. Rejections may occasionally include unsolicited feedback. Contributors are paid (a set rate and by negotiation) and receive a print copy of the magazine.
WE SAY: We looked at a PDF of

this 32-page literary magazine, which is printed in newspaper format. A bold and striking cover announces the contents, which are laid out across four columns per page for prose, and three columns for poems. The effect is one of immediacy and freshness. Work appears in English and in Scottish Gaelic, and always embraces Scotland as landscape and culture.

NOTTINGHAM REVIEW, THE

DIGITAL AND E-ZINE
07929 364186
thenottinghamreview@gmail.com
www.thenottinghamreview.com
Editor: Spencer Chou
Established 2015. Mainly fiction, recently expanding to include poetry. All online content freely available to all.
GENRES: Literary. Strictly no non-fiction.
SUBMISSIONS: Open to all. Submit by email to thenottinghamreview@ gmail.com. Guidelines at www. thenottinghamreview.com/submit. Usually responds within four weeks. Rejections may include occasional unsolicited feedback. Unpaid.
WE SAY: Relative newcomer *The Nottingham Review* is a beautiful-looking digital magazine available in multiple formats. The design is simple – professional and contemporary. There are no images in the inner pages, just text with plenty of white space. The cover is uncluttered: one large, simple image. Where possible, there are live links to information on contributing writers, so readers can easily find out more. Each issue has a theme, and the stories are engaging nuggets of the everyday, followed by enthusiastic comments on the web-browser version. We

think this is one to watch.
See also: prose publisher p100

NUTSHELL
PRINT AND DIGITAL
editorial@nutshellmagazine.com
www.nutshellmagazine.com
Editors: Faye Fornasier,
Paul McGrane, Sophie Wardell,
Jack Houston
Established 2008. Mixed form, with
art and illustration featuring heavily.
Available direct from publisher
website; by post and email order;
and at independent bookshops
and local literary events. All
content available to all.
GENRES: Literary fiction; poetry.
SUBMISSIONS: Open to all.
Submit by email to editorial@
nutshellmagazine.com. Usually
responds in over six months. No
feedback offered with rejections.
Contributors receive a print copy of
the magazine.
WE SAY: A new issue of *Nutshell
Magazine* comes out about once
a year, and all print issues have
(unsuprisingly) sold out, so we
looked at the digital versions.
The reason for the gap between
issues becomes apparent when
you see the effort that goes into
them: the design is refreshed each
time, with 98 pages of full-colour
bespoke illustrations and carefully
selected and displayed stories and
poems. It's difficult to pinpoint
the aesthetic looked for – as the
editors say themselves, the style
is ever evolving, and if they like
a submitter's work enough, they
may ask for a different submission,
based on art they'll supply.

OCTAVIUS MAGAZINE
DIGITAL
info@octaviusmagazine.com
www.octaviusmagazine.com
Editor: Samuel Best
Established 2011. Mixed form.
Available by post and email order;
at selected/local chain bookshops;
and at national and local literary
events. All online content is freely
available to all.
GENRES: Literary fiction; poetry.
No non-fiction.
SUBMISSIONS: Open to all.
Submit by email to submissions@
octaviusmagazine.com.
Submission guidelines at www.
octaviusmagazine.com/submit.
Usually responds within four weeks,
with feedback only if requested.
Unpaid.
WE SAY: A digital magazine
with a minimalistic design. Very
modern, with simple navigation,
the site updates regularly. There
are no writer biographies; the
lyrical and engaging work is left to
speak for itself, and the magazine
encourages experiments with
technique and discourse. Out of
the ordinary content from up-and-
coming writers.

OFF LIFE: COMICS FOR A LOST GENERATION
PRINT AND DIGITAL
info@offlife.co.uk
www.offlife.co.uk
Editor: Daniel Humphrey
Off Life is 'the UK's only street-
press comic', offering a space for
indie comics and illustrators, with
open submissons for each issue.
Looks for 'comments on modern
life'. Preferably no fantasy or
superheroes or sci-fi.

OGHAM STONE, THE
PRINT
oghamstoneul@gmail.com
theoghamstoneul.com

Editors: students and faculty. Journal produced by the University of Limerick. Publishes fiction, creative non-fiction, memoir, poetry, short graphic fiction, visual arts and photography.

PAPER AND INK
PRINT

paperandinkzine@outlook.com
paperandinkzine.co.uk
Editor: Martin Appleby

Established 2013. Mixed form. Available direct from the publisher website and from independent bookshops.

GENRES: Drama and criticism; literary fiction; poetry. No non-fiction.

SUBMISSIONS: Open to all. Submit by email to paperandinkzine@outlook.com. Guidelines at www.paperandinkzine.co.uk/#!submissions/c24vq. Usually responds within one to three months. Rejections may occasionally include unsolicited feedback. Contributors receive a print copy of the magazine.

WE SAY: *Paper and Ink* is a basic paper-and-ink magazine: folded spine, black-and-white illustrations and photography. It has a distinctly punk attitude, taking a stand against the literary establishment and all things digital. It's simple, but well put together; we like the directness of the themes for each issue ('damn the man'; 'shitty jobs'; 'hangovers').

PENNILESS PRESS MAGAZINE
DIGITAL

10 Albert Road, Grappenhall, Warrington, Cheshire K1C 2X9
01925 602430
info@pennilesspress.com
www.pennilesspress.co.uk

Editors: Alan Dent, Ken Clay
Mixed form.

GENRES: Literary fiction; poetry; biography and true stories; history; society, education and politics; literary criticism.

See also: Penniless Press Publications (prose publisher) p104

PENNY DREADFUL, THE ☆
PRINT

Clonmoyle House, Coachford, Cork,
The.P.Dreadful@Gmail.com
thepennydreadful.org
Editors: Marc O'Connell,
John Keating

Mixed form. Annual subscription £26. Available direct from publisher website, selected/local chain bookshops, independent bookshops and at local literary events.

GENRES: Drama and criticism; graphic/comics; literary fiction; poetry; and reviews, specifically literary pieces that can include elements of biography.

SUBMISSIONS: Open to all. Submit through Submittable via thepennydreadful.org/index.php/submit/ (guidelines in the same place). Usually respond within four weeks. Rejection may occasionally include unsolicited feedback. Unpaid.

WE SAY: A perfect-bound magazine, with a professional design on high-quality paper – and a particularly dark ethos. The issue we checked out (No. 5) had a cover featuring a woman with blank, black eyes, a knowing smile and a red hood with horns – fair warning about the edgy, occasionally humorous writing inside. Contemporary, Irish and living up to its name, the work featured well-written stuff – but be warned: it's

not a comfort read.
See also: The Dreadful Press (prose publisher p80 and poetry publisher p27)

PLANET AND PLANET EXTRA
PRINT AND E-ZINE
PO Box 44, Aberystwyth,
Ceredigion SY23 3ZZ
01970 611 255
submissions@planetmagazine.org.uk;
website@planetmagazine.org.uk
www.planetmagazine.org.uk
Articles, poetry, reviews (Wales focus, as this journal is 'The Welsh Internationalist'). Paid.

PLATFORM FOR PROSE
ONLINE SHOWCASE
editor@platformforprose.com
www.platformforprose.com
Established 2015. Mixed form: shorts, flash and poetry. Available direct from publisher website. Forthcoming anthologies (e-books) will be available from Amazon. Some online content freely available to all.
GENRES: Contemporary short fiction. No children's or young adult fiction, sci-fi or fantasy.
SUBMISSIONS: During submissions windows, submit by email to editor@platformforprose. com. Guidelines at www. platformforprose.com/submissions. Usually responds within four weeks. No feedback currently offered with rejections. Unpaid.
WE SAY: Despite the name, this showcase *does* include some poetry. It's an easy to navigate, good-looking site with a healthy mixture of short stories, flash fiction and poems. It also recently branched out into audio presentation and included comment sections under the content so that readers can express their pleasure at the work.

POPSHOT MAGAZINE
PRINT AND DIGITAL MAGAZINE
hello@popshotpopshot.com
www.popshotpopshot.com
Editor: Jacob Denno
Established 2008. Mainly fiction. Annual subscription £10. Publication available direct from publisher website; in chain bookshops nationwide and from bookshop websites.
GENRES: Literary fiction; poetry. No non-fiction.
SUBMISSIONS: Open to all. Submit through Submittable at www. popshotpopshot.com/submit (guidelines at same address). Usually responds within four weeks, – no feedback unless requested. Contributors receive a print copy of the magazine.
WE SAY: An A5, 64-page literary magazine printed on matt paper. The modern formula of contemporary illustration mixed with poetry, short stories and flash fiction feels fresh and original. Each illustration is quirky and unique, specifically commissioned to appear alongside each piece of writing. Our favourite was 'Through the Flowers', a short story complemented by pop-art flowers with eyeballs at their centre. Wonderfully weird. The magazine has taken off in 18 countries around the world.

PUSH – THE WRITING SQUAD
ONLINE PLATFORM
steve@writingsquad.com
www.sqpush.com
Editor: Steve Dearden
Established 2001. Mixed form. All online content freely available to all.

GENRES: Literary fiction; poetry; travel; new journalism.
SUBMISSIONS: Submissions from members only or by invitation only.
WE SAY: An online magazine that features articles and creative writing for young adults. The design is contemporary, the colour scheme bright but not overwhelming, and the work is clearly laid out. Content includes poetry and prose, lyrical and contemporary.

PYGMY GIANT, THE
E-ZINE
thepygmygiant@gmail.com
thepygmygiant.com
UK flash fiction and non-fiction under 800 words, with the site updated each Monday and Thursday. 'All good short fiction should have a big, big personality'.

QUAINT MAGAZINE
PRINT
quaintlitmag@gmail.com
quaintmagazine.com
Editors: Kia Groom, Soleil Ho
Mixed form. Submissions open to female-identified and genderqueer/non-binary folk only.

QUEENS HEAD, THE
PRINT AND E-ZINE
www.thequeenshead.wtf
Fiction, poetry and non-fiction. Limited print-run batches of 50.
GENRES: Speculative; magical realism; slipstream; experimental poetry (preferably no erotica or political poetry); history; pop culture (slightly askance).

RIPTIDE JOURNAL
PRINT
Dept of English, Queen's University of Exeter, Exeter, Devon EX4 6QH
07895 012300
editors@riptidejournal.co.uk
www.riptidejournal.co.uk
Editors: Dr Virginia Baily, Dr Sally Flint
Established 2006. Mainly fiction, but includes poetry and life-writing. Available direct from publisher website; by post and email order; from independent bookshops; and at local literary events. Stockists listed on the website. Some content available online to all.
GENRES: Children's fiction; drama and criticism; erotica; fantasy/sci-fi; graphic/comics; horror; romance. No non-fiction.
SUBMISSIONS: Open to all. Submit by email to editors@riptidejournal.co.uk. Guidelines at www.riptidejournal.co.uk/contribute/. Usually responds within four to six months. No feedback offered. Contributors are paid a set rate and receive a print copy and discount purchase price on the magazine.
WE SAY: Only technically a journal, *Riptide* is a series of anthologies published as volumes as opposed to issues. Each volume contains a healthy amount of work (23 pieces in Vol 10: 'The Suburbs', which is the one we looked at), and has a gloss laminate cover and decent paper. The inside is pure book: (no illustrations, a prelims page, contents, thanks, and the work), but the cover design is very much that of a journal, with a single piece of art in a wide, white frame, and brief information about the contents below. This volume had an introduction from Michael Rosen, and some recognisable names in the contributors' list.
See also: Dirt Pie Press (poetry publisher p26 and prose publisher p79)

SABLE

PRINT AND E-ZINE
info@sablelitmag.org
www.sablelitmag.org
Managing editor: Kadija Sesay
An established and important publication, Sable LitMag is a showcase magazine for writers of colour, featuring work from internationally renowned and new writers. The magazine also offers training and support, and created the Writer's HotSpot: the first international creative writing residencies for people of colour. Originally solely a literary magazine, Sable has recently been recreated as a cultural magazine, 'underwritten by literary factors'. Types of work accepted include fiction, poetry, in translation, memoir, travel narratives (Blackpackers), essays, classic review and more. Online only slots include reviews, listings and microfiction.
SUBMISSIONS: Open to all writers of colour. Submit by email to editorial@sablelitmag.org. Full guidelines at www.sablelitmag.org/submissions.

SARASVATI ☆

PRINT
24 Forest Houses, Halwill, Beaworthy, Devon EX21 5UU
publishing@indigodreams.co.uk
www.indigodreams.co.uk
Editors: Dawn Bauling,
Ronnie Goodyer
Established 2005 (ltd company since 2010). Mainly poetry, some prose. Subscription £16/year for four issues. Available direct from publisher website; by post and email order; from nationwide chain bookshops; from independent bookshops; and from Amazon.

The Editors won the Ted Slade Award for Services to Poetry 2015 (organised by Poetry Kit).
GENRES: All styles considered.
SUBMISSIONS: Open to all. Submit by post (IDP, 24 Forest Houses, Halwill, Beaworthy, Devon EX21 5UU) or by email (publishing@indigodreams.co.uk). Guidelines at www.indigodreams.co.uk. Usually responds within four weeks. No feedback offered with rejection.
WE SAY: One of Indigo Dreams' publications, Sarasvati is an A5, 56-page quarterly magazine, perfect bound with a glossy full-colour cover. We liked the fact that every poet had at least three pages dedicated to their (high quality) work. The magazine has an international readership and IDP fosters a community of readers.
For what They Say, see Indigo Dreams Publishing Ltd (poetry publisher) p37. See also The Dawntreader (mixed-form literary magazine p139) and Reach Poetry (poetry magazine) p191

SEIN UND WERDEN

E-ZINE
9 Dorris Street, Manchester M19 2TP
seinundwerden@gmail.com
www.kissthewitch.co.uk/seinundwerden/sein.html
Editor: Rachel Kendall
Established 2004 (previously print). Mixed form. All online content available to all.
Shortlisted for the 2015 British Fantasy Awards – best magazine/periodical.
GENRES: Crime/thriller/mystery; fantasy/sci-fi; horror; literary fiction; surreal; art, fashion and photography; music, stage and screen; travel.
SUBMISSIONS: Open to all. Submit

by email to seinundwerden@
gmail.com. Guidelines at www.
kissthewitch.co.uk/seinundwerden/
submissions.html. Usually responds
within one to three months.
Rejection may occasionally include
unsolicited feedback. Unpaid.
WE SAY: We looked at *Sein und
Werden*'s 'Mappa Monday'. The
online publication is presented
as a map, with the contents page
structured like a map key, and
it provides a collection of short
stories and poems. It takes a
contemporary approach whilst
experimenting with different forms
within the content.
**See also: Sein und Werden Books
(poetry publisher p51 and prose
publisher p110)**

SENTINEL LITERARY QUARTERLY
PRINT AND E-ZINE
www.sentinelquarterly.com
Mixed form, accepting poetry,
short stories, novel extracts,
reviews and interviews, plays and
essays. Note that a different email
address applies for each area of
submission.

SHOOTER LITERARY MAGAZINE
PRINT
377 Oakeshott Avenue,
London N6 6ED
shooterlitmag@gmail.com
www.shooterlitmag.com
Editor: Melanie White
Established 2014. Mixed form:
short stories, poetry and short non-
fiction. Annual subscription £19.99
(UK); £34.99 (international) (for
two issues). Available direct from
publisher website; by post and
email order; at selected/local chain
bookshops (eg Foyles Charing

Cross); and at national and local
literary events. Only subscribers/
purchasers can access online
content. An e-book version of the
magazine is made available when
print editions sell out.
Shooter was nominated for
Saboteur Awards' Best Magazine
2015.
GENRES: Drama and criticism;
fantasy/sci-fi; literary fiction;
poetry; biography and true stories;
health and lifestyle; humour;
society, education and politics;
literary journalism (essays, memoir,
reported/researched narrative
pieces). Varies according to theme.
SUBMISSIONS: Open to all,
during submissions windows –
submissions must relate to the
issue theme and be of a literary
standard. Submit by email to
submissions.shooterlitmag@
gmail.com. See guidelines at
shooterlitmag.com/submissions.
Usually responds within one to
three months. Rejections may
occasionally include unsolicited
feedback. Contributors are
paid a set rate and receive a
print copy of the magazine.
WE SAY: A very professional
publication. We looked at
Issue 2 as an e-book. The team
have mastered the art of the
beautifully designed e-book,
including coloured dividing
pages and backgrounds, pull-
quotes, images and a stunning
cover. Stories and poems on the
theme of 'union' were variously
pensive, sexual, philosophical and
humorous. A great magazine.

SLEEPY HOUSE PRESS
E-ZINE
info@sleepyhousepress.com
www.sleepyhousepress.com

A showcase site looking to build a community of writers. Accepts all types of fiction and poetry for publication online and also runs workshops. The aim of this press is to make connections rather than just see your work published. This is just starting out so currently looking for volunteers and donations.

SONOFABOOK MAGAZINE
PRINT
146 Percy Road, London W12 9QL
0208 7432467
info@cbeditions.com
www.cbeditions.com
Editor: Charles Boyle
Established 2015. Mixed form. Available direct from publisher website and at independent bookshops.
GENRES: Literary fiction, non-fiction, poetry.
SUBMISSIONS: Currently only writers closely associated with CB Editions are published in the magazine.
For a fuller description of this press see CB Editions (poetry publisher p22 and prose publisher p74)

SOUTHWORD JOURNAL ☆
E-ZINE
Munster Literature Centre,
Frank O'Connor House,
84 Douglas Street, Cork
+353 021 431 2955
info@munsterlit.ie
www.munsterlit.ie
Editors: Patrick Cotter, Danielle McLaughlin, Matthew Sweeney, Colm Breathnach
Established 2001. Mixed form. All online content available to all.
GENRES: Literary fiction; poetry; literary criticism; Litríocht as Gaeilge.

SUBMISSIONS: Submit via Submittable at southword. submittable.com/submit (guidelines at the same address). Usually responds within one to three months. No feedback offered with rejections. Contributors are paid a set rate.
WE SAY: *Southword* recently moved from print to digital only. The website is not particularly attractive, but is very easy to navigate, and the work featured is extremely high quality in both English and Irish. *Southword* also pays extremely well. Stories and poems are literary and ideally have some connection to Ireland.
See also: Southword Editions (poetry publisher) p58

SPONTANEITY
E-ZINE
ruth.mckee@gmail.com
spontaneity.org
Editor: Ruth McKee
Established 2013. Mixed form. All online content available to all.
GENRES: Literary fiction; poetry; creative non-fiction.
SUBMISSIONS: Open to all. Submit by email to editor@spontaneity. org. Guidelines at spontaneity.org/ submit/. Usually responds within four weeks. Rejections may include occasional unsolicited feedback. Unpaid.
WE SAY: The contents page of *Spontaneity*'s latest issue is laid out like a series of newspaper articles, linking to work inspired by art (visual and written) that has previously appeared on the site. It's easy to fall down a rabbit-hole of reactions as you discover what prompted each piece. It's a unique approach to a literary magazine, and the resulting work is intense,

lyrical, personal and experimental. If you're a writer who likes to work to prompts, this is one for you.

STAND MAGAZINE
PRINT
School of English, Leeds University, Leeds LS2 9JT
Stand@leeds.ac.uk
www.people.vcu.edu/~dlatane/stand-maga
Editor: Jon Glover
Established 1952, and has published many writers who went on to be established figures, as well as paving the way for translated Russian and Eastern European work. Works in close association with the School of English at the University of Leeds. Mixed form work published: new writing, poetry, fiction, criticism. Only hard copy submissions accepted.
GENRES: Inventive; radical; experimental.

STEPAWAY MAGAZINE
DIGITAL AND E-ZINE
editor@stepawaymagazine.com
www.stepawaymagazine.com
Editors: Darren Richard Carlaw, Elena Kharlamova
Established 2011. Poetry and flash fiction. All online content available to all. Winner of the Walking Visionaries Award 2015 (Walk21).
GENRES: Literary fiction; poetry; travel – literature that evokes the sensory experience of walking in specific neighborhoods, districts or zones within a city.
SUBMISSIONS: Open to all. Submit by email to submissions@stepawaymagazine.com. Guidelines at stepawaymagazine.com/about. Usually responds within one to three months,

with feedback only if requested. Unpaid.
WE SAY: A 36-page digital magazine with selected contents on a theme. Its design is simple and professional. The magazine features poetry and short stories about walking and navigating urban spaces, with a contemporary lyrical aesthetic.

STINGING FLY, THE ☆
PRINT
PO Box 6016, Dublin 1, Ireland
stingingfly@gmail.com
www.stingingfly.org
Editors: Thomas Morris, Declan Meade
Established 1997. Mainly fiction. Subscription €30/year. Available direct from publisher website, in selected/local chain bookshops and Independent bookshops and at local and national literary events.
GENRES: Literary fiction; poetry; essays; reviews.
SUBMISSIONS: Open to all. Submit by post to PO Box 6016, Dublin 1, Ireland. Usually responds within one to three months. Rejections may occasionally include unsolicited feedback. Contributors are paid a set rate and receive a print copy and a discount purchase price on the magazine.
WE SAY: We looked at Issue 33/Vol 2 of this magazine, 'In the Wake of the Rising', which at 288 pages, resembles a hefty anthology. A matt laminate cover, with a striking graphic design of old photographs The contents consist of critical and artistic responses to the Easter Rising, in the centenary year of the event, and so is politically and historically rooted. The work included is sometimes serious,

sometimes experimental – one poem is entirely in tweets. The layout is clean and inviting – crucial when a magazine has as much to say as this one does. A great read. **See also: prose publisher p113**

STREETCAKE MAGAZINE
DIGITAL
streetcakemagazine@gmail.com
www.streetcakemagazine.com
Editors: Nikki Dudley, Trini Decombe
Established 2008. Mixed form. All online content available to all.
GENRES: Crime/thriller/mystery; fantasy/sci-fi; literary fiction; poetry. No non-fiction.
SUBMISSIONS: Open to all. Submit by email to streetcakemagazine@gmail.com. Guidelines at www.streetcakemagazine.com/submissions.html. Usually responds within one to three months. Rejection may include occasional unsolicited feedback. Contributors receive a digital copy. Unpaid.
WE SAY: A long-established digital magazine, *Streetcake* keeps its issues short and sweet. We looked at Issue 45. The cover is a simple, bright image; the contents cleanly laid out and leaning towards the experimental.

STRUCTO
PRINT AND DIGITAL
editor@structomagazine.co.uk
structomagazine.co.uk
Editor: Euan Monaghan
Established 2008. Mixed form. Annual subscription £14 (two issues). Available direct from publisher website; from independent bookshops; and on other bookshop websites. All online content is available to all.
GENRES: Literary fiction; poetry; slipstream; literary interviews.

SUBMISSIONS: Open to all, during submissions windows. Submit via Submittable (guidelines at link at structomagazine.co.uk/submissions/). Usually respond within four weeks or up to three months. Rejections may occasionally include unsolicited feedback. Contributors receive print copy/ies and a discount purchase price on the magazine.
WE SAY: A striking cover image, overlaid by the *Structo* logo, continues on the inner cover pages. The text layout is accented by judicial use of dropcaps and plenty of white space. The content alternates, poetry and prose, with highlights such as an interview with Ursula le Guin accented.
See also: Structo Press (poetry publisher p58 and prose publisher p115)

SYNAESTHESIA MAGAZINE ☆
DIGITAL
synaesthesiamagazine@gmail.com
www.synaesthesiamagazine.com
Editors: Annabelle Carvell, Carlotta Eden
Established 2013. Very mixed form (fiction, poetry, interview, articles, music). All online content available to all.
GENRES: Literary fiction; poetry; art, fashion and photography; music, stage and screen; science, technology and medicine; travel – article subjects can be dependent on the issue theme.
SUBMISSIONS: Open to all, during submissions windows. Submit through Submittable at synaesthesia.submittable.com/submit. Guidelines at www.synaesthesiamagazine.com/#!submissions/ck0q. Usually responds within one to

three months. Tries to provide feedback (however little) for every submission, to make up for not being able to pay writers/artists. **WE SAY:** A 76-page quarterly magazine, *Synaesthesia* is a feast for all senses. Bold edgy photographs and paintings compliment every piece of work; video and music are also incorporated into the digital design. This is a thoroughly modern magazine, and the writing is punchy, sharp and beautiful. The editors look for work that evokes the feeling of synaesthesia, so submissions should be uniquely descriptive and engaging. Each issue has a different theme ('Eat'; 'Thunder and Lightning'). A pleasure to read.

TEARS IN THE FENCE
PRINT
Portman Lodge, Durweston, Blandford Forum, Dorset DT11 0QA
tearsinthefence@gmail.com
tearsinthefence.com
Editor: David Caddy
Established 1984. Mainly poetry, reviews and interviews. Annual subscription £25 for three issues. Available direct from publisher website; by post and email order; and at local literary events. Nominated for Best Poetry Magazine Pulitzer Award and nominated for Best Poetry Editor Pulitzer Award.
GENRES: Drama and criticism; poetry; art, fashion and photography; travel; literary fiction.
SUBMISSIONS: Open to all. Submit by email to tearsinthefence@gmail.com. Guidelines at tearsinthefence.com/how-to-submit/. Usually responds within one to three months, with feedback offered for

a fee. Contributors receive a print copy of the magazine.
WE SAY: A long-established magazine that has maintained a simple print style and a striking monochrome look. Pages are closely printed, and included work ranges from the contemporary and experimental to the more traditional.

TEST CENTRE
PRINT AND AUDIO
77a Greenwood Road, London E8 1NT
admin@testcentre.org.uk
www.testcentre.org.uk
Editors: Jess Chandler, Will Shutes
Established 2011. Mainly publishes poetry. Available direct from publisher website; from selected/local chain bookshops; independent bookshops; and at local literary events. Nominated for Most Innovative Publisher in the 2015 Saboteur Awards.
GENRES: Literary fiction; poetry. No non-fiction.
SUBMISSIONS: Open to all. Submit by post (77a Greenwood Road, London E8 1NT) or by email (admin@testcentre.org.uk). Usually responds within one to three months. Rejection may occasionally include unsolicited feedback. Contributors receive a print copy of the magazine.
WE SAY: A4, 64 pages, with a stab-stapled spine. 'Test Centre Six' (the issue we looked at) has a heavy cardboard cover with monochrome artwork. Released in a limited edition series, *Test Centre* features fiction and poetry from contributing writers, and from authors under the Test Centre book imprint.

See also: Test Centre (poetry publisher) p60

THREE DROPS FROM A CAULDRON

E-ZINE
threedropspoetry@gmail.com
threedropspoetry.co.uk
Editor: Kate Garrett

Publishes poetry and flash fiction (or hybrids) involving myth, legend, folklore, fable and fairytale. Poetry and flash are published on the site four times a week.

UNDER THE RADAR ☆

PRINT
mail@ninearchespress.com
www.ninearchespress.com
Editors: Matt Merritt, Jane Commane

Established 2008. Mainly poetry, some short fiction. Annual subscription £18 (soon to be £22). Available direct from publisher website; by post and email order; at chain bookshops nationwide; at independent bookshops; at literary events; from Amazon; and through Inpress Books.

Winner of the 2014 Sabotage Award for Most Innovative Publisher.

SUBMISSIONS: Open to all, during submissions windows. Submit through Submittable at ninearchespress.submittable. com/submit. Guidelines at ninearchespress.com/magazine. html. Usually responds within one to three months. No feedback if rejected. Unpaid.

WE SAY: *Under the Radar* is Nine Arches Press' flagship publication, and a great way to be noticed by the press if you want to publish a collection. Primarily poetry, with some short fiction and reviews, *Radar* is well designed and balanced. The editors are always eager to discover new poets, so have a policy of not featuring the same poets in consecutive issues, giving you a better chance of being discovered.

See also: Nine Arches Press (poetry publisher) p43

[UNTITLED] ☆

PRINT AND DIGITAL
untitledfalkirk@gmail.com
untitledfalkirk.blogspot.co.uk
Editor: Craig Allan

Established 2012. Mixed form. Available direct from publisher website; by post and email order; at selected/local chain bookshops; at independent bookshops; and at local literary events. All online content is available to all.

GENRES: Crime/thriller/mystery; fantasy/sci-fi; graphic/comics; literary fiction; poetry; art, fashion and photography; society, education and politics.

SUBMISSIONS: Open only to writers either working, living or originally from Falkirk. Will also consider work from those who have significantly contributed to the arts in Falkirk regardless of their location. Submit only during submissions windows, by email to untitledfalkirksubmissions@gmail. com. Usually responds within four weeks. Rejections may occasionally include unsolicited feedback. Contributors receive a print copy of the magazine.

WE SAY: A 40-page quarterly magazine, which we looked at in digital format. The magazine pops up as a PDF in scribd. Illustrations include sketchs and line drawings. The poetry is largely experimental and free verse. That this is a niche magazine doesn't detract from the skill of the writing, nor from the way the work has been presented. Its local remit means the stories and poetry sit alongside listings of local events.

See also: Untitled Falkirk (poetry publisher) p61

VISUAL VERSE

DIGITAL / ONLINE ANTHOLOGY
OF ART AND WORDS
visualverse@thecurvedhouse.com
www.visualverse.org
Editors: Preti Taneja,
Kristen Harrison

Established 2013. Mixed form. All content available to all.
GENRES: Fantasy/sci-fi; historical fiction; literary fiction; poetry; art, fashion and photography. Welcomes all genres with a literary register.
SUBMISSIONS: Submit through the submissions form at visualverse.org/submit (guidelines at same address). Cannot respond individually with acceptance/rejections – if accepted, pieces appear on the site within one week. Editors sometimes edit in collaboration with the writer. Contributors receive extensive publicity and the opportunity to be published in related projects and other journals.
WE SAY: *Visual Verse* gives their writers a gorgeous monthly picture prompt and one hour to respond to it. The work is carefully curated and cleanly presented, and each month's selection shows an extraordinary breadth of imagination. The editors also promote their writers, and maintain an easy-to-search archive. *VV* is a unique publication with an extensive readership – a great way to challenge yourself and get your work read.

THEY SAY

Visual Verse is an anthology of art, poetry, short fiction and non-fiction. Each month, we supply a compelling image as a prompt and invite writers – published or unpublished – to submit a piece in response. There is a catch: you must write it within one hour and it must be between 50 and 500 words. *Visual Verse* is about experiencing the rush of writing without overthinking, and letting your instinct conjure up something unexpected. The image is the starting point, the rest is up to you.

WALES ARTS REVIEW ☆
E-ZINE / DIGITAL
www.walesartsreview.org
Editor: Gary Raymond
Established 2012. Mainly non-fiction. All online content available to all. Some published fiction has been released as an anthology.
GENRES: Literary fiction; art, fashion and photography; music, stage and screen; society, education and politics.
SUBMISSIONS: Submit by email to gary@walesartsreview.org. Guidelines at www.walesartsreview.org/contact/. Usually responds within four weeks. Rejections may include occasional unsolicited feedback. Unpaid.
WE SAY: *Wales Arts Review* is a professional e-zine, complete with eyecatching headlines, sliding images and daily updates. The focus is on reviews but creative writing and illustrations are also included – there's a handy link that take you straight to the stories, including work from some of Wales' best writers.

WASAFIRI MAGAZINE ☆
PRINT
The Open University, 1-11 Hawley Crescent, London NW1 8NP
020 7556 6110
wasafiri@open.ac.uk
www.wasafiri.org
Editors: Susheila Nasta (founding editor), Sharmilla Beezmohun (deputy editor)
Established 1984. Mixed form. Subscription approx £50, and can only be purchased via publisher Taylor and Francis. Single issues are also available by post and email order, and at independent bookshops and local literary events. Only subscribers/purchasers can access online content.
GENRES: Crime/thriller/mystery; drama and criticism; erotica; fantasy/sci-fi; graphic/comics; horror; historical fiction; literary fiction; poetry; romance; art, fashion and photography; biography and true stories; children and teenagers; history; society, education and politics; travel and literary criticism.
SUBMISSIONS: Open to all. Submit by post (to The Editor, *Wasafiri*, The Open University in London, 1-11 Hawley Crescent, London NW1 8NP) or by email (wasafiri@open.ac.uk). Guidelines at www.wasafiri.org/submit.asp. Usually responds in over six months. Rejections may include occasional unsolicited feedback. Contributors are paid a set rate, and receive a print copy and a discount purchase price on the magazine.
WE SAY: Perfect-bound, 100-page almost-A4 literary magazine, *Wasafiri* has a glossy, contemporary design that usually features photographic artwork on the cover. Chockful of international contemporary writing, the magazine opens with articles, interviews and art commentary (complete with full colour pictures), followed by short fiction and poetry. It ends with plenty of in-depth reviews of books from around the world. As befits an international magazine, plenty of the writing inside is translated. The issue we looked at had a particular focus on Brazilian culture.

WHITE REVIEW, THE
PRINT AND E-ZINE
editors@thewhitereview.org
www.thewhitereview.org

Mixed form. Serious-minded but accessible work, with an emphasis on contemporary arts and literature.

WINAMOP.COM
E-ZINE
editor@winamop.com
www.winamop.com
Established 2003. Mixed form. All online content available to all.
GENRES: Drama and criticism; historical fiction; literary fiction; poetry; biography and true stories; music, stage and screen.
SUBMISSIONS: Open to all. Submit by email to editor@winamop.com. Guidelines at winamop.com/guidelines.htm. Usually responds within four weeks. Rejections may include occasional unsolicited feedback.
WE SAY: *Winamop* is an established, home-brew e-zine, featuring work from a community of regular contributors, which it is actively looking to expand. The design is somewhat old-fashioned, but wins points for being easy to navigate and read. The supportive vibe and encouraging submissions blurb ('if you think it's good enough, likely so will we') make it a very welcoming and inclusive publication.

WORD BOHEMIA
E-ZINE
enquiries@wordbohemia.com
wordbohemia.co.uk
Mixed form. Relaunching in 2016.

WRITE ON! MAGAZINE
DIGITAL
Writing West Midlands, Unit 204, The Custard Factory, Gibb Street, B9 4AA
0121 246 2774
www.writeonmagazine.org
Editors: William Gallagher,

Joanne Penn
Established 2013. Mainly fiction. All online content available to all.
GENRES: Children's fiction; fantasy/sci-fi; poetry; YA; teenage.
SUBMISSIONS: Open to young people aged 8-20 living in the West Midlands. Submit by email to joanne@writingwestmidlands.org. Guidelines at www.writeonmagazine.org/get-involved/. Usually responds within one to three months, and always provides feedback to anyone or any pieces that they choose not to publish.
WE SAY: Run by Writing West Midlands for younger writers, *Write On!* is a digital magazine for readers who want a quick, refreshing dip into some high quality work. The editors don't patronise or make excuses for their young (aged 8-20 years) writers: they simply showcase some extraordinary up-and-coming talent – one short poem or story per page and just a splash of colour, letting the pieces speak for themselves.

Poetry magazines and e-zines

These magazines are all dedicated to poetry only – any prose they publish is strictly poetry-related, in the form of interviews, news, reviews or articles.

There are some beautifully produced and accessible print poetry magazines, including at least one that specialises in printing performance poetry. We're also pleased to include many e-zines and digital magazines in this section – pleased, because social media comments demonstrate that people love a good poem provided they can connect with it. They just need to find the right one, and online magazines make that more of a possibility. Apart from in a widely circulated magazine (like *Mslexia*), you're far more likely to have your poetry read online than in a print magazine – although there's still nothing quite like the thrill of seeing your work in print.

These days the quality of the material published in some e-zines is so high that even the lofty Forward Prize organisers bent to pressure in 2016 and allowed poetry nominations from 20 online magazines on a first-come-first served basis. A pretty measley concession, granted, but an indication of the growing status of this sector.

Poetry magazines and e-zines

ACUMEN LITERARY JOURNAL

PRINT

6 The Mount, Higher Furzeham Road, Brixham, South Devon TQ5 8QY

01803 851098

patriciaoxley@gmail.com

www.acumen-poetry.co.uk

Editor: Patricia Oxley

Established 1985. Annual subscription £15. Available direct from publisher website; by post and email order; at local literary events; and on Amazon.

Award-winning publication.

SUBMISSIONS: Open to all. Submit by post or by email to 6 The Mount, Higher Furzeham Road, Brixham, South Devon TQ5 8QY or patriciaoxley6@gmail.com. Usually responds within four weeks. Feedback only if requested. Contributors receive a print copy.

WE SAY: *acumen* is one of our leading poetry magazines, combining poetry with reviews and articles. A5 and perfect bound, it's well designed, with sleek, eye-catching covers and quality writing that has the knack of being serious but readable, inviting responses to previous issues and opening up discussion through reviews and essays. We looked at Issue 80, in which Editor Patricia Oxley describes the process of choosing the included poems. Frequently and fairly described as one of the most wide-ranging, inclusive poetry journals around, this should be a prime target for any serious poet.

See also: acumen (poetry publisher) p15

AGENDA MAGAZINE

PRINT AND ONLINE BROADSHEETS

The Wheelwrights, Fletching Street, East Sussex TN20 6TL

editor@agendapoetry.co.uk

www.agendapoetry.co.uk

Editor: Patricia McCarthy

Established 1959. Annual subscription £28.

SUBMISSIONS: Open to all, during submission windows. Submit by email to submissions@agendapoetry.co.uk. Usually responds within one to three months. Rejection may occasionally include unsolicited feedback.

WE SAY: *Agenda* is a perfect-bound publication with an anthology aesthetic. Although the page count varies, each ssue is book-length and the title and theme are chosen to reflect the submissions. We looked at Vol 49, No 1: 'Callings'. The matt-cover is usually the work of a chosen artist (who is featured in the publication and online) on a block-colour background. The magazine presents lyrical, accessible poems, essays and reviews on cream paper, and offers free supplements as Broadsheets on its website..

See also: Agenda Editions (poetry publisher) p15

ANGLE: JOURNAL OF POETRY IN ENGLISH

DIGITAL

anglepoetry.co.uk

Editors: Ann Drysdale, Peter Bloxsom, Philip Quinlan

Prefers poetry in received or nonce forms, but open to considering any work which has a strong element of rhythm or 'music'.

ANIMA
PRINT
www.animapoetry.uk
Editor: Marcus Sly
Established 2014. Annual subscription £15 (including postage). Available direct from publisher website.
GENRES: Spirituality and beliefs.
SUBMISSIONS: Open to all. Submit through Submittable at anima. submittable.com/submit. Usually responds within four to six months. Rejection may occasionally include unsolicited feedback. Contributors receive a print copy (but must contribute postage costs).
WE SAY: We looked at a PDF of the first issue of *Anima*, which is a relatively new publication. The print version of the 72-page A5 magazine is perfect bound, with a solid colour cover, and the title and butterfly logo embossed in white. The theme was spiritual, the poems curated and displayed in a way that takes the reader on a journey. There is a feeling of being offered stories in poetry form, compounded by the inclusion of 'epilogue' poems in their own section at the end. With very little information about the contributing poets, this is all about the poetry, and presenting it in such a way that it stands on its own.
See also: Anima Poetry Press (poetry publisher) p16

ANTIPHON
DIGITAL AND E-ZINE
editors@antiphon.org.uk
www.antiphon.org.uk
Editors: Rosemary Badcoe, Noel Williams

Established 2011. Free access – all online content available to all. Includes recordings of poets reading their work on the blog.
SUBMISSIONS: Open to all. Submit through Submittable at antiphon. submittable.com/submit. Guidelines at antiphon.org.uk/index.php/ submissions. Usually responds within one to three months. Rejection may occasionally include unsolicited feedback. Unpaid.
WE SAY: We looked at Issue 17, 59 pages. *Antiphon* is designed to be downloaded in a PDF format, but the layout would look impressive in print too, being clear and professional. It uses full-colour images to signpost the poetry, repeating a detail from a painting to each section of the magazine: a very effective visual prompt when scrolling through. The poems are fresh and contemporary.

ARTEMIS POETRY ☆
PRINT
3 Springfield Close, E Preston, West Sussex BN16 2SZ
01903 783816
editor@poetrypf.co.uk
www.secondlightlive. co.uk
Editors: Dilys Wood and guest editors
Established 2002. Subscription £11 annual, including postage and packing. Back copies £5. Available by post and email order.
SUBMISSIONS: Open to women only. Submit by post to 3 Springfield Close, East Preston, West Sussex, BN16 2SZ. Usually responds within one to three months, only to successful submissions. Unpaid.
WE SAY: Issues of *ARTEMISpoetry* are generally around 60 pages long, and the magazine features the work of new and established

women writers only, and particularly that of older poets. The cover design is a little crowded (and has been relatively unchanged for years) with the layout containing so much colour and so much text that at first glance it's not recognisable as a magazine cover. The contents count, though – publisher Second Light is a formidable organisation and *ARTEMIS* is packed with worthy essays and interviews alongside the poetry, again bringing much-needed attention to female poets.

BLACK LIGHT ENGINE ROOM, THE
PRINT
12 Harrogate Crescent, Middlesbrough TS5 6PS
theblacklightenginedriver@hotmail.co.uk
Editor: P.A. Morbid
Established 2010. Poetry, reviews, interviews. Subscription £18 (UK), £20 (Europe), £30 (rest of the world) for three issues per year. £30 (UK), £40 (Europe), £50 (rest of the world) for both *Black Light Engine Room* and Dark Matter chapbooks (see p19). Available by post and email order; and at local literary events.
SUBMISSIONS: Open to all. Submit by email to theblacklightenginedriver@hotmail.co.uk. Usually responds within one to three months. No feedback offered with rejection. Contributors receive a print copy.
WE SAY: A 17-page A4 stapled magazine, on slightly shiny paper, with a wildly eye-catching and colourful wrap-around cover design. We looked at Issue 13, where the front page showed an illustrated cat gazing out at

the reader, and the back cover showed the back of the cat. The poetry within is intense, but each page contains around four poems, sometimes by different writers, which can make it difficult to focus on just the one poem.
See also: The Black Light Engine Room Press (poetry publisher) p19

BLACKBOX MANIFOLD
E-ZINE
www.manifold.group.shef.ac.uk
Editors: Alex Houen, Adam Piette
Reviews, short essays, and poems (particularly poems with prose, narrative, or sequences).

BLITHE SPIRIT
PRINT
britishhaikusociety.org.uk/journal
Editor: David Serjeant
Haiku – submissions open to members only.

BURNING BUSH 2
DIGITAL
burningbushrevival@gmail.com
theburningbushrevivalmeeting.wordpress.com
Editor: Alan Jude Moore
Established 2012. All online content freely available to all.
GENRES: Poetry, literary, flash, reviews and interviews.
SUBMISSIONS: During submissions windows, submit by email to burningbushrevival@gmail.com. Guidelines at burningbush2.org/contact/Issue-1-poems/. Usually responds within four to six months. No feedback offered if rejected. Unpaid.
WE SAY: *The Burning Bush 2* is a magazine that lets the work speak for itself. It forgoes illustration, colour or any complex design completely, and as a result is a

stark, black-and-white publication that is reminiscent of photocopied litzines, but with a modern twist. The reading experience is more like a book than a magazine, with new poets from around the world displayed alongside stalwarts of the contemporary poetry scene.

CANTO POETRY
E-ZINE
editors@cantopoetry.co.uk
www.cantopoetry.co.uk
Sister journal of *Riptide* (mixed-form literary magazine, see p166).Themed poems, that offer conviction, along with sensibility and musicality.

BUTCHER'S DOG POETRY MAGAZINE
PRINT
c/o New Writing North, 3 Ellison Terrace, Ellison Place, Newcastle upon Tyne NE1 8ST
submissions@
butchersdogmagazine.com
www.butchersdogmagazine.com
Editors: Degna Stone, Luke Allan, Sophie F Baker, Jake Campbell, Amy Mackelden, Andrew Sclater

Established 2012. Poetry, reviews, interviews. Subscription £11 per annum + p&p. Available direct from publisher website, in selected/local chain bookshops and independent bookshops, and at literary events.
Butcher's Dog was selected for The Pushcart Prize 2016.
SUBMISSIONS: Submit through Submittable to butchersdog. submittable.com/submit. Usually responds within one to three months. No feedback offered if rejected. Contributors receive a print copy and a discount purchase price on the magazine.
See also: Butcher's Dog (poetry publisher) p21

THEY SAY

Butcher's Dog is a biannual poetry magazine showcasing exciting new work by poets from all over the UK – with a special focus on the poetry and poets of the North. Every issue has a different combination of editors and each limited edition magazine is a beautiful object created with care and attention. There is no set theme, we just want you to send us your best work. If you haven't read *Butcher's Dog* yet we strongly recommend that you do before submitting. If you like what you read chances are we'll like your poems too.

WE SAY: *Butcher's Dog* is bright and beautiful, made from quality materials, with a staple spine, and featuring 20-25 poets in each issue. The design is lovely and very professional, with stylish illustrated covers and plenty of white space. Small, but well formed, with a great reputation in the poeting world.

COMPASS MAGAZINE, THE
E-ZINE
editors@thecompassmagazine.co.uk
www.thecompassmagazine.co.uk
Editors: Lindsey Holland,
Andrew Forster
Established 2015. Poetry, reviews,
poetics. All online content freely
available to all.
SUBMISSIONS: Submit by email
to editor@thecompassmagazine.
co.uk. Guidelines at www.
thecompassmagazine.co.uk/
submissions-2/. Usually responds
within one to three months. No
feedback with rejection. Unpaid.
WE SAY: A stylish e-zine, *The
Compass* is a fully designed site (as
opposed to created from a simple
template). The range of content
– reviews, interviews, articles and
poems – means the home page
is quite crowded, but it's easy to
navigate. This is a poetry zine run
by poets for the poetry community.

CTL+ALT+DEL
E-ZINE/PRINT
rhys.trimble@gmail.com
theabsurd.co.uk/cad
Contemporary poetry e-zine that
can be printed from the website
and folded into a print version.

DIAMOND TWIG
E-ZINE
9 Eversley Place, Newcastle
upon Tyne NE6 5AL
0191 276 3770
diamond.twig@virgin.net
Editor: Ellen Phethean
Primarily a book publisher, but
also publishes one poem a month
online.
**For fuller descriptions of this press,
see also poetry publisher p25 and
prose publisher p79**

ENVOI POETRY JOURNAL
PRINT
Meirion House, Tanygrisiau, Blaenau
Ffestiniog, Wales LL41 3SU
01766 832112
www.cinnamonpress.com
Editors: Jan Fortune, Adam Craig
Established 2005. Poetry, reviews
and interviews. £20 subscription
for discounts on all publications as
well as free benefits. Publication
available direct from publisher
website; at chain bookshops
nationwide; in independent
bookshops; at local literary events;
on Amazon; and via Inpress Books.
GENRES: Historical; literary; poetry;
experimental; cross-genre.
SUBMISSIONS: During submissions
windows, submit by email to
envoi@cinnamonpress.com.
Guidelines at www.cinnamonpress.
com/index.php/envoi (see the
website for open submissions
periods). Usually responds within
one to three months. Standard
email/letter rejection in most
cases, but may offer feedback to
those who have come close to
publication.
WE SAY: We looked at Issue
172, a large-format, perfect-
bound magazine, with a matt
laminate cover and a clean
modern appearance. The journal
underwent a redesign in the past
year, and now uses its red and
blue logo colours to great effect
against black and white/sepia
images. The journal rightly prides
itself on having an eye for setting
out poetry on the page, but
we found the articles were hard
to read across the wide space.
Features, reviews and articles
are at the rear of the magazine,
which makes for a lovely,
uninterrupted read of the poetry,

which is mainly strong in images and lyricism.

For a fuller description of this press, including what They Say, see also Cinnamon Press (prose publisher p75 and poetry publishers p23).

ERBACCE ☆

PRINT
erbacce@blueyonder.co.uk
erbacce-press.com
Editor: Alan Corkish
Established 2004. Available direct from publisher website; by post and email order; at independent bookshops; at national and local literary events; and from Amazon. Note: erbacce is a cooperative in which poets volunteer to support other poets via their royalties.
SUBMISSIONS: Open to all. Submit by post (Dr Andrew Taylor, 5 Farrell Close, Melling, Liverpool, L31 1BU UK) or by email (erbacce@blueyonder.co.uk). Guidelines on the website. Usually responds within four weeks. Rejections may occasionally include unsolicited feedback. Contributors receive a copy of the journal and a discount price on further copies.
For a fuller description of this press see erbacce-press (poetry publisher) p29

FROGMORE PAPERS, THE ☆

PRINT AND E-ZINE
21 Mildmay Road, Lewes, East Sussex BN7 1PJ
frogmorepress@gmail.com
www.frogmorepress.co.uk
Editor: Jeremy Page
Established 1983. Poetry, reviews, interviews. Subscription £10 per year. Available by post and email order. All online content is available to all.

GENRES: Poetry.
SUBMISSIONS: During submissions windows, submit by post to The Frogmore Papers, 21 Mildmay Road, Lewes, BN7 1PJ. Usually responds within one to three months, no feedback offered with rejection. Contributors receive a print copy.
WE SAY: *The Frogmore Papers* print magazine is A5 and 42 pages long, with a thick board cover printed with a pleasingly textured image that appears to be a detail from a painting (Issue 85). It has a stapled spine, but the weight of a perfect-bound publication, courtesy of the high-quality paper. The reviews included throughout are unobtrusively short and at the bottom of the page, meaning that, apart from the occasional line drawing, the pages are almost entirely given over to the poetry itself.

FUSELIT

PRINT MAGAZINE
contact@drfulminare.com
www.sidekickbooks.com
Editors: Kirsten Irving, Jon Stone
Poetry focussed magazine (along with art and format twists) from the team behind the ultra-creative Sidekick Books. On hiatus throughout 2016.
For a fuller description of this press, including what They Say, see Sidekick Books (poetry publisher) p53

HIGH WINDOW JOURNAL, THE

E-ZINE
submissions@the highwindow.uk
thehighwindowpress.com
Editors: David Cooke,

Anthony Costello, Natalie Rees
Poetry focused e-zine containing poetry, essays, features, reviews and translations. Includes an 'American Poet' section, to encourage mutual discovery between UK and Irish, and US poets. Operate submissions windows.
See also: The High Window Press (poetry publisher) p36

IOTA POETRY
PRINT
58 Dale Road, Matlock, Derbyshire DE4 3NB
info@templarpoetry.com
www.templarpoetry.com
Founded 25 years ago. Features around 20 poets per issue, and includes a short portfolio of each poets' work. Also includes features and reviews. £1 submissions fee.
See also: Templar Poetry (poetry publisher) p60

JOURNAL, THE
PRINT
17 High Street, Maryport, Cumbria CA15 6BQ
01900 812194
smithsssj@aol.com
thesamsmith.webs.com
Editor: Sam Smith
Established 1996. Subscription £11 (UK only). Available direct from publisher website; and by post and email order.
SUBMISSIONS: Publication history required. Submit by post (17 High Street, Maryport, Cumbria CA15 6BQ) or by email (smithsssj@aol. com). Usually responds within four weeks. No feedback offered with rejection. Contributors receive a print copy.
WE SAY: A 36-page poetry magazine with a minimalist design, and a fluid approach to layout – two poems by one poet are featured on the same page, with the shorter poem in a box, for example, and reviews are split into columns with example poems highlighted. *The Journal* favours contemporary poetry, and though it doesn't include author biographies, it does list the poet's location/nationality next to their names with the poems.
See also: Original Plus (poetry publisher) p43

LITTER MAGAZINE
E-ZINE
xeqalan@hotmail.com
www.leafepress.com/litter
Editor: Alan Baker
Established 2000. Poetry, reviews, interviews. All online content available to all.
SUBMISSIONS: Solicited work only. No feedback offered with rejections.
WE SAY: *Litter Magazine*, while a great resource for poetry, leaves the casual reader wondering how recently it's been updated. A poetry review never goes out of date, but the lack of dates makes for a feeling of being out-of-time. The site itself is quite home-brew but care has clearly been taken to ensure the poems are laid out correctly – with the more experimental poem structures, this is important. The insights offered by the reviews are well worth a read.
See also: Leafe Press (poetry publisher) p39

LONG POEM MAGAZINE
PRINT
20 Spencer Rise, London NW5 1AP
020 7485 4928

186

mail@longpoemmagazine.org.uk
www.longpoemmagazine.org.uk
Editors: Linda Black, Lucy Hamilton

Established 2007. Poems and sequences over 75 lines, with one related essay per issue. Subscription £14.50/year (UK). Available direct from publisher website; and by post and email order.

GENRES: Travel.

SUBMISSIONS: During submissions windows, submit by email to mail@longpoemmagazine.org.uk. Guidelines at www.longpoemmagazine.org.uk/page3.htm. Usually responds within one to three months. No feedback offered with rejection. Contributors receive a print copy.

LUNAR POETRY

PRINT, DIGITAL AND SPOKEN WORD ALBUMS
Lunar Poetry Bookshop, I'klectik Art-Lab, Old Paradise Yard, 20 Carlisle Lane, Lambeth, London SE1 7LG. 07952 928 253
editor@lunarpoetry.co.uk
www.lunarpoetry.co.uk
Editor: Paul McMenemy

Established 2014. Poetry and criticism. Annual subscription £40 for 12 issues. Available direct from publisher website, and at independent bookshops and local literary events. Only subscribers/purchasers can access all online content.

SUBMISSIONS: Open to all. Submit by email to editor@lunarpoetry.co.uk. Usually responds within one to three months. Feedback on rejections only if requested. Contributors receive a print copy.

WE SAY: *Lunar Poetry* has a glossy, fairly flimsy, cover, and the 84 inner pages are printed on rather thin paper. But based on the undoubted quality of the contents, this tells us that *Lunar* is lacking money, not skill. We loved the cover illustration, which is a well-wrought cartoon of an astronaut with a typewriter. Plenty of well-curated poetry and a number of in-depth reviews populate the pages. *Lunar Poetry* is obviously aiming for the stars.

MAGMA ☆

PRINT AND DIGITAL
23 Pine Walk, Carshalton SM5 4ES
magmapoetry@ntlworld.com
www.magmapoetry.com
Editors: rotating editorship

Poetry and poetry-related features, in themed issues. Annual subscription £18.95 (including P&P). Available direct from publisher website; in selected/local chain bookshops; and in independent bookshops. Online, only subscribers/purchasers can access full content, with some content available to all.

SUBMISSIONS: Open to all. Submit through Submittable at magmapoetry.com/contributions/ (guidelines available at same address). Usually responds within one to three months. Rejection may occasionally include unsolicited feedback. Contributors receive a print copy.

WE SAY: *Magma* is square – 74 large square pages, in fact – and this alone gives it an edge. The colour is full cover, and the inner pages are punctuated with greyscale images and large black headline boxes. We looked at the digital version, but could easily imagine the weight of the magazine in print: modern and hefty. The shape allows space for long lines and experimental, concrete poetry to be displayed. The editors change for each issue, so the contents will vary, but whatever you send, you know it will look good in print.

MODERN POETRY IN TRANSLATION
PRINT
The Queen's College, Oxford OX1 4AW
deborah@mptmagazine.com
www.mptmagazine.com
Editor: Sasha Dugdale
Poems must be in English translation – no poems originally written in English accepted.

NORTH MAGAZINE, THE ☆
PRINT
0114 346 3037
office@poetrybusiness.co.uk
www.poetrybusiness.co.uk
Editors: Ann Sansom, Pete Sansom
Established 1986. Poetry, reviews, critical articles. Annual UK subscription £15 (£19 rest of the world). Available direct from publisher website; by post and email order; and at Cornerhouse (Manchester) and Salts Mill (Saltaire).
SUBMISSIONS: Open to all, during submissions windows. Submit by post to *The Poetry Business*, Bank Street Arts, 32-40 Bank Street, Sheffield, S1 2DS. Online submissions accepted from overseas only. Usually responds within one to three months. No feedback with rejection. Contributors receive a print copy of the magazine.
WE SAY: *The North Magazine* has come a long way over the years, graduating from a black-and-white, stapled A4 zine to the far

slicker incarnation it is today, with a bold, muted pallette on the cover, high-quality production values, and contents that include poems, articles, reviews and features. *The North* has a strong mix of established and new poets in its pages: an aspirational magazine to submit to.
See also: Smith|doorstop books (poetry publisher) p54

OPEN MOUSE, THE
E-ZINE
theopenmouse.wordpress.com
Editor: Colin Will
Established 1996. Single poems (around 100 per year). All online content available to all.
SUBMISSIONS: Open to all. Submit by email to colin.will@zen.co.uk. Guidelines at theopenmouse. wordpress.com. Usually responds within four weeks. No feedback offered with rejection.
WE SAY: Self-described as 'a site for poems', *The Open Mouse* is developed from a basic wordpress template, which means it's an easy scroll through poems that are added twice a week. The tastes of the Editor, and idiosyncrasies of the site, mean that the poetry included is accessible and fairly traditional in style (no concrete poetry or strange spacing), nothing requiring footnotes and explanations – which makes this well-curated site a pleasure to read.

PENNINE PLATFORM
PRINT
Frizingley Hall, Frizinghall Road, Bradford, West Yorkshire BD9 4LD
01274 541015
www.pennineplatform.co.uk
Editor: Nicholas Bielby
Established 1975. Annual

subscription £10.50. Available direct from publisher website; by post and email order; at local literary events; and at Amazon and other bookshop websites.

SUBMISSIONS: Open to all. Submit by post to *Pennine Platform*, Frizingley Hall, Frizinghall Road, Bradford BD9 4LD. Usually responds within four to six months. All submissions receive critical feedback. Contributors receive a print copy.

WE SAY: A 60-page, A5 poetry magazine with a simple yet artistic design. We looked at Issue 77, which focusses on rhyming metric poetry and free verse, with an introduction from editor Nicholas Bielby exploring the use of these forms. The resulting choices are a fine collection. We came away from *Pennine Platform* feeling that we'd learnt something.

See also: Graft Poetry (poetry publisher) p35

PICKLED BODY, THE

E-ZINE
thepickledbody@gmail.com
www.thepickledbody.com
Editors: Dimitra Zidous,
Patrick Chapman

Themed poetry and art, presenting 'work from the surreal to the sensual and points inbetween'.

PN REVIEW

PRINT
Carcanet Press, 4th Floor, Alliance House, 30 Cross Street, Manchester M2 7AQ
0161 834 8730
info@carcanet.co.uk
www.pnreview.co.uk
Editor: Michael Schmidt

A Carcanet Press publication, and one of the heavy-weights in terms of poetry publication. A top-tier magazine that includes poetry, and poetry related reviews, interviews and academic features.

SUBMISSIONS: Hard-copy submissions only (except for individual subscribers, who can submit electronically). Submissions no longer than ten pages of work. Decisions usually made within eight weeks. See the website for full guidelines.

See also: Carcanet Press (poetry publisher) p22

POEMS IN WHICH

E-ZINE
poemsinwhich@gmail.com
www.poemsinwhich.com
Editors: Rebecca Perry,
Alex MacDonald, Amy Key,
Wayne Holloway, Nia Davies

Established 2012. Poetry, in which... All content is freely available to all. Winner of Best Magazine in the 2013 Saboteur Awards.

SUBMISSIONS: Open to all. Submit by email to poemsinwhich@gmail.com. Guidelines at www.poemsinwhich.com/about/. Usually respond within one to three months. Rejection may occasionally include unsolicited feedback. Unpaid.

WE SAY: The design of *Poems in Which* is simple: no blaring colours or images, easy-to-find contact details. The site's USP – that every poem must be a 'poem in which' something happens – means that the often experimental, sharply contemporary styles of the poems featured are grounded: there's always something for the reader to grasp. It also makes for some memorable titles. The magazine is edited by some of the UK's best up-and-coming poets.

POETRY LONDON ☆

PRINT

The Albany, Douglas Way, London
SE8 4AG

020 8691 7260

admin@poetrylondon.co.uk

www.poetrylondon.co.uk

Editors: Jess Chandler, Ahren Warner,
Tim Dooley, Martha Kapos

Established 1988. Poetry, reviews,
interviews with poets. Subscription
UK: £25/year; Europe: £33/year;
outside Europe: £40/year. Available
direct from publisher website and
at chain bookshops nationwide.

SUBMISSIONS: Open to all. Submit
by post or by email to Poetry
London, The Albany, Douglas
Way, London SE8 4AG or admin@
poetrylondon.co.uk. Usually
responds within one to three
months. Rejection may occasionally
include unsolicited feedback.
Contributors are paid a set rate
and receive a discount purchase
price on the magazine.

WE SAY: One of the major titles in
poetry publishing, *Poetry London*
is as much about profile as poetry,
judging from the portaits of poets
it uses as cover images. It contains
poetry from around the world,
along with features and articles.
It also boasts a comprehensive
poetry listings section. It's a
coup to get your work into this
magazine.

**See also: Poetry London (poetry
publisher) p47**

POETRY SCOTLAND

PRINT

91-93 Main Street, Callander, Scotland
FK17 8BQ

sallyevans35@gmail.com

www.poetryscotland.co.uk

Editor: Sally Evans

A broadsheet magazine containing
nothing but poetry, with a focus on
Scottish writing. Open only to UK
residents, and adamant that work
is chosen on merit, not on previous
publication history, so a good
one for beginners to approach.
Poems in English, Gaelic, Scots
and occasionally Welsh and other
languages all considered.

SUBMISSIONS: Submit via email to
sallyevans35@gmail.com (subject
line: 'Poetry Scotland poems').
Any subject, any style. No more
than six poems. Response times
vary.

POETRY SPACE SHOWCASE ☆

PRINT AND DIGITAL

www.poetryspace.co.uk

Editor: Susan Sims

Subscription ('Friend of Poetry
Space') £15 per year. Available
direct from publisher website and
on Amazon. All online content is
available to all.

SUBMISSIONS: Open to all. Submit
by email to susan@poetryspace.
co.uk. Usually responds within
one to three months. Rejections
may include occasional unsolicited
feedback. Unpaid.

WE SAY: The *Poetry Space
Showcase* is slightly hidden in
the Poetry Space website and
is less showy than the name
suggests: a single, easy-on-the-
eye web page, followed by the
featured poems. But showiness
isn't everything, and this is still a
professional, understated site. A
different photograph heralds the
start of each new poem, which
all share the virtues of striking
imagery and memorable
metaphors.

**See also: Poetry Space (poetry
publisher) p48**

POETRY WALES ☆
PRINT AND DIGITAL
57 Nolton Street, Bridgend CF31 3AE
01656 663018
info@poetrywales.co.uk
www.poetrywales.co.uk
Editor: Nia Davies
Established 1965. Poetry, reviews, articles. Annual subscription £27. Available direct from publisher website; by post and email order; and at local literary events. Only subscribers/purchasers can access online content.
SUBMISSIONS: Open to all. Submit through Submittable at poetrywales.submittable. com/submit. Usually responds within four to six months. No feedback offered with rejections. Contributors are paid a set rate and receive a print copy of the magazine.
WE SAY: Perfect-bound 96-page magazine on thick quality paper. The copy we looked at (Vol. 51, No. 1) featured a landscape photo on the matt cover, and explored how Patagonia and Wales might imagine each other. The content included some translated poetry, as well as in-depth articles alongside the many poems, which ranged from strict structure to free-verse.
See also: Seren Books (prose publisher p52 and poetry publisher p110)

POETRY&PAINT
PRINT, DIGITAL AND E-ZINE
24 Sherbrooke Way, Worcester Park, KT4 8BP
0789 688 0996
poetryandpaintsubmissions@gmail.com
www.poetryandpaint.wordpress.com
Editor: Camina Masoliver
Established 2013. Poetry and visuals (art, fashion photography) anthology magazine. Available on lulu.com (www.lulu.com/spotlight/Carmina).
SUBMISSIONS: During submissions windows, submit by email to poetryandpaintsubmissions@gmail. com. Guidelines at poetryandpaint. wordpress.com/submissions. Usually responds within four to six months. No feedback offered with rejections. Contributors receive a digital copy.
WE SAY: The cover of *Poetry & Paint* – an A5 magazine, 66 pages long – is quite plain. It's on the inner pages where the name starts to make sense. The illustrations are bright and beautiful and compliment the chosen poems well. The designers have opted for a slightly odd font, which takes some getting used to, but does fit the artistic aesthetic.

PULSAR POETRY MAGAZINE
E-ZINE
34 Lineacre, Grange Park, Swindon Wiltshire SN5 6DA
pulsar.ed@btinternet.com
www.pulsarpoetry.com
Editor: David Pike
Established 1994. Poetry and reviews. All online content freely available to all.
GENRES: Hard-hitting work with message and meaning. Not keen on religious or epic poems.
SUBMISSIONS: Open to all – up to three unpublished poems, but no simultaneous submissions. Submit by post or by email to *Pulsar* Editor, 34 Lineacre, Grange Park, Swindon, Wiltshire, SN5 6DA or pulsar.ed@btinternet.com. Usually responds within four weeks. No feedback offered with rejection. Contributors receive exposure.
WE SAY: *Pulsar Poetry* has a simple,

but unconventional, old-fashioned layout, on a yellow background with rather a small font. With dropdown menus and menu-bars now the norm, its not easy to find the poems, but once found navigation is easy, and the content clearly signposted. The poetry and discourse are modern and the zine works hard to promote its poets and other publications.

QUAIT
PRINT
114 Sandy Lane, Cholton, Manchester M21 8TZ
www.sinewavepeak.com
Editor: Luke Allan
Established 2011. Concrete and formal poetry – each issue dedicated to a different poetic form. Available direct from publisher website and at independent bookshops. Only subscribers/purchasers can access online content.
SUBMISSIONS: Open to all. Submit by post or by email to 114 Sandy Lane, Cholton, Manchester M21 8TZ or luke@sinewavepeak.com. Usually responds within four weeks. Rejection may occasionally include unsolicited feedback. Contributors receive a print copy and a discount purchase price on the magazine.
For a fuller description of this press, including what They Say, see sine wave peak (poetry publisher) p55

RAUM POETRY
PRINT
info@roomspoetry.com
www.raumpoetry.com
Keen to experiment with unconventional poetry as well as traditional forms.

REACH POETRY ☆
PRINT
24 Forest Houses, Halwill, Beaworthy, Devon EX21 5UU
publishing@indigodreams.co.uk
www.indigodreams.co.uk
Editors: Ronnie Goodyer, Dawn Bauling
Established 2005 (ltd company since 2010). Subscription £48/year for 12 issues. Available direct from publisher website; by post and email order; at chain bookshops nationwide; at independent bookshops; and on Amazon. Editors won the Ted Slade Award for Services to Poetry 2015.
GENRES: Biography and true stories; history; music, stage and screen; travel.
SUBMISSIONS: Open to all. Submit by post (IDP, 24 Forest Houses, Halwill, Beaworthy, Devon EX21 5UU) or by email (publishing@indigodreams.co.uk). Guidelines at www.indigodreams.co.uk. Usually responds within four weeks. No feedback offered with rejection. Contributors receive a monthly monetary prize, shared by the top three as voted for by readers.
WE SAY: *Reach Poetry* is an A5, 52-page monthly magazine, perfect bound with a glossy full colour cover. Poets with work in the magazine are in for an interactive experience, as it has a popular letters page, and encourages readers to vote for their favourite poems. The style of poetry is wide-ranging – many different forms appeared in the Issue we read.
For what They Say, see Indigo Dreams Publishing Ltd (poetry publisher) p37. See also *The Dawntreader* p139 *and Sarasvati* p167 (mixed-form literary magazines)

RIALTO, THE ☆

PRINT
PO Box 309, Aylsham, Norwich
NR11 6LN
info@therialto.co.uk
www.therialto.co.uk
Editor: Michael Mackmin
Assistant editors: Rishi Dastidar,
Holly Hopkins, Fiona Moore,
Abigail Parry

Established 1984. Poetry,
poetry news and views. Annual
subscription £24 (overseas
£24+£12 shipping; concessions
£19). Available direct from
publisher website and at a few
selected/local chain bookshops
and independent bookshops.
SUBMISSIONS: Open to all. Submit
by post (*The Rialto*, PO Box 309,
Aylsham, Norwich NR11 6LN) or
Submittable (therialto.submittable.
com/submit). Guidelines on the
website. Usually responds within
one to six months. Returns may
include occasional unsolicited
feedback. Contributors are paid a
set rate.
WE SAY: Perfect-bound, 64-page
A4 magazine with an artistic edge.
The screamingly bright cover
of Issue 83 featured a full-page
illustration of reds, oranges and
yellows, on a bold blue ground.
Inside on thick white paper, poems
are laid out with clear thought as
to their shape and size, so there's
no feeling of overcrowding, and
even the title page has a couple
of poems on it (Wordsworth and
Hopkins).
**See also: The Rialto/Bridge
Pamphlets (poetry publisher) p49**

THEY SAY

When we started *The Rialto*
we wanted to create a place,
at a time (1984) when there
were fewer poetry magazines,
where beginning writers,
of any age, could find a
welcome for their work
alongside their established
peers. That's still our aim.
Nearly all the poems in the
magazine are unsolicited,
and we look out for fresh
names. Hannah Lowe calls
The Rialto 'the poetry magazine
to read'.
From early on we've thought
about gender balance – the
current issue has 31 female
and 31 male poets, the
previous issue 19 male and 28
female. We'd welcome more
contributions from ethnically
diverse writers.

193

SHEARSMAN MAGAZINE

PRINT
50 Westons Hill Drive, Emersons
Green, Bristol BS16 7DF
0117 957 2957
editor@shearsman.com
www.shearsman.com/shearsman-
magazine

Editor: Tony Frazer

Established 1981 (2003 in its
current form). Poetry and literary
criticism. Available direct from
publisher website, by post and
email order, at selected/local chain
and independent bookshops and
on Amazon and other bookshop
websites.

SUBMISSIONS: Open to all, during
submissions windows. Submit
by post (Shearsman Books Ltd.,
50 Westons Hill Drive, Emersons
Green, Bristol BS16 7DF), by
email (editor@shearsman.com) or
through the online submissions
portal at www.shearsman.com/
how-to-contact-shearsman-books.
Usually responds within four to six
months. No feedback offered if
rejected. Contributors receive two
free copies of the magazine.

WE SAY: An 108-page A5
publication chockful purely of
poetry. We looked at a PDF of
Shearsman so can't comment as
to the quality of print, but the
design is clean and effective. A
single line draws attention to
the poet's name and the poem
title, the sans-serif font of which
makes a nice comparison with the
more traditional serif used for the
poems.

Eduardo Milán
Selected Essays

THEY SAY

The press and magazine have
a clear inclination towards
the more exploratory end
of the current spectrum
of contemporary poetry.
However, quality work of
a more conservative kind
will always be considered
seriously, provided that
the work is well-written.
What I do not like at all is
sloppy writing of any kind; I
always look for some rigour
in the work, although I will
be more forgiving if the
writer is trying to push the
boundaries. I like mixing
work from both ends of the
spectrum in the magazine,
and firmly believe that good
writing can, and should,
cohabit with other forms of
good writing.

**See also: Shearsman Books ltd
(poetry publisher) p52**

SHADOWTRAIN
E-ZINE
shadow2train@yahoo.com
www.shadowtrain.com
Editor: Ian Seed
Established 2006. Poetry and reviews. All online content available to all.
SUBMISSIONS: Open to all. Submit by email to shadow2train@yahoo.com. Guidelines at www.shadowtrain.com/id6.html. Usually responds within four weeks. No feedback offered with rejections. Contributors receive exposure.
WE SAY: An e-zine with a simple design that is easy to navigate; it refers to its issues as carriages, and the train is long... *Shadowtrain* takes a contemporary approach to poetry, featuring work that experiments with various poetic forms, and which covers a diverse range of subject matter.

SOUTH POETRY MAGAZINE
PRINT
PO Box 4228, Bracknell RG42 9PX
south@southpoetry.org
www.southpoetry.org
Editors: Patrick Osada, Anne Peterson, Chrissie Williams, Andrew Curtis, Peter Keeble
Established 1990, published twice annually. Poetry, reviews, profiles. Annual subscription £12 (or £22 for two years). Available by post and email order; and at the Foyle's Charing Cross and Royal Festival Hall branches in London.
SUBMISSIONS: Open to all, during submissions windows. Submit by post to *South Poetry Magazine*, PO Box 4228, Bracknell, RG42 9PX. Hard copies only, please. Full guidelines at www.southpoetry.org/content/submissions. Individual responses not possible. Successful submitters' names are posted on the website eight to ten weeks after the deadline for that issue's submissions. Contributors receive a print copy.
WE SAY: *South Poetry* has stuck to the same format for years, including the use of a striking black-and-white cover photograph. Contents include a profile and sample work from an established poet, a wide selection of anonymously submitted new poetry, and reviews. We looked at an online example so can't comment on the print layout, but the style of poems selected is wide-ranging.

STRIDE MAGAZINE
E-ZINE
editor@stridemagazine.co.uk
www.stridemagazine.co.uk
Editor: Rupert Loydell
Established 1982. Poetry (including prose poems), articles and reviews. All online content available to all.
SUBMISSIONS: Submit by email to editor@stridemagazine.co.uk. Usually responds within four weeks. No feedback offered with rejections.
WE SAY: The homepage of *Stride*'s website is not pretty, but it works: submissions info to the left and a list of contents, starting with the most recent additions, to the right. Start clicking through to the articles and poetry, and it's clear that the focus for *Stride* is entirely on the work. No menus, nothing distracting – just a clear font and careful layout for each item. Reviews and articles are smart, opinionated and in-depth, and the poetry ranges from traditional to concrete (there are some beautiful shapes on the page).

SYMMETRY PEBBLES
E-ZINE
submissions@symmetrypebbles.com
symmetrypebbles.wordpress.com
Contemporary poetry and art, with
an interest in new, exciting, risk-
taking poets. Preference is towards
'experimental, surreal, satirical, anti,
free-thinking, brave, occasionally
blunt and dangerous poetry'.

TENDER JOURNAL
DIGITAL
www.tenderjournal.co.uk
Established 2013 as a platform for
work by female-identified writers
and artists. Illustrated, 'made by
women', and published three or
four times a year in PDF form.

WOLF, THE
PRINT
editor@wolfmagazine.co.uk
www.wolfmagazine.co.uk
Editor: James Byrne
Founded 2002, and quickly
became a leading poetry
magazine. Publishes international
translations, critical prose and
interviews. Poetry aesthetic
leans towards experimental over
mainstream, and serious over light
verse.

YOUR ONE PHONE CALL
E-ZINE
youronephonecall@yahoo.co.uk
youronephonecall.wordpress.com
Editor: Dai Shotter
'Poetry with a knife edge'. A Wales-
based literary zine, publishing 'top
notch' poetry.

Prose magazines and e-zines

We define prose quite widely for this section: short stories, long short stories, flash fiction, creative non-fiction and more. Any magazine that publishes work that's literary, but not poetry, is included. However, the majority of these magazines focus on what we would normally think of as straight short stories. There are also some stunning publications for writers (and readers) of genre fiction.

Prose magazines and e-zines

AESOP MAGAZINE

PRINT AND DIGITAL
18 and a half Sekforde Street,
London EC1R 0HL
editor@aesopmagazine.com
www.aesopmagazine.com
Editor: Max Raku
Established 2015. Mainly fiction.
Free magazine. Print publication
available to all, via direct
distribution outside major central
London stations and in offices,
members clubs and universities
in the City of London. Available
digitally by email.
GENRES: Crime/thriller/mystery;
drama and criticism; historical
fiction; literary fiction; romance;
biography and true stories; humour.
SUBMISSIONS: Open to all. Submit
through the form at
www.aesopmagazine.com/
submissions.html (guidelines at the
same address). Usually responds
within one to three months,
with feedback only if requested.
Contributors receive a print copy
and a digital copy.
WE SAY: We looked at Issue 1. At
33-pages and A4 sized, *Aesop*
offers a selection of short stories
every month, against a bright
and charmingly colourful layout
of illustrations in a wide range of
styles that mean this free mag will
catch the eye of both children and
adults. Fonts and colours vary story
to story – a bold approach, as this
could look cluttered, but *Aesop's*
designers make it work, and each
story really stands out as a result.
The writing is for all ages, too.
**See also: poetry publishers p15 and
prose publishers p67**

ALT HIST

PRINT AND DIGITAL
althist.editor@gmail.com
althistfiction.com
Historical fiction and alternate
history. A rare outlet for short
historical fiction. Looking for
entertaining, well-written stories
with a historical setting.

BLACK STATIC

PRINT, DIGITAL AND E-ZINE
5 Martins Lane, Witcham, Ely,
Cambridgeshire CB6 2LB
andy@ttapress.com
www.ttapress.com
Editor: Andy Cox
Established 1994 (under the title
The Third Alternative – renamed
and given horror focus in 2005).
Mainly fiction. See ttapress.com/
shop/ for subscription rates.
Publication available direct from
the publisher website; by post and
email order; in chain bookshops
nationwide; in independent
bookshops; and at literary events.
All online content is freely available
to all.
GENRES: Horror and dark fantasy;
book reviews; film reviews;
interviews; comment.
SUBMISSIONS: Submissions open
to all. Stories of up to 10,000
words. Submit via Submittable
at tta.submittable.com/submit
(guidelines at same address).
Usually responds within four weeks.
Contributors receive money and a
copy of the magazine. Rejections
may occasionally include
unsolicited feedback.
WE SAY: A blocky, dark,
foreboding, laminated cover,

proper spine and 96-pages of high-production values (beautiful design interwoven with shadowy, creepy, black-and-white illustrations), *Black Static* is the acknowledged bible of horror writing – for good reason. You'll recognise many names in this magazine, and it's a mark of genre quality to get your work in alongside them. The stories range from shivery to terrifying, interspersed with a great array of non-fiction: reviews, comments, interviews etc. A magazine that knows what it's about and how to present it.
See also: TTA Press (prose publisher) p118

BOOKANISTA
E-ZINE
editors@bookanista.com
newvoices@bookanista.com
www.bookanista.com
Editors: Farhana Gani, Mark Reynolds
Welcomes general submissions from publishers and established writers for articles, interviews and short fiction. For open subs, try their New Voices for short fiction.

CRIMEWAVE
PRINT
5 Martins Lane, Witcham, Ely, Cambridgeshire CB6 2LB
andy@ttapress.com
www.ttapress.com
Editor: Andy Cox
Established 1999. Short stories. Published irregularly – see ttapress.com/shop/ for subscription rates. Publication available direct from the publisher website; by post and email order; in chain bookshops nationwide; in independent book-shops and at literary events. All online content is freely available to all. Award-winning stories.

GENRES: New modern crime and mystery.
SUBMISSIONS: Submissions open to all. Stories of up to 10,000 words. Submit via Submittable at tta.submittable.com/submit (guidelines at same address). Usually responds within four weeks. Rejections may occasionally include unsolicited feedback. Contributors receive money and a copy of the magazine.
WE SAY: Released every two years or so, *Crimewave* is more an anthology series than a magazine. Containing 240-pages of short stories, novels and novelettes, it's an American Royal-size paperback, with a wrap-around cover design. Like TTA Press's other publications, *Crimewave* is a mainstay of genre fiction, and names that crop up here are established or emerging writers in the field – an aspiration for any crime-writer's CV.
See also: TTA Press (prose publisher) p118

DUBLIN REVIEW, THE
PRINT
PO Box 7948, Dublin 1, Ireland.
order@thedublinreview.com
www.thedublinreview.com
Editor: Brendan Barrington
Established 2000. Mixed form: fiction and non-fiction. See thedublinreview.com/subscribe for subscription information. Available direct from publisher website; by post and email order; and from Amazon.
GENRES: Literary fiction; essays; memoir; travel writing; criticism; reportage.
SUBMISSIONS: Open to all. Submit by post to Submissions, The Dublin Review, PO Box 7948, Dublin 1, Ireland. Guidelines at

thedublinreview.com/submissions. Usually responds within one to three months. No feedback offered with rejection. Contributors are paid a set rate and receive a discount purchase price on the magazine.

WE SAY: Collectors' quality covers, with the issue number wrought large against a plain coloured background, and contributors and contents listed below. *The Dublin Review* has a classic literary journal

CASKET OF FICTIONAL DELIGHTS, THE ☆

E-ZINE (ONLINE PUBLICATION)
12 Glenshiel Road, London SE9 1AQ
07553 131635
joanna@thecasket.co.uk
www.thecasket.co.uk
Editors: Joanna Sterling, Menna Bonsels, Lucy Durneen

Established 2011. Fiction and multimedia. All online content available to all. Winner of CityLit 'Between the Lines' 2009.
GENRES: Crime/thriller/mystery; drama and criticism; historical fiction; literary fiction; romance. No non-fiction.
SUBMISSIONS: Open to all. Submit through the online form at www.thecasket.co.uk/submissions/. Guidelines at www.thecasket.co.uk/submissions/general-terms-conditions/. Usually responds within one to three months. Feedback not usually offered with rejection.
WE SAY: *The Casket* is a quirky looking site; a bit steam-punk and certainly original – no wordpress template here! There's the odd typo on the homepage, but the stories are well-curated, easy to find, clearly laid out and often have an audio version – and they frequently feature original and refreshing voices.

The Casket of Fictional Delights

THEY SAY

Established in 2011 to showcase short stories and flash fiction when these genres were poorly represented in the UK. We publish writers from around the world and diverse backgrounds. We are looking for stories that will intrigue, amuse and provoke thought in the reader. We harness technology to deliver our stories to as wide an audience as possible. Many of the short stories are recorded by professional actors or voiceover artists and published on iTunes. We are consistently ranked in the top 20 of the short story category on iTunes. Our target readership is adults, mainly in the age range of 30-50.

look. The balance of personal history, essay, reportage and short story varies from issue to issue, and the publishers favour long work (up to 12,000 words).

EAST OF THE WEB
E-ZINE
submissions@eastoftheweb.com
www.eastoftheweb.com/short-stories
Fiction – short stories across multiple genres, rates by age and length for easy browsing.

FLASH: THE INTERNATIONAL SHORT-STORY MAGAZINE ☆
PRINT
Department of English, University of Chester, Parkgate Road, Chester CH1 4BJ
01244 513152
flash.magazine@chester.ac.uk
www.chester.ac.uk/flash.magazine
Editors: Peter Blair, Ashley Chantier
Established 2008. Mainly fiction. Subscription £9/year. Available direct from publisher website, post and email order.
GENRES: Literary fiction, with reviews and literary criticism.
SUBMISSIONS: Open to all. Submit by email to flash.magazine@ chester.ac.uk. Guidelines at www. chester.ac.uk/flash.magazine/ submissions. Usually responds within four weeks, no feedback with rejection. Contributors receive a print copy of the magazine.
WE SAY: Perfect-bound 111-page magazine that includes flash fiction, essays and reviews. The cover is matt, with a photographic image on the front and appropriately flashy silver spine and back. Reasonable quality white paper inside, and no illustrations, but plenty of very short fiction. After the original fiction, there's

a section called 'Flash presents', which presents classic work (Virginia Woolf, in the issue we looked at – Vol. 7 No. 2), followed by an essay on her work. Then several reviews and advertisements thoughtfully kept to the last few pages.

FLIGHT JOURNAL
E-ZINE
www.flightjournal.org
Publishes bold, short fiction. A journal born of Flight 1000, a Spread the Word Associates scheme. Spread the Word is the London writer's development agency, which identifies and supports talented writers from a diversity of backgrounds.

GREEN BOOK, THE
PRINT
brian@swanriverpress.ie
swanriverpress.ie
Editor: Brian Showers
Established 2003. Non-fiction commentaries, articles, reviews. Available direct from publisher website; by post and email order; from independent bookshops and online book dealers; and at national literary events and local literary events.
GENRES: Literary criticism and history based around Irish gothic, supernatural and fantastic. No fiction.
SUBMISSIONS: Open year-round. Usually responds within four weeks. Rejection may occasionally include unsolicited feedback. Contributors receive a print copy.
WE SAY: 108 pages, perfect bound, with a glossy cover that always features white text against a background of green, with a photo image in the middle, *The Green*

Book is a scholarly affair, simply and well put together. It contains a mixture of new and old writing (Rudyard Kipling appears in the issue we looked at), with reviews appearing last.

GHASTLING, THE

PRINT AND DIGITAL
editor@theghastling.com
www.theghastling.com
Editor: Rebecca Parfitt

Established 2014. Fiction.
Print available on Amazon and via the publication website; all online content available to all.
GENRES: Graphic/comics; horror; literary fiction; the macabre and peculiar. No non-fiction.
SUBMISSIONS: During submissions windows, submit by email to editor@theghastling.com. Usually responds within one to three months. No response by indicated time means a rejection. Unpaid at the moment.
WE SAY: *The Ghastling* calls itself a 'modern-day pennydreadful', but its production values are far higher than that implies. Slightly smaller than A4, with a page count that varies depending on the contents (it started out at 54 pages and has climbed from there), this magazine is perfect bound, using quality materials with a design that harks back to woodcut prints, but with touches of colour and contemporary art mixed in. The cover images so far have been unnerving – and that sense of slowly unveiled horror perfectly invokes the stories within.

See also: The Ghastling Press (prose publisher) p87

THEY SAY

Devoted to ghost stories, the macabre and the oh-so-strange. This magazine delights in the spooky and peculiar and publishes both fiction and artwork. Like the Victorian curiosity shop, we love to display work that comes from the 'darker side', makes us feel uneasy and holds our curious gaze – almost mesmeric... Think 'circus-weird' and you've got our attention. Please note: psychological horror is our thing – we do not accept or enjoy reading gory horror or gory horror porn. No. Don't even try it. It's not our ouija-board-style.

See also: Swan River Press (prose publisher) p115

HALO LIT MAG
E-ZINE
submissions@halolitmag.co.uk
www.halolitmag.co.uk
New – launched December 2015.
Flash fiction by women writers.

INCUBATOR, THE
DIGITAL / E-ZINE
15 Cairndore Vale, Newtownards,
Co Down, BT23 8PF
editor.theincubator@gmail.com
theincubatorjournal.com
Editor: Kelly Creighton
Established 2014. Mainly fiction.
Available via publisher website, all
content available to all.
GENRES: Crime/thriller/mystery;
drama and criticism; literary fiction;
poetry; memoir; essays; one-scene
plays; book reviews.
SUBMISSIONS: Open to writers
with a connection to Ireland.
Submit during submissions
windows by email to editor.
theincubator@gmail.com.
Guidelines at theincubatorjournal.
com/submissions. Usually
respond within four weeks.
No feedback offered with
rejection. Unpaid.
WE SAY: We looked at Issue 8,
on issuu.com. *The Incubator* has
a colour photo-image cover
(dying tea roses, in this case),
with no headlines. 86 pages
long, with the work divided
cleanly into interview, short
stories, book review and finally,
poems. The design inside is
minimal and uncluttered – the
only decoration is a curlier font
for contributors' names and titles.

INTERZONE
PRINT, DIGITAL AND E-ZINE
5 Martins Lane, Witcham, Ely,
Cambridgeshire CB6 2LB
andy@ttapress.com
www.ttapress.com
Editor: Andy Cox
Founded 1982, and taken over
by TTA Press in 1994. Fiction,
interviews, reviews. See ttapress.
com/shop/ for subscription rates.
Publication available direct from
publisher website; by post and
email order; in chain bookshops
nationwide; in independent
bookshops; at literary events;
and from Amazon, Apple, and
Weightless Books. All online
content freely available to all.
Winner of British Science Fiction
Association award and British
Fantasy Award; nominated for the
Hugo Award.
GENRES: Sci-fi and fantasy; book
reviews; film reviews; interviews;
comment.
SUBMISSIONS: Submissions open
to all. Stories of up to 10,000
words. Submit via Submittable
at tta.submittable.com/submit
(guidelines at same address).
Usually responds within four
weeks. Rejections may occasionally
include unsolicited feedback.
Contributors receive money and a
copy of the magazine.
WE SAY: *Interzone* is full-colour,
with each story illustrated. Perfect
bound, laminated and 100 pages
long, it's the longest-running sci-fi
magazine in the UK. Its design
has moved with the times, while
also remaining rather retro. The
cover has a blocky style, with the
sort of stunning cover art that wins
awards. This is an extremely high-
quality publication, with content
to match: stories, commentary,

reviews and interviews. Big names and big awards go hand in hand.
See also: TTA Press (prose publisher) p118

LONG STORY, SHORT JOURNAL
E-ZINE
longstoryshortjournal@gmail.com
longstoryshort.squarespace.com
Editor: Jennifer Matthews
Established 2012. All online content available to all.
GENRES: Literary fiction. No non-fiction.
SUBMISSIONS: Open to all, but stories must be 4000 words or longer. No upper limit. Submit by email to longstoryshortjournal@gmail.com. Guidelines at longstoryshort.squarespace.com/submissions. Usually responds within one to three months. Rejection may occasionally include unsolicited feedback. Unpaid.
WE SAY: One lengthy short story each month appears on the simple professionally designed site. The contents page displays a photo and an introduction to each story; the stories themselves run down the page unimpeded by adverts. If you'd prefer a PDF to print out, *Long Story, Short* welcomes requests by email for that format. With its descriptive and engaging content, this e-zine encourages readers to sit down and take their time to read good writing.

NECESSARY FICTION
E-ZINE
editor@necessaryfiction.com
www.necessaryfiction.com
Editors: Steve Himmer,
Michelle Bailat-Jones (translations),
Helen McClory (fiction),
Susan Rukeyser (reviews)

Book reviews, short stories, 'Research Notes' and occasional interviews and essays, updated throughout the week. Particularly supportive of independent publishers in their reviews, and all areas of writing are open to submissions.

NUMBER ELEVEN MAGAZINE
E-ZINE
numbereleveneditor@gmail.com
numberelevenmagazine.com
Editor: Graham Connors
Quarterly publication for short stories, flash fiction, graphic novel artwork and illustrations.

OBLONG MAGAZINE
DIGITAL AND OCCASIONAL PRINT
editor@oblongmagazine.com
oblongmagazine.com
Editor: Jo Beckett-King
Established 2012. Fiction. All online content available to all. Oblong is primarily an online magazine, but has published print editions in the past and hopes to publish more in the future.
GENRES: Literary. No non-fiction.
SUBMISSIONS: Open to all, during submissions windows. Submit through Submittable at oblongmagazine.submishmash.com/. Guidelines at oblongmagazine.com/submit/. Usually responds within four to six months. Rejection may occasionally include unsolicited feedback. Contributors receive a print copy where available, otherwise unpaid.
WE SAY: The *Oblong* website eschews decoration and teasers of featured work. Each piece of flash fiction appears in chronological order, on the home page. It's not the sleekest site, but the look does echo a design that works in the

print version. All print issues of *Oblong* have sold out (a mark in its favour?), so we can't comment on the production quality, but we like the brown paper cover design (think parcel paper). The flash fiction is well curated; we were struck by the melancholy and depth of the pieces.

OPEN PEN MAGAZINE
PRINT
464 Commercial Road, London E1 0JN
info@openpen.co.uk
www.openpen.co.uk
Editor: Sean Preston
Established 2011. Mainly fiction. Available at independent bookshops.
GENRES: Drama and criticism; literary. No non-fiction.
SUBMISSIONS: Open to anyone who hasn't yet had a book published. Submit by email to submissions@openpen.co.uk. Guidelines at www.openpen.co.uk/submit/. Usually responds in up to three months, with feedback only if requested. Contributors receive a print copy of the magazine.
WE SAY: Free 20-page magazine, with a matt cardboard cover featuring a bright eye-catching illustration, and a stapled spine, *Open Pen* is crammed with short fiction. Apart from one small advert and a call for submissions, all the pages are given to stories that are intense bursts of quality short fiction. The editor's letter and masthead are relegated to the inner cover.

PAPAYA PRESS
PRINT AND MIXED-MEDIA
papayapressinfo@gmail.com
papayapress.tumblr.com
Based in the North of England,

Papaya Press produce small one-off zines and mixed-media publications, working with artists and writers. Previous publications include *[Re]fit*, 'a response to the appropriation of space and gentrification of Berlin'.

RED LINE, THE
DIGITAL
redlineshared@gmail.com
www.overtheredline.com
Editors: Joshua Osto, Stephen Lynch
Established 2013. Mainly fiction. All online content available to all.
GENRES: Literary, preferring fiction that shows the standards and originality associated with 'literary' work; reviews and articles about the craft of the short story.
SUBMISSIONS: During submissions windows, submit via Submittable at theredline.submittable.com/submit. Guidelines at overtheredline.com/submissions/. Usually responds within one to three months. Rejections can be standard or positive, encouraging resubmissions and explaining the process – but feedback is given only if requested. Contributors receive money (set rate – one writer receives £50 or equivalent).
WE SAY: *The Red Line*'s covers are eye-catching and well designed – and all different in style depending on the theme of the issue. The inner pages look a little clunkier: a largish font has been used, at the request of readers, but the text looks squashed in the red framing boxes, and it's difficult to read headings laid over dark images. However, the black-and-white photos used to illustrate each story (fading as the text begins) are used to great effect, as is the jaunty slash of red under the story titles.

SHORELINE OF INFINITY ☆
PRINT, DIGITAL AND E-ZINE
0131 208 1900
editor@shorelineofinfinity.com
www.shorelineofinfinity.com
Editor: Noel Chidwick
Established 2015. Mainly fiction.
Available direct from publisher
website, post and email order.
Only subscribers/purchasers can
access online content.
GENRES: Fantasy/sci-fi; reviews;
commentary on science fiction
related topics.
SUBMISSIONS: Open to all, during
submissions windows. Submit
via the online manager at www.
shorelineofinfinity.com/submissions
(guidelines at same address).
Usually responds within one to
three months. Standard rejection
may occasionally include unsolicited
feedback. Contributors are paid a
set rate and receive a digital copy
of the magazine.
WE SAY: A 108-page magazine.
We looked at Issue 1 in PDF
format. The front cover design is
quirky and near classic sci-fi – think
stars, and spacemen, but with
deliberately clunky photoshopped
characters. The mono illustrations
inside, a different illustration with
each story, are less distinctive. It's
beautifully laid out, apart from the
strangely low-resolution logo. As
well as stories, *Shoreline* includes
interesting reviews of sci-fi novels.
Fairly new on the scene, but on
the up.
**See also: The New Curiosity Shop
(prose publisher) p98**

SHORT ANTHOLOGY, THE
PRINT
editors@theshortanthology.com
www.theshortanthology.com
Editors: Will Martin, Kat Phan

Established 2014. Fiction.
Available direct from publisher
website and independent
bookshops.
GENRES: Children's fiction; crime/
thriller/mystery; drama and
criticism; erotica; fantasy/sci-fi;
horror; historical fiction; literary
fiction; romance; YA. No non-
fiction.
SUBMISSIONS: Submissions by
invitation only. Usually responds
within four weeks. Rejection may
occasionally include unsolicited
feedback. Contributors receive a
print copy of the magazine.
WE SAY: *The Short Anthology*
features fiction inspired by
photographs. It is perfect bound,
smaller than A5 and 78-pages-
worth of satisfyingly thick paper.
The first issue of *The Short
Anthology* is beautifully designed,
with a full page dedicated to
each story title, and printed end
papers reproducing one of the
photographs in black and white.
The highlight, though, is the
photography: rather than printing
the images on to the page, the
photographs are glued to the
pages, as if in a photo album.
It looks professional, but is a
reminder of how much handmade
effort has gone into each copy of
the magazine.

SHORT FICTION MAGAZINE ☆
PRINT
University of Plymouth, Faculty of Arts
6 Portland Villas, Devon PL4 8AA
01752 585 106
anthony.caleshu@plymouth.ac.uk
www.shortfictionjournal.co.uk
Editor: Tom Vowler
Established 2007. Short fiction.
Available direct from publisher
website and at national and local

literary events. All online content available to all.

GENRES: Literary. No non-fiction.

SUBMISSIONS: Open to all, during submissions window only. Submit by email to shortfiction2010@gmail.com. Guidelines at www.shortfictionjournal.co.uk/?page_id=29. Usually responds within one to three months, but only to writers whose work is being accepted. Contributors receive a print copy of the magazine.

WE SAY: 164-pages of thick, slightly shiny, paper; perfect bound, with a David Shrigley picture on the cover (we looked at Issue 9), *Short Fiction* is a heavyweight of short story publishing. The contents read like a guide to established short story writers whose work you should be paying attention to (think Alison Moore, Rhoda Greaves, Toby Litt, Alex Preston...). Subtitled 'The Visual Literary Journal', this issue is filled with black-and-white images alongside the text, plus a full-colour art supplement. There's a playfulness in the layout of the text as well: bolds; italics; font size variation and speech bubbles are all welcome additional to the rather experimental stories.

SOUTH CIRCULAR, THE
DIGITAL
hello@thesouthcircular.com
www.thesouthcircular.com
Editor: Aoife Walsh
Established 2011. Short stories. Quarterly. Only purchasers can access content (€3 per issue, PDF and ePub).

Award-nominated: Danielle McLaughlin's story 'Five Days to Polling Day' (Issue 8, December 2013) was nominated for the 2014 writing.ie Short Story of the Year Award as part of the Bord Gais Irish Book Awards.

GENRES: Literary. No non-fiction.

SUBMISSIONS: Open to all, during submissions windows. Submissions welcome from anywhere in the world, but must be English language. Submit by email to submissions@thesouthcircular.com. Guidelines at www.thesouthcircular.com/submit/. Responds within one to three months to successful submissions only. Contributors are paid a set rate and receive a digital copy of the magazine.

WE SAY: We looked at Issue 5: 40 pages of simple and effective design. The cover image is from Irish-Swedish design duo, M&E Design, and is eye-catching and rather beautiful. That the magazine only features four stories means they can use the space to display the text properly. Each story has a title page, and has been laid out with care. A lattice effect image bookends them. The contributors to this magazine are usually emerging writers, so this is a good submission opportunity for less-established writers.

SPELK
E-ZINE
spelkfiction@gmx.com
www.spelkfiction.com
Editor: Gary Duncan
Established 2014. Flash fiction. All online content available to all.

GENRES: Crime/thriller/mystery; literary. No non-fiction.

SUBMISSIONS: Open to all. Submit by email to spelkfiction@gmx.com. Guidelines at spelkfiction.com/submit-2/. Usually responds within four weeks. Rejection may occasionally include unsolicited feedback.

WE SAY: *Spelk*'s layout is a simple template. The homepage features the most recent published story, a basic menu and an alphabetical list of contributors linking to their featured stories, so you can hunt for your favourite writers. The browse function is a bit awkward – if you click on the archives, only the last story posted in the month appears, giving the false impression that *Spelk* only updates once a month. In fact, it's more like once a week, so readers keep coming back for a regular hit of sharp flash fiction – and the fiction is edgy, packing a punch in 500 words or fewer.

STORGY MAGAZINE ☆
DIGITAL AND E-ZINE
59 Montague Road, Hanwell, London W7 3PG
07792 411560
storgy@outlook.com
www.storgy.com
Editors: Tomek Dzido, Anthony Self, Sally-Anne Wilkinson, A. Suiter Clarke
Established 2013. Fiction. All online content available to all
GENRE: Literary. No non-fiction.
SUBMISSIONS: Open to all. Submit by email to storgy@outlook.com. Guidelines at storgy.com/touch-us/. Usually responds within one to three months. No feedback offered with rejection. Contributors receive a digital copy.
WE SAY: *Storgy* is a prime example of what an e-zine can be. The fonts are clear, the site is slick and the home page is loaded with images, but not overwhelming. We get the impression that a lot of thought has gone into making the reading experience a pleasant one: *Storgy* has nearly 6,000 Likes on Facebook, so this e-zine clearly has readers. One thing we do miss is a comprehensive archive list, but you could argue that this just gives the new work a sense of immediacy.
See also: Storgy (prose publisher) p114

TIMEZONE MAGAZINE
PRINT
www.timezonemagazine.co.uk
Editor: Marie Doinne
Established 2012. Fiction. Available direct from publisher website, post and email order, independent bookshops and BFI Bookshop (London).
GENRES: Fantasy/sci-fi; literary. No non-fiction.
SUBMISSIONS: Submit during submissions windows, adhering to the chosen theme. Submit by email to timezonemagazine@gmail.com. Guidelines available at www.timezonemagazine.co.uk/#!submissions/cn5v. Usually responds within four to six months. No feedback offered with rejection. Contributors receive a print copy of the magazine.
WE SAY: *Timezone* is a slim B5 publication (i.e. tall and skinny), and each issue is published as a limited edition. It features a screenprinted image on the cover, and illustrations accompany each of the three stories – and it's bilingual. Much love has clearly gone into this magazine, and it shows in the quality of the end product.

UNTHOLOGY
PRINT AND DIGITAL
PO Box 3506, Norwich NR7 7QP
information@unthankbooks.com

www.unthankbooks.com
Editors: Robin Jones, Ashley Stokes

Brought to you by the editors at Unthank Books, *Unthology* is a published twice a year. Each 'issue' is an anthology containing short stories, reportage, essays or novel extracts from anywhere in the world, it welcomes 'the classic slice-of-life well told just as much as the experimental, the shocking and the strange'. A series of books rather than a journal, really.

SUBMISSIONS: Open to all, all year round, but please only submit once every six months. Submit by email to unthology@unthankbooks.com. Guidelines at www.unthankbooks.com/unthology.html.

See also: Unthank Books (prose publishers) p120

Part 3:
Competitions

Conquering competitions

Entering writing competitions can feel like casting your precious words into an abyss, only to watch them drop out of sight without so much as a faint splash. Nevertheless, it can be a worthwhile endeavour.

For winners, there is the actual prize money, of course, plus the glow of achievement and validation, and the notch on your CV. But even if you don't win, there's the camaraderie on social media amongst people who have entered, and the flurry of anticipation when the longlists are announced. More importantly, there is the insight that can be gained from reading the winners' work and critically applying that same eye to your own work. And bear in mind that when the competition is run by a small press or magazine, the entrance fees play a vital part in helping the press to survive.

Here are a few tips to improve your chances of winning:

- We've said it before, but please (please) read the rules carefully, and stick to them. If they call for anonymous entries, make sure your name is confined to a cover sheet only. If they call for entries by post rather than email, then post your work. If the competition is for unpublished work only, make sure your story hasn't appeared anywhere – if you win, you will be found out and disqualified. Managing a competition is hard work; don't give the organisers and judges any reason to exclude you.
- Don't go for the obvious idea. Try stepping out of your comfort zone of gender, race, sexuality, setting. Judges will be reading hundreds of entries so it helps if there is something (other than your brilliant writing) that makes your entry stand out.
- Avoid rushing to finish an original poem or story just minutes before the deadline. Give yourself time to step away from it for a few days – the longer the better – and edit it at least once more before you submit.
- Check that your story is actually telling a story and that your poem has something to say. Judges often comment that story entries read like an extract from a longer manuscript; or that a poem doesn't seem to have a point.
- Cut the padding. Start your story as late as possible in the narrative. With poems, ask yourself whether you really need that opening stanza. Judges, far more than normal readers, need to be ensnared by your very first line.
- Obviously you will check carefully for typos and punctuation

mistakes, but look out for clichés and obvious word pairings too. Clichés leap off the page for sifters and judges, so spend time identifying and rewriting each one.

And if the results come through and your entry isn't on the longlist?

- Don't take it personally. Remember that when there's a panel of judges, the winners are often the result of argument and compromise. With a single judge, individual taste plays a part, too.
- Don't abandon the work. Reread it critically. Could you make it stronger? If so, redraft it and try again. If it's already as good as it can be, try again with a different competition – or submit it to one of the many magazines we've helpfully listed in this book for that purpose,

Good luck!

A3 REVIEW, THE

writingmaps.submittable.com/submit
Themed monthly contest.
CATEGORIES: Poetry; flash fiction; graphic stories; comics. No more than 150 words; no larger than A6 panel.
ENTRY FEE: $5 (approx £3) per submission.
PRIZES: £150 first prize; £75 second prize; £50 third prize.

AESTHETICA MAGAZINE

www.aestheticamagazine.com/creative-writing-award
CATEGORIES: Poetry (up to 40 lines per poem); short fiction (up to 2,000 words).
ENTRY FEE: £15+VAT for two poems or one story. Multiple entires allowed.
PRIZES: £500 (poetry winner); £500 (short fiction winner); publication in the *Aesthetica Creative Writing Anthology*; a selection of books from Vintage and Bloodaxe Books; one-year print subscription to *Granta*; full membership to The Poetry Society (Poetry Winner); consultation with Redhammer Management (Short Fiction Winner); a complimentary copy of the Anthology.

ALMOND PRESS

www.dystopianstories.com/terms-and-conditions/
CATEGORIES: Short stories (under 5,000 words).
PRIZES: £100 first prize; shortlisted works published in electronic and print format; visibility.

AMBIT MAGAZINE

www.ambitmagazine.co.uk
CATEGORIES: Poetry; short fiction (no more than 1,000 words).
ENTRY FEE: £6 per poem; £8 per story.
PRIZES: Each category £500 first prize, £250 second prize, £100 third prize; publication; invitation to read at launch party.

ARACHNE PRESS LIMITED

www.arachnepress.com
CATEGORIES: Poetry; short story.
PRIZES: Publication; selection of books; badge.

ARTEMIS POETRY / SECOND LIGHT PUBLICATIONS

www.secondlightlive. co.uk
CATEGORIES: Long poems (over 50 lines, no upper limit); short poems (up to 50 lines).
ENTRY FEE: £6 per long poem; £4 per short poem (or £9 for three/£14 for eight).
PRIZES: Each category £300 first prize, £100 second prize, £50 third prize, book prize for commended; publication.

AS YET UNTITLED

www.elbow-room.org/competition
CATEGORIES: Poetry; short fiction; visual arts.
PRIZES: Each category £200 first prize, £50 second and third prize; publication in anthology; featured in exhibition and live event.

BARE FICTION
www.barefictionmagazine.co.uk
CATEGORIES: Poetry (max 40 lines); short story (max 3,000 words); flash fiction (max 500 words); debut poetry collection (between 16 and 20 pages).
ENTRY FEE: £5 per poem (£3 subscribers); £6 per flash fiction (£4 subscribers); £8 per short story (£6 subscribers); £20 per poetry collection.
PRIZES: Poetry, flash fiction and short story: £500 first prize, £200 second prize, £100 third prize, £25 highly commended; publication. Poetry collection: first prize £1,000, plus collection publication and 50 complimentary copies; second and third prizes pamphlet publication and 30 complimentary copies.

BLACK & WHITE PUBLISHING LTD
www.blackandwhitepublishing.com
CATEGORIES: Novel.
PRIZE: Publication.

BLACK PEAR PRESS
www.blackpear.net
CATEGORIES: Short story (up to 1,500 words).
ENTRY FEE: £5 per story.
PRIZES: First prize £75; second prize copies of two BPP publications; longlist and other selected stories published in anthology.

BRITTLE STAR
www.brittlestar.org.uk/competition
Runs bi-annually.
CATEGORIES: Poetry (no longer than 60 lines); short fiction (no longer than 2,000 words).
ENTRY FEE: £4.50 for first entry, £3.50 subsequent entries.

PRIZES: Each category £250 first prize, £50 second prize, £25 third prize; publication; invitation to launch and prize-giving.

CANDLESTICK PRESS
www.candlestickpress.co.uk
Very occasional competitions linked to their website and Facebook page. Prizes vary.

CASKET OF FICTIONAL DELIGHTS, THE
www.thecasket.co.uk
CATEGORIES: Flash fiction.
PRIZES: Publication; recording of flash fiction for publication on iTunes.

CATERPILLAR, THE
www.thecaterpillarmagazine.com
CATEGORIES: The Caterpillar Poetry Prize (no line limit); The Caterpillar Short Story Prize (no more than 2,000 words).
ENTRY FEE: €12 per poem/story.
PRIZES: €1,000 for the best poem; €1,000 for the best story.

CHOC LIT
www.choclitpublishing.com/html/ search_for_a_star.html
CATEGORIES: Novel (between 60,00 and 100,000 words).
ENTRY FEE: £10.
PRIZE: Publication.

CINNAMON PRESS
www.cinnamonpress.com/index.php/ competitions/our-awards
CATEGORIES: Poetry (see 'mini competitions on website); debut poetry collection (10 poems up to 40 lines each); poetry pamphlet (15-25 poems up to 50 lines each); debut novel/novella (first 10,000 words); short story (2,000-4,000 words).

ENTRY FEE: £10 for pamphlet prize; £12 per entry for novels, stories, and full poetry collections.
PRIZES: Novel/novella: £500 plus publishing contact. Poetry collection: £300 plus publishing contract; 25 runners up published in anthology. Poetry pamphlet: publishing contract plus 30 copies of pamphlet x 4. Short story: £500 first prize; £100 second prize; £50 third prize; publication of winners and up to 10 runners' up stories.

COMMA PRESS

www.commapress.co.uk
New writer showcase.
CATEGORIES: Short story (between 2,000 and 6,000 words).
PRIZES: Paid publication.

CRO MAGNON, THE

www.thecromagnon.com
CATEGORIES: Poetry (single poem); Poetry (collection/pamphlet); short story (up to 3,000 words); flash fiction; theatre. Newly established.
ENTRY FEE: Short story £5; check the website for updates on other categories.
PRIZES: £100 and publication; shortlisters all published. Future prizes to range from £100 – £500 and will include publication; professionally produced theatre performance of work.

CUCKOO CHRONICLE

chronicle.cuckoowriters.com
Cuckoo Young Writers Awards, part of the Northern Writers Awards.
CATEGORIES: Prose, poetry or creative non-fiction (writers aged 14-18).
PRIZE: £300.

DOG HORN PUBLISHING

www.doghornpublishing.com
CATEGORIES: Poetry (single poem); poetry (collection/pamphlet); novel; short story; flash fiction
PRIZES: Publication; professional feedback/mentoring; introduction to agent/publisher.

DREADFUL PRESS, THE

www.thepennydreadful.org/index.
php/novellaprize/
CATEGORIES: Novella (between 15,000 and 35,000 words).
ENTRY FEE: €10 per manuscript, maximum two manuscripts per entry.
PRIZES: €2,000 and publication.

ELBOW ROOM

www.elbow-room.org/competition
CATEGORIES: Poetry; short fiction; visual arts.
PRIZES: Each category £200 first prize, £50 second and third prize; publication in anthology; featured in exhibition and live event.

ERBACCE

www.erbacce.com
The Annual erbacce-prize for Poetry.
CATEGORIES: Poetry (single poem); poetry (collection/pamphlet).
PRIZES: Publication; publishing contract; free copies with 20% royalties.

EYEWEAR PUBLISHING

www.eyewearpublishing.com
Melita Hume Prize and Sexton Prize for Poetry.
CATEGORIES: Melita Hume (collection between 48 and 100 pages). Sexton (collection by an American poet between 48 and 100 pages).
ENTRY FEE: Melita Hume £10; Sexton Prize $27.

PRIZES: Melita Hume £1,500 and publication; Sexton $1,000 and publication.

FAIR ACRE PRESS

www.fairacrepress.co.uk/competitions
CATEGORIES: Poetry pamphlet (up to 30 pages, no page longer than 30 lines), separate categories for previously published and unpublished poets.
ENTRY FEE: £12
PRIZES: Each category winner: publication; editorial advice; pre-publication reading at Wenlock Poetry Festival; complimentary copies; entry to Michael Marks Award and Poetry Books Society Pamphlet Choice; copies sent out for review.

FISH PUBLISHING

www.fishpublishing.com
CATEGORIES: Poetry (up to 300 words); YA novel (5,000 words or first chapter); short story (max 5,000 words); flash fiction (max 300 words); short memoir (max 4,000 words).
ENTRY FEE: Fees vary, according to whether entering online or by post, and whether or not entrants include critiques. See website.
PRIZES: Poetry: €1,000 first prize; week-long residency second prize. YA Novel: publication. Short story: €3,000 and week-long fiction writing workshop, first prize; week-long retreat plus travel expenses second prize; €300 third prize. Flash fiction and Short memoir: €1,000 first prize; Fish online writing course, second prize. Ten stories from each short category appear in the prize anthology, with published authors receiving five copies each and invitations to read at West Cork Literary Festival.

FITZCARRALDO EDITIONS

www.fitzcarraldoeditions.com/prize
The Fitzcarraldo Editions Essay Prize.
CATEGORIES: Book-length essays (submit a proposal of up to 5,000 words for a eassy that will be minimum 25,000 words).
PRIZES: £3,000; writing retreat; publication; introduction to agent/ publisher.

FLASH: THE INTERNATIONAL SHORT-STORY MAGAZINE

www.chester.ac.uk/flash.magazine
CATEGORIES: Flash fiction.
PRIZES: Up to £249.

FROGMORE PRESS, THE

www.frogmorepress.co.uk
The Frogmore Poetry Prize
CATEGORIES: Poetry (no longer than 40 lines).
ENTRY FEE: £3 per poem.
PRIZES: £250 and two-year subscription to *The Frogmore Papers* – first prize; £75 and one-year subscription – first runner up; £50 and one-year subscription – second runner-up. Shortlisters receive a selection of books.

GALLEY BEGGAR PRESS

www.galleybeggar.co.uk
CATEGORIES: Short story (up to 6,000 words).
ENTRY FEE: £10 per submission.
PRIZES: Winner chooses between £500 or year-long editorial support for a writing project.

GATEHOUSE PRESS

www.gatehousepress.com
New Fictions Prize.

CATEGORIES: Short fiction (stories between 10,000-13,000 words).
PRIZES: Publication; professional feedback/mentoring.

INDIGO DREAMS PRESS

www.indigodreams.co.uk
CATEGORIES: Poetry (collection/pamphlet) and single poem.
PRIZES: Publication.

INK, SWEAT & TEARS

www.inksweatandtears.co.uk
In association with Cafe Writers Commission.
CATEGORIES: Poetry pamphlet (12 page plus a proposal).
ENTRY FEE: £10
PRIZES: £2,000 and publication, plus 100 copies of the pamphlet.

INTERPRETER'S HOUSE, THE

www.theinterpretershouse.com/
competition
Open House.
CATEGORIES: Poetry (50 lines max).
ENTRY FEE: £3 for single poems, £10 for three poems.
PRIZES: £500 first prize; £150 second prize; £100 third prize; seven highly commended; publication.

JOTTERS UNITED LIT-ZINE

jottersutd.wix.com/jotters-united
CATEGORIES: Poetry; short story (max 2,000 words).
PRIZES: Publication; selection of books.

LONDON MAGAZINE, THE

www.thelondonmagazine.org/
category/tlm-competition/
CATEGORIES: Poetry (up to 40 lines); short story (up to 4,000 words, no flash fiction).
ENTRY FEE:£7 first poem; £5 per subsequent poem. £10 per story.

PRIZES: Poetry £300 first prize, £200 second prize; £150 third prize. Short story £500 first prize, £300 second prize, £200 third prize. Publication.

MAGMA

www.magmapoetry.com/competition
CATEGORIES: Short poems (Editor's Prize: up to 10 lines); poetry (Judge's Prize: 11-50 lines).
ENTRY FEE: £5 single poem, or £15 for four poems.
PRIZES: Judge's Prize: £1,000 first prize, £300 second prize, £150 third prize. Editor's Prize: £1,000 first prize, £300 second prize; £15 special mentions x10. Publication.

MOTH, THE

www.themothmagazine.com
CATEGORIES: Ballymaloe International Poetry Prize (no line limit; entry fee €12 per poem); The Moth Short Story Prize (stories up to 6,000 words; entry fee €12 per story); The Moth Art Prize (portfolio of 5-10 2D artworks; entry fee €20 per portfolio).
PRIZES: Poetry €10,000 first prize, €1,00 runner-up x3, publication. Short story €3,000 first prize, writing retreat second prize (w/€250 stipend), €1,000 third prize, publication. Art month-long retreat with €1,000 stipend.

MOTHER'S MILK BOOKS

www.mothersmilkbooks.com/index
php/writing-prize
CATEGORIES: Poetry (40 lines max); prose (1,200 words max); children's poetry (40 lines max).
ENTRY FEE: A purchase of any product through the Mother's Milk Online Store.

PRIZES: £100, plus publication, back issue of *Juno*, complimentary copy of anthology (prose and poetry; £10 book token, plus publication, mounted print of poem and complimentary copy of anthology (children's poetry).

MSLEXIA

www.mslexia.co.uk/competitions
Women writers only.
CATEGORIES: Poetry (single poem); poetry pamphlet (20-24 pages of 18-20 poems); novel (first 3,000 words for book of at least 15,000 words); short story (up to 2,200 words).
ENTRY FEE: £7 for up to three poems; £20 per pamphlet; £25 per novel entry; £10 per short story.
PRIZES: Poetry: first prize £2,000; second prize £400; third prize £200; special prize for previously unpublished £500; publication for all. Poetry pamphlet: £250 and publication by Seren. Novel: £5,000 for the winner. Short story: first prize £2,000; second prize £500; third prize £250; three finalists £100; publication for all.

MYRIAD EDITIONS

www.myriadeditions.com/competitions
First Drafts and First Graphic Novel Competition.
CATEGORIES: Narrative fiction (up to 5,000 words from a novel or short story collection in progress); graphic novel (15-30 pages of a work in progress).
ENTRY FEE: £10.
PRIZES: First Drafts: writing retreat; professional feedback; mentoring. First Graphic Novel: professional feedback/mentoring; introduction to agent/publisher; writing retreat; possible publication.

NEW WELSH REVIEW/READER

www.newwelshwritingawards.com
The New Welsh Writing Awards.
CATEGORIES: Non-fiction long-form essay (5,000 to 30,000 words).
ENTRY FEE: Free.
PRIZES: First prize: £1,000, e-book publication; professional feedback/mentoring; introduction to agent/publisher. Second prize: writing retreat (week). Third prize: residential weekend. All three receive a year's subscription. Runners-up: considered for publication.

NINE ARCHES PRESS

campus.poetryschool.com/primers-guide-your-poems-into-print/
Primers – with The Poetry School
CATEGORIES: Poetry pamphlet (initial six poems; further 14 if shortlisted).
ENTRY FEE: £14 per submission.
PRIZES: Publication; professional feedback/mentoring.

NORTH MAGAZINE, THE

www.poetrybusiness.co.uk/competition-menu/competition
The Poetry Business Book & Pamphlet Competition
CATEGORIES: Collection/pamphlet (20-24 pages of poems; full-length manuscript if shortlisted).
ENTRY FEE: £25.
PRIZES: Equal share of £2,000; pamphlet publication x3; book publication x1; launch readings; magazine publication.

NOTTING HILL EDITIONS

www.nottinghilleditions.com/essay prize-intro
The Notting Hill Editions Essay Prize
CATEGORIES: Essays (between 2,000 and 8,000 words on any subject).

ENTRY FEE: £20 (includes a copy of previous competition winners book).
PRIZES: £20,000 first prize; £1,000 runners-up x5. Publication.

PENNY DREADFUL, THE

www.thepennydreadful.org/index
.php/novellaprize/
CATEGORIES: Novella (between 15,000 and 35,000 words).
ENTRY FEE: €10 per manuscript, maximum two manuscripts per entry.
PRIZES: €2,000 and publication.

PENNYSHORTS

www.chiplitfest.com/short-story-
competition-rules
Sponsors ChipLitFest Short Story competition.
CATEGORIES: Short stories (not exceeding 3,000 words).
ENTRY FEE: £5 per submission
PRIZES: £500 first prize, £100 second prize, £50 third prize.

POETRY LONDON

www.poetrylondon.co.uk/competition
CATEGORIES: Poetry (up to 80 lines).
ENTRY FEE: £7 per poem (£3 for subscribers).
PRIZES: £1,000 first prize; £500 second prize; £200 third prize, and publication in magazine. commendations £75 and online publication x4.

POETRY SPACE

www.poetryspace.co.uk/poetry-space-
competition
CATEGORIES: Poetry (up to 40 lines).
ENTRY FEE: £5 per poem.
PRIZES: £250 first prize; £100 second prize; £50 third prize. Publication for top twenty

poems, plus complimentary copy for poets.

POETRY WALES

www.poetrywales.co.uk
CATEGORIES: Poetry pamphlet (20-24 pages long).
PRIZES: Up to £250 and publication.

RIALTO, THE

www.therialto.co.uk
The RSPB and The Rialto Nature Poetry Competition.
CATEGORIES: Poetry (single poem) Poetry (collection/pamphlet)
ENTRY FEE (SINGLE POEM): £6 for first poem, £3.50 for subsequent poems.
PRIZES (SINGLE POEM): £1,000 first prize, £500 second prize; writing retreat worth £550 third prize; day out with Mark Cocker.

SHORELINE OF INFINITY

www.shorelineofinfinity.com
CATEGORIES: Short story.
PRIZES: £80; publication.

SHORT FICTION MAGAZINE

www.shortfictionjournal.co.uk
CATEGORIES: Short fiction (up to 6,000 words).
ENTRY FEE: £7 per story.
PRIZES: £500 plus publication for first prize; £200 second prize; shortlisted stories published online.

SMITH|DOORSTOP BOOKS

www.poetrybusiness.co.uk/
competition-menu/competition
The Poetry Business Book & Pamphlet Competition
CATEGORIES: Collection/pamphlet (20-24 pages of poems; full-length manuscript if shortlisted).
ENTRY FEE: £25.

PRIZES: Equal share of £2,000; pamphlet publication x3; book publication x1; launch readings; magazine publication.

SOUTHWORD JOURNAL/ EDITIONS

www.munsterlit.ie

CATEGORIES: Gregory O'Donoghue Poetry Prize; The Seán Ó Faoláin Short Story Competition; The Fool for Poetry Chapbook Competition.

PRIZES: Poetry: first prize €1000, a week's residency, publication and a trip to Cork, Ireland; second prize €500 and publication; third prize €250 and publication. Ten runners-up paid €30 publication fee. Poetry pamphlet: first prize €1000; second prize €500. Both receive 50 complimentary copies of their chapbook. Short story: first prize €2,000, publication and week-long residency; second prize €500 and publication; four shortlisted writers receive publication fee of €120.

STINGING FLY, THE

www.stingingfly.org

The Davy Byrnes Short Story Award, run every five years.

CATEGORIES: Short story

PRIZES (AS OF 2014): €15,000 first prize; €1,000 for five runners-up; publication.

STORGY

www.storgy.com

CATEGORIES: Short story (max 5,000 words).

ENTRY FEE: £5.

PRIZES: £500 first prize; £25 book vouchers for runners-up x2; publication; signed book.

SYNAESTHESIA MAGAZINE

www.synaesthesiamagazine. com/#!competitions/c1a9m

CATEGORIES: Poetry (no longer than 50 lines); Poetry collection/ pamphlet; short story; flash fiction.

PRIZES: Up to £100; publication; books.

[UNTITLED] / [UNTITLED FALKIRK]

untitledfalkirk.blogspot.co.uk

CATEGORIES: Poetry (single poem); poetry (collection/pamphlet); short story.

PRIZES: Publication; writing opportunities.

WALES ARTS REVIEW

www.walesartsreview.org

CATEGORIES: Short story; flash fiction; non-fiction.

PRIZES: Various prizes.

WASAFIRI MAGAZINE

www.wasafiri.org/wasafiri-new-writing-prize.asp

Open to anyone without a complete book in the category entered.

CATEGORIES: Poetry; fiction; life writing. 3,000 word limit or five poems max.

ENTRY FEE: £6 (one category); £10 (two categories); £15 (three categories).

PRIZES: £300 for the winner of each category; publication.

WAYWISER PRESS, THE

www.waywiser-press.com/ hechtprize.html

The Anthony Hecht Poetry Prize (US-based office).

CATEGORIES: Book-length poetry collection.

ENTRY FEE: $27.

PRIZES: $3,000; publication; invitation to read.

WRECKING BALL PRESS
www.wreckingballpress.com
CATEGORIES: Poetry collection/
pamphlet)
PRIZES: Publication.

We hope this guide will be useful for you during your publishing journey. If you know of a publisher that should have been included (or one that has closed down since the publication of this book), please contact us so that we can include/omit them from the next edition.
postbag@mslexia.co.uk

With special thanks to...

Charlotte Barker, who worked so hard and ploughed through endless amounts of admin to help us pull this information together.

All the indie press editors, assistants and publicity directors who helped us compile this guide by filling out forms, answering questions, sending us sample copies and spreading the word. We appreciate your time and effort and hope that some great writers use these pages to discover you.

All those websites and organisations, including Short Stops (shortstops. info), Paul McVeigh's blog (paulmcveigh.blogspot.co.uk), Inpress and the Poetry Library, which do so much to spread the word about indie publishers and submission slots and which were invaluable sources of information.

All those writers who also helped us discover presses through the sheer enthusiasm of sharing their work on social media.

Index